T0287093

LIFE IN TECHNICOLOR

A CELEBRATION OF

Published by ECW Press
665 Gerrard Street East
Toronto, ON M4M 1Y2
416-694-3348 / info@ecwpress.com

Library and Archives Canada Cataloguing in Publication

Wild, Debs, author
Coldplay: life in technicolour / Debs Wild, Malcolm Croft.
Co-published by Carlton Books Ltd.
ISBN 978-1-77041-486-0 (hardcover)

1. Coldplay (Musical group). 2. Rock musicians—England—Biography. I. Croft, Malcolm author. II. Title.

ML421.C688W66 2018 782.42166092'2 C2018-903505-6

Editorial Director: Roland Hall
Design: Russell Knowles
Picture Research: The Authors
Additional Picture Research: Steve Behan
Production: Yael Steinitz

Printed and bound in Canada
5 4 3 2

LIFE IN TECHNICOLOR

A CELEBRATION OF

DEBS WILD
& MALCOLM CROFT

A NOTE FROM PHIL HARVEY

"Debs, there is no doubt in my mind that none of this would have happened without you. Literally. God knows what would have happened if you hadn't been in the audience that night in Manchester. Make sure you put that in your book!!!"

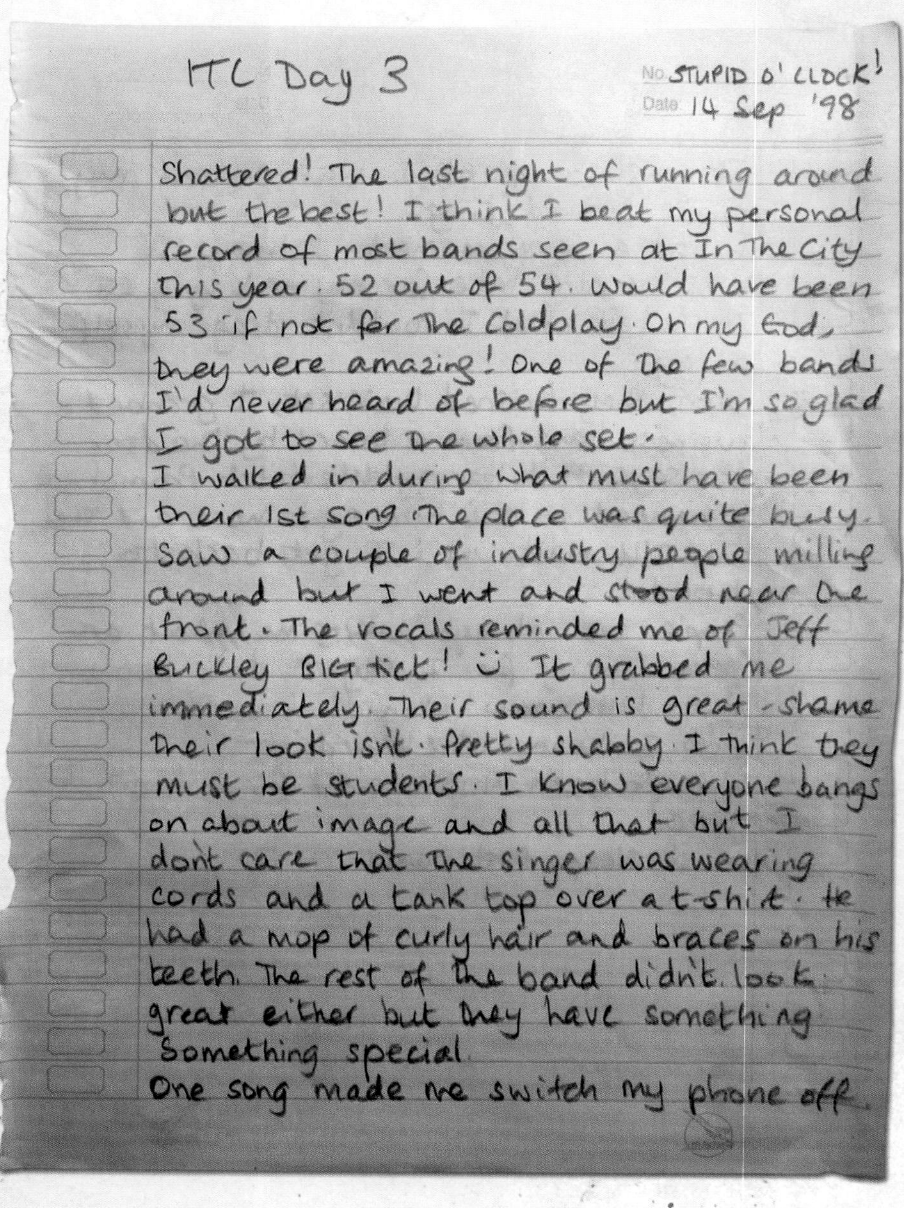

ITC Day 3

No STUPID O'CLOCK!
Date 14 Sep '98

Shattered! The last night of running around
but the best! I think I beat my personal
record of most bands seen at In The City
this year. 52 out of 54. Would have been
53 if not for The Coldplay. Oh my God,
they were amazing! One of the few bands
I'd never heard of before but I'm so glad
I got to see the whole set.
I walked in during what must have been
their 1st song. The place was quite busy.
Saw a couple of industry people milling
around but I went and stood near the
front. The vocals reminded me of Jeff
Buckley BIG tick! :) It grabbed me
immediately. Their sound is great - shame
their look isn't. Pretty shabby. I think they
must be students. I know everyone bangs
on about image and all that but I
don't care that the singer was wearing
cords and a tank top over a t-shirt. He
had a mop of curly hair and braces on his
teeth. The rest of the band didn't look
great either but they have something
Something special.
One song made me switch my phone off.

ABOVE AND OPPOSITE Debs's diary entry immediately after seeing Coldplay for the first time at The Cuban Cafe, Manchester on 14 September, 1998.

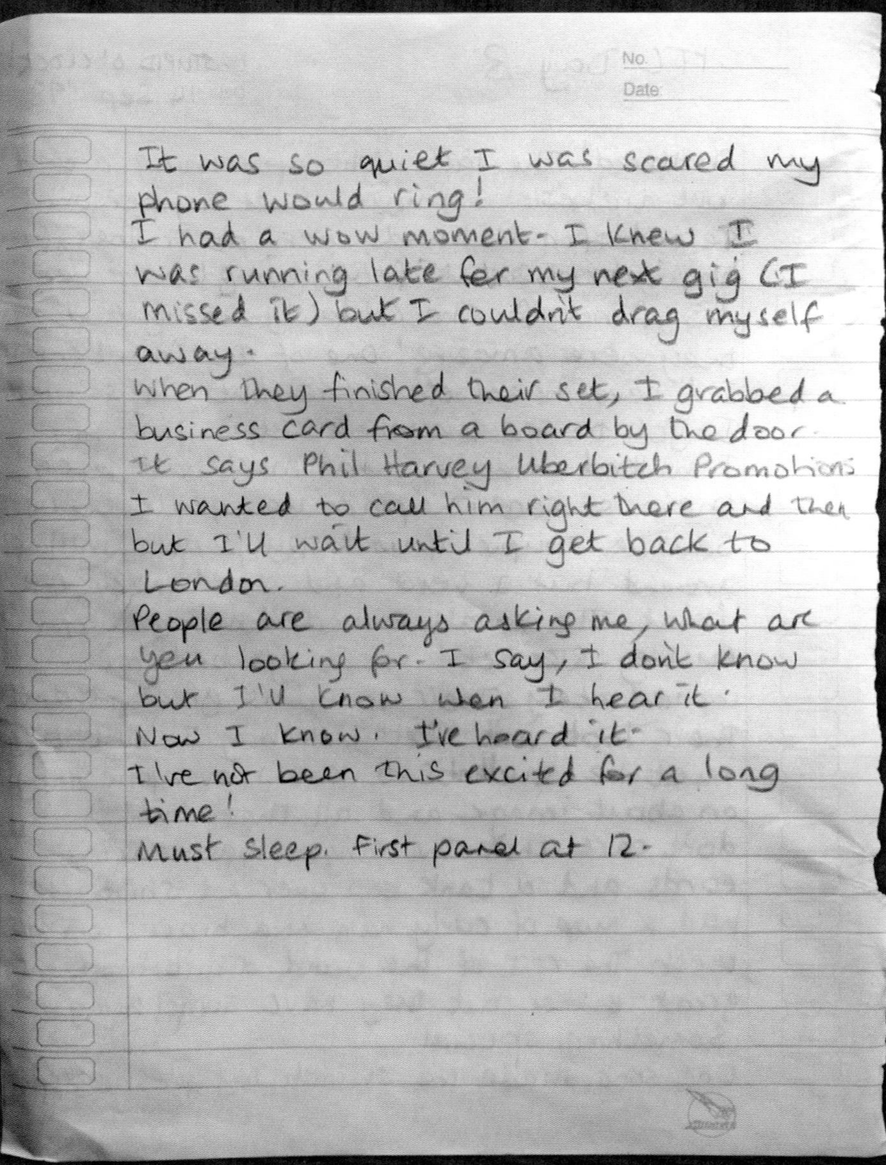

No.
Date

It was so quiet I was scared my phone would ring!
I had a wow moment - I knew I was running late for my next gig (I missed it) but I couldn't drag myself away.
When they finished their set, I grabbed a business card from a board by the door. It says Phil Harvey Uberbitch Promotions
I wanted to call him right there and then but I'll wait until I get back to London.
People are always asking me, what are you looking for. I say, I don't know but I'll know when I hear it.
Now I know. I've heard it.
I've not been this excited for a long time!
Must sleep. First panel at 12.

> “There is no doubt in my mind that all of this would still have happened but I'm immensely proud that it all started from that night.”

Debs Wild

INTRODUCTION

Twenty years ago Guy, Jonny, Will and Chris formed Coldplay. Today they are arguably the biggest band in the world. They have achieved their dreams and so much more. How can we possibly cover it all?

When we sat down to write this book, we found ourselves asking the question "What is it about Coldplay that makes them special enough to have continued on such an upward trajectory for so long?"

As their manager Dave Holmes says, "It's a pretty incredible story. Twenty years on and it's still going. They're in their own lane."

From their earliest rehearsals at Jonny and Chris' flat at 268 Camden Road to selling out Wembley Stadium four nights in a row, all roads have led to where they are today. The band's determination to succeed has been evident since day one. "Chris and I used to pore over unofficial biographies of bands," Phil Harvey told us. "Anything we could grab our hands on and study the progressions, decision-making and the personnel – and we loved it." It was because of this that we decided to celebrate the band on such a momentous occasion – twenty years together.

After all that time, Coldplay are still a band who wear their hearts on their sleeves, have genuine chemistry together, and the music they create, makes them stronger than ever. Their songwriting has allowed them to remain relevant through the ever-changing musical landscape. There's nothing manufactured here.

"I think the band's success is in part to do with their refusal to accept that it is only the four of them against the world. Or that they deserve all the credit," says friend, actor and writer Simon Pegg. "They are very much the heart of a collective that includes so many people and their graciousness has served to endear them to everyone around them. I think it's partly why they are still making music. You can't burn out if nobody wants to set fire to you."

To their fans, Coldplay have always been likeable. They are not rock stars in the old mould, they do not court controversy: they are four best friends (five, if you include fifth member Phil) simply sharing their love of music with like-minded souls. There's no pretence, just passion. The group are comfortable simply being Coldplay – a word that only means one thing: Guy, Jonny, Will and Chris.

Life in Technicolor is a celebration of their first twenty years, as told by the people who were there. The band's next journey will be full of surprises they tell us, so now, on the eve of their anniversary, it feels like a good time to go back and remember just how far they've come.

DEBS WILD &
MALCOLM CROFT

Happy Birthday

I Love you debs
Love
CHRIS

Happy Birthday!
Lots of love, Guy xx

To Debs
You are the best!
love [illegible]

Dear Debs
Happy Birthday Lovely.
Lots of love, Willxxx

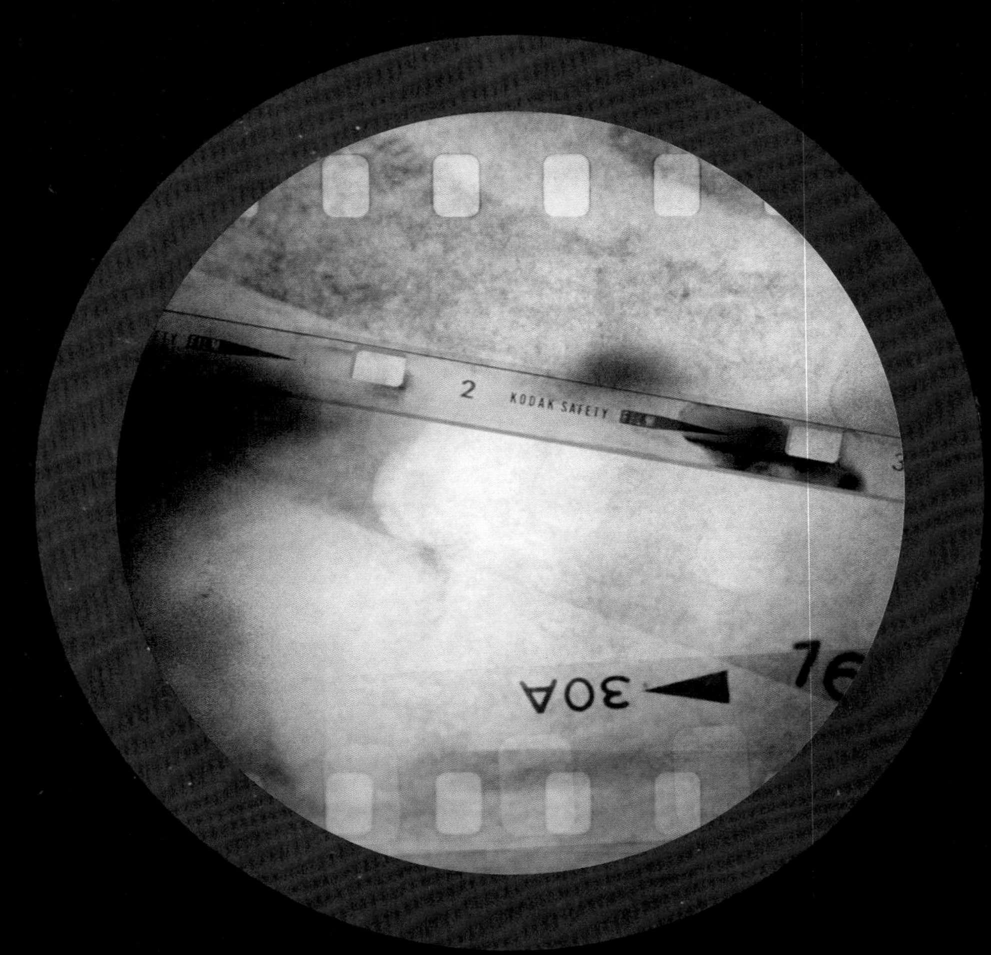
2
KODAK SAFETY

CHAPTER ZERO

CAN ANYBODY STOP THIS THING?

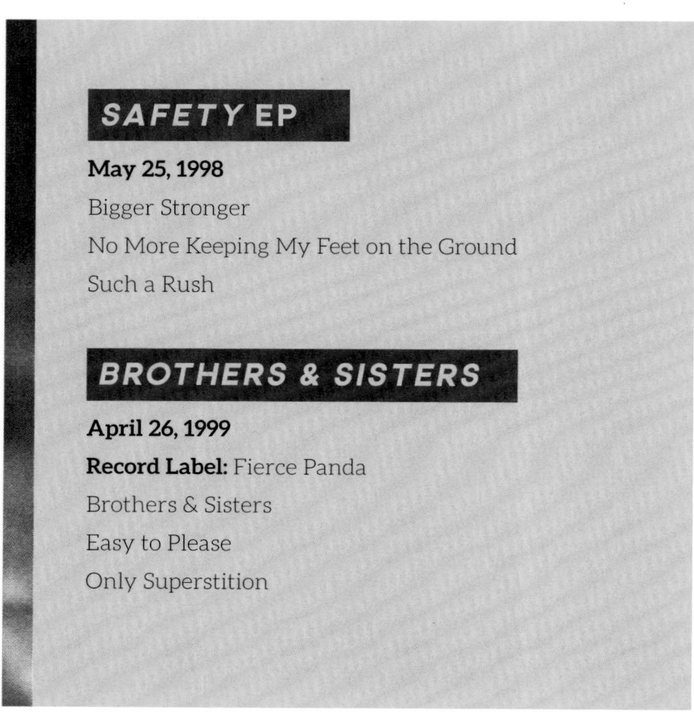

SAFETY EP

May 25, 1998

Bigger Stronger

No More Keeping My Feet on the Ground

Such a Rush

BROTHERS & SISTERS

April 26, 1999

Record Label: Fierce Panda

Brothers & Sisters

Easy to Please

Only Superstition

The 20-year story of Coldplay's ascension to global success is nothing short of a modern-day fairy tale. But, let's go back to the start, to September 1996, when four students met at University College of London (UCL) and became friends. This is where Big Fat Noises, Starfish and, finally Coldplay burst spectacularly to life.

ORIENTATION AND FORMATION

It was at UCL, at the heart of London's Euston area, where Coldplay first shook hands. Chris, who travelled to London from Devon "to try and meet Jonny, Guy and Will" had enrolled in Classical Studies. Will was reading Anthropology, Jonny Astronomy and Mathematics, and Guy began with Engineering before switching to Architecture, then ditching studies altogether when the band were beginning to gain record label interest.

The new friends began to hang out together in the student halls of residence, Ramsay Hall, along with Tim Crompton, Kris Foof and Mat Whitecross, the future director of the band's music videos and film. Chris and Will first met on a coach going to a hockey game, as they played for the university squad. The pair discovered they both played guitar, and soon after busked a selection of cover songs together in nearby Covent Garden.

Jonny, who had arrived at UCL from Mold, North Wales, recounts where he was the first time he met nearly all of his future bandmates: "I remember meeting Will for the first time and Chris too. Chris was running up and down the corridor with this really long curly mop [of hair]. I thought he was a bit

> "Chris was running up and down the corridor with this really long curly mop and I thought he was a bit mad."
>
> Jonny

RIGHT Chris, Jonny, Will and Guy photographed by their friend Kris Foof at the Wye College Ball in 1998.

OPPOSITE The rough artwork for Big Fat Noises' debut EP, *Panic*.

mad, a bit wacky. Will was very nice."

Their stay at Ramsay Hall in their first year of studies cemented the band's friendship, and provided a creative environment for the foursome. "One of the great things about being at university was the fact that there was time on our hands. You could structure your day around playing music," said Will. "And that's what we did."

"I remember in the first week or so people sitting around and playing music. I remember specifically jamming with Chris; there was amazing acoustics on this big stairwell and we just sat and played guitars. There was one jam where I was on the very bottom floor lying down at the bottom of the stairs, and Chris was on the fifth floor – sort of like a five-floor musical experience," said Will.

The four students used their time in Ramsay Hall to great effect. "We met each other because we were living in the halls of residence," Guy explained. "It was this block of rooms, everyone had their own room, and downstairs was the bar and the pool table, so everyone met in and around that area, and people would introduce themselves to each other. I can remember meeting them all over a pint." Over pool and talk of football, a keen friendship emerged. "What was quite important for us was we all knew each other for about a year before we played any music together, so we did have this friendship which was based purely on friendship rather than being musicians, which I think is key to why we've managed to remain so close for so long."

While a friendship was forming, not all connections between the foursome were instant. "Guy thought I was an idiot," recalled Chris. "But then he worked out I had this old Fender Rhodes in my room. It was only then Guy showed an interest."

The band started playing music together properly, and often, in their second year, using Jonny and Chris' flat at 268 Camden Road as a rehearsal space.

Out-of-town friends used to visit often, including Gavin Aherne, James "Pix" Pickering, John Hilton and Phil Harvey. There was a bus from Oxford and Phil was on it pretty regularly.

Phil's memories of meeting Chris' future bandmates were that Jonny was "wise, kind and gentle," Will was "strong and witty," and Guy was "handsome, mysterious and busy." "Chris was like a sun in a solar system," Phil said. "He just happened to get the right pieces of rock to come into his gravitational pull at the right time."

In 1997, still in their infancy, Jonny, Guy and Chris decided to make a demo but they were missing a band member – a drummer. At this point in time, the band were using the short-lived moniker Big Fat Noises.

DRUMS. HERE IT COMES

Will was the last of the four boys to join the band, and it was at his first rehearsal with Jonny, Chris and Guy that they all began to feel complete. But while Will had experience playing drums as a teenager, he wasn't a drummer. When Chris had mentioned they were on the lookout for someone who could play, Will suggested his roommate. "They came to my house, because I lived with a guy with a drum kit," Will recalled. "He was a good drummer, but he didn't turn up – he was at the pub or something – so I just said I'd give it a go." With one drum roll he was in the band. "It was the most lazy and technically inept fill-in that I could have possibly managed, but it's just about the chemistry. They recorded it, and it kind of went from there. I played on one song on that EP, and in the beginning of the next year they said, 'Do you want to be in the band?' I said, 'Absolutely.' I was desperate to be in a band. I would have played kazoo," explained Will. "I remember being in Jonny's bedroom and just remember listening to Chris play those quiet songs and thinking, 'These are really good.'"

The first "Coldplay" rehearsal was in January 1998. Jonny remembered it well, "In my bedroom in the flat Chris and I shared in Camden, the two of us and Guy waited for Will to turn up. We were worried, Will hadn't played the drums much for years. He strolled in nonchalantly and played with incredible confidence and grace. We were now complete."

A cut-out colour photograph of Will was added to the artwork of November 26, 1997, *Panic* EP, which featured Chris, Jonny and Guy in black and white. The band submitted a copy to the *NME* Unsigned Showcase event that Ultrasound went on to win.

BELOW Promo poster for the band's first gig as Starfish at The Laurel Tree in Camden, London, in 1998.

BELOW RIGHT The original setlist for Starfish's first gig at The Laurel Tree.

FIRST GIG

The four members toyed with the name Trombelese – which came from mishearing the lyrics "strong beliefs" in 'Freed From Desire' by Gala – before settling on a marginally better one for their first ever gig. Will had called the local promoter, whose card he had been given, asking for a slot and was offered one sooner than expected. A name was needed desperately, so they chose one in haste.

"Unfortunately, we were called Starfish," Will remembers. "There's not much to say about that, other than I'm glad we changed the name!"

That first gig was on January 16, 1998, in the upstairs room at The Laurel Tree pub, Camden, a stone's throw away from Chris and Jonny's flat. The name of the night was Jellybabies. Will and Jonny designed and printed 100 flyers in the university's computer room to ensure as many friends came as possible. Fellow Ramsay Hall resident, and friend, Kris Foof remembers the night. "It was a terrible venue with an awful sound. The crowd, largely friends, were packed like sardines downstairs, spilling over into the street outside, and there was a queue to get into the live room upstairs. The fashion of Starfish was questionable, but those six songs played that night sounded like songs you had already heard – full of depth, character and progressions."

Starfish's setlist contained the songs 'If All Else Fails', 'So Sad' (played twice), 'Panic', 'Vitamins', 'High Speed' and 'Ode to Deodorant'. The band got paid £40 each for this six-song set. "'Panic' [later re-invented as 'Don't Panic'] is a song that is very special to me," said Will, "because it was the first song I ever played with the band, even before they were called Starfish." The original version isn't immediately recognizable as the same song but bears some of the same lyrics.

Phil was at the gig too. "There were a lot of people there," he

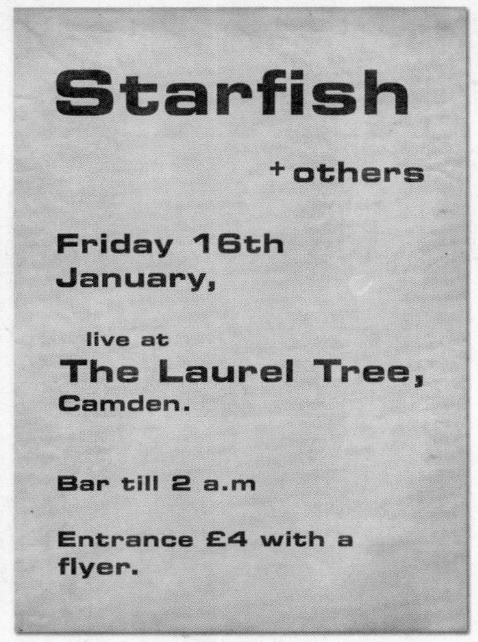

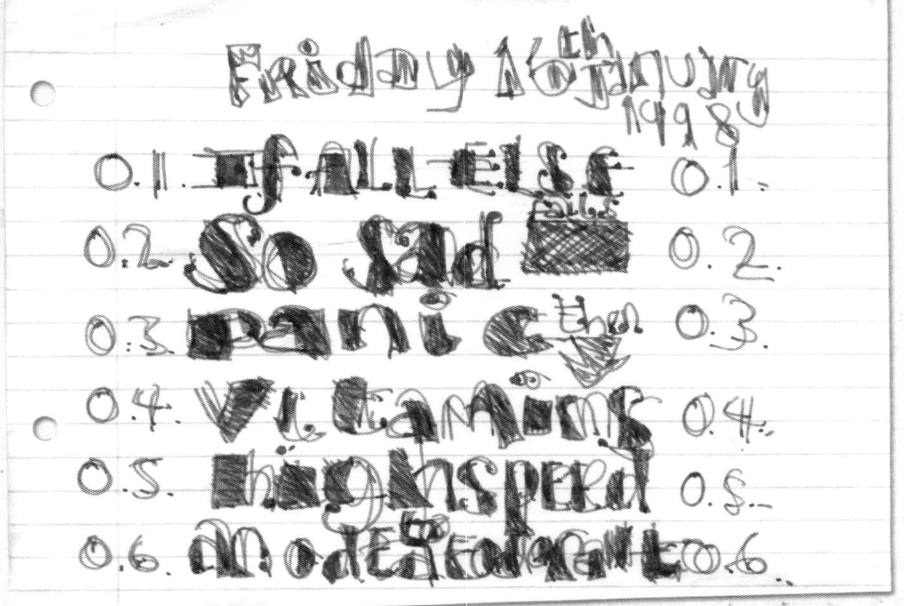

ABOVE Downstairs at The Laurel Tree in Camden before the band's first gig as Starfish.

BELOW Early gig, 1998.

THE COLDPLAY

The final name change came courtesy of close friend and fellow UCL student Tim Crompton. Tim was in the process of putting a band of old schoolmates together (later called Bettina Motive). While killing time waiting for a delayed removal van, he had considered the name after he found a copy of Philip Horky's book, *Child's Reflections, Cold Play*. Tim had a list of potential band names but Cold Play was quickly rejected; the future bandmates didn't like it, so they discarded it. Starfish were happy to pick it up.

RIGHT The cover of Philip Horky's book *Child's Reflections, Cold Play*.

said. "I went as a friend. I was at University and I remember it was on the same day as one of my exams. I walked out of the exam early to catch the bus to London, because I just wanted to see the gig. They were all very nervous. Chris' gawky front-man persona was cranked up to 11 then. He was very self-deprecating. I was obviously really impressed, because from that moment I could really see myself getting involved."

All four members shared the same passion for music and were determined to be the best, even during these formative days. Their ambition saw them draw up a band plan, which they stuck to a wall in Jonny and Chris' flat. "We were very calculated about how we were going to do this thing," recalls Guy. "We had this

BELOW Early rehearsal: Guy and Chris at 268 Camden Road.

ridiculously pompous list of 1 to 10 of what we were going to do and number 10 was 'get record deal'. We did systematically go through that list and tick things off."

In 2005, Jonny referred back to the list, "We planned to get signed within five gigs – we thought that's how long it would take us. It took ten, I think. We didn't ever get frustrated," he said, not revealing whether they naively believed it was going to be that simple or just that they had such staunch self-belief.

Despite taking more than double the number of gigs to attain their record deal – an impressive feat considering how difficult it is to 'break into' the music industry – their dedication from the beginning was unflinching.

"We were determined to do it from the start," said Jonny, "and from the moment I met Chris I really did think that we could go all the way."

The newly named Coldplay rehearsed almost every night. "We used to play in bathrooms, the basement, even in the park," said Chris. "Anywhere we could find to play. We occasionally played in the lift. Then we moved house and our ambition became enormous."

The sofa in the Camden flat where they rehearsed as students was so old that the springs were poking through. Will used to sit on that sofa to play drums. Every time he stood up, his trousers got caught on the broken springs and tore.

As the band progressed around the local music scene, they faced an issue with a promoter. It made sense that the group would turn to Phil for advice.

"At the same time that I was boring myself stupid studying Latin and Greek up at Oxford," Phil said, "I used to work a couple of nights a week in the local nightclubs, setting up and promoting student nights. It was pretty basic stuff, but it gave me a vague idea of what it is to hire a venue, book a band and try and make a little money."

"One day Chris was telling me about how one of the local Camden promoters had a bit of a vice-like grip on the band and wasn't coughing up any money," Phil said. "So, I suggested the band put on their own event. We booked a local venue called Dingwalls and printed up thousands of flyers. I think in the end we got about 400 people in there, which was a big deal. As I remember, it was the money from that night which allowed me to pay back my Dad and my Oxford room-mate who had lent me the funds to get the *Safety* EP made. We sold the first 50 copies that night, so all in all I suppose that was the time that I officially became manager". The disgruntled promoter went on to say the band would never play Camden again.

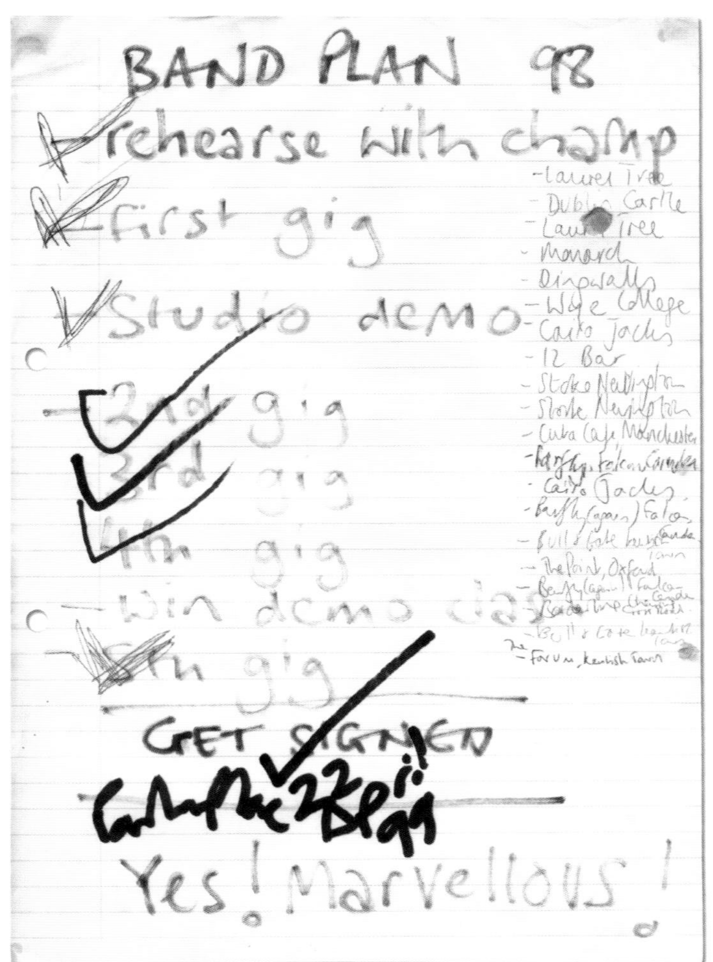

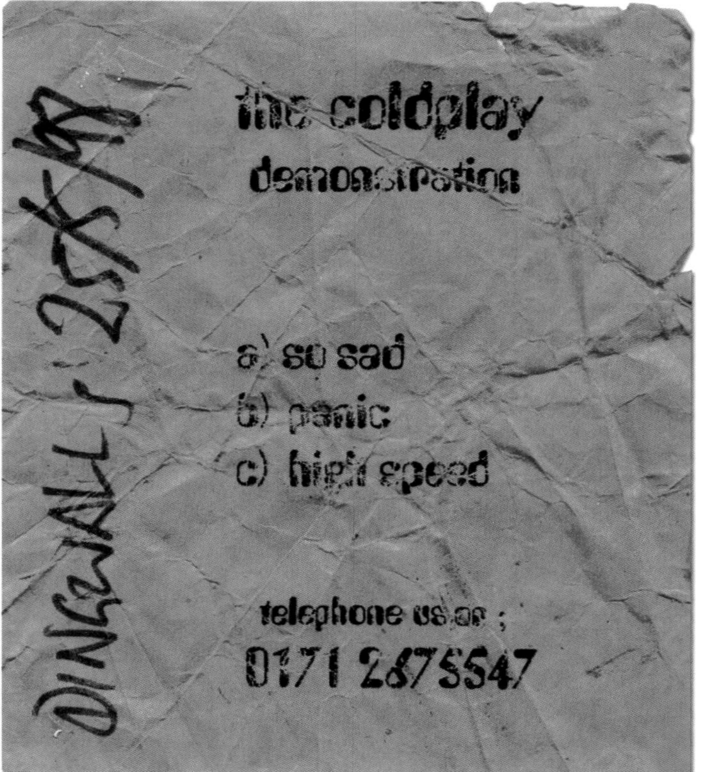

LEFT Chris' handwritten band plan that was pinned to a wall at 268 Camden Road.

BELOW An early demo tracklisting.

THE SAFETY EP

The *Safety* EP was recorded by Nikki Rosetti at Sync City Studios, in Tottenham, over two days: February 1 and 2, 1998. The studio cost £1,500 for the recording, pressing and artwork (a photo of Chris taken by art student, John Hilton, a school friend of Tim Crompton's).

Rosetti met the band some time before the session to discuss what they wanted to achieve. They had a plan to record an ambitious number of tracks. As Rosetti recalled: "I remember a certain urgency toward the end of the session, especially from Chris who wanted to get as much as possible recorded."

A version of 'Vitamins' with just Chris on vocals and acoustic guitar emerged from the end of the first day's session, taking the final total to eight tracks over two days. "We could probably have done just one take of each song," Rosetti said. "They were that ready."

Phil remembers very distinctly hearing their first demo for the first time. "Getting back on a Sunday evening and sitting with Chris and Jonny in their flat listening to the unmixed music. The last track 'Such a Rush' ended and I turned to them and said something ridiculous like 'I could go into any record company in London with this tape and get us whatever we wanted.' I hardly knew what a record company was, let alone what we actually might want from one, but it was the right sentiment. I was 100 per cent into the music, which was enough for me to stumble through."

When the band played London's Dublin Castle on Sunday February 22, 1998, Coldplay were on last and due to borrow the drum kit from the middle-billed band, who had their set cut short because they overran. In protest they left with their kit, leaving Will with only a snare and hi-hat to play. He improvised and the gig went ahead with Dan Green, the front-of-house engineer, on sound duties. They would cross paths again some time later.

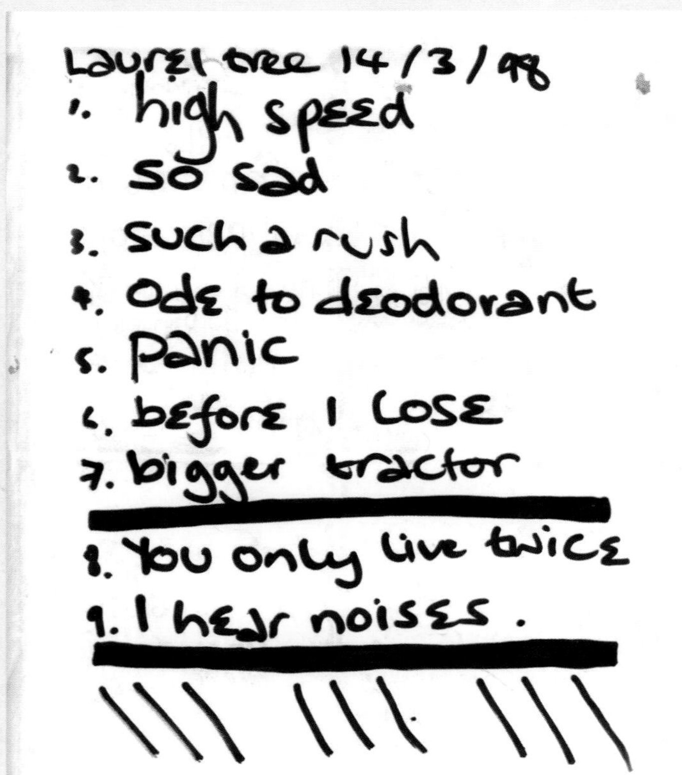

ABOVE Flyer for the band's gig at The Dublin Castle, February 22, 1998.

LEFT Thae setlist for their second gig at The Laurel Tree in 1998.

RIGHT Front and back of the *Safety* EP cover. The photograph was taken by friend John Hilton.

Keane's songwriter and keyboard player Tim Rice-Oxley, a friend of the group and fellow UCL student, saw Coldplay's second gig at The Laurel Tree on March 14, just two months after their debut appearance. "They were incredibly slick and the songs already seemed very honed and well-written," he said. Even the tongue-in-cheek cover of 'You Only Live Twice'... Chris already seemed to know just how to pitch everything."

On Tuesday May 19, 1998, Phil took delivery of a box of 500 copies of the *Safety* EP (now worth more per copy than it cost to produce). Phil sold the first copy to his Oxford flatmate for £3, the bulk were distributed to family, friends and a select few music industry types, and the rest sold at their gigs. "350 copies

Coldplay

SAFETY e.p.

Coldplay

SAFETY

BIGGER STRONGER
NO MORE KEEPING MY FEET ON THE GROUND
SUCH A RUSH

Coldplay

BIGGER STRONGER
NO MORE KEEPING MY FEET ON THE GROUND
SUCH A RUSH

All songs written by Coldplay
Produced by Coldplay & Nikki Rosetti
Engineered by Nikki Rosetti
Recorded at Sync City Studios
Management: Phil Harvey
Photography by John Hilton
Sleeve design by Kut & Payste Studios, London

© Coldplay 1998
℗ Coldplay 1998
For further information on Coldplay, contact Phil on 0777 55 24 245 or 0171 267 5547

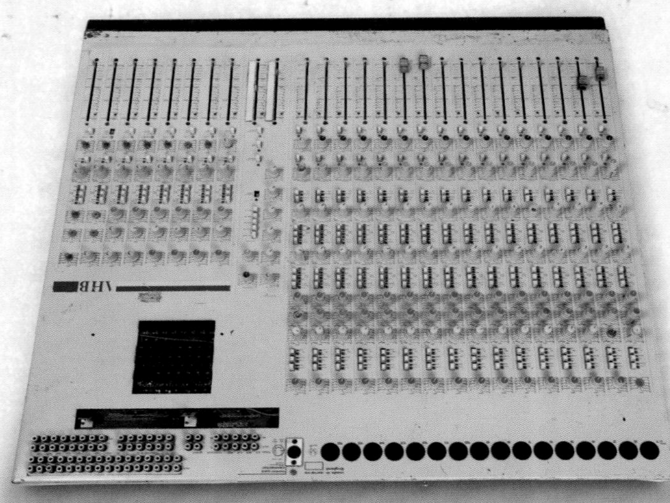

went to various music people, probably only 150 went on the open market," Phil said.

To give himself a sense of validation Phil was reading the industry trade paper *Music Week* – "If I'm reading *Music Week*, I must be a proper music manager," he said.

Phil began cold-calling A&R people on a regular basis. He had a list of names written in a book. The list was split into three segments based on a label's roster.

Despite this organization, Phil wasn't getting anywhere with the record companies. When he called, either people hadn't listened to it – or worse, they had and didn't like it.

More gigs were lined up throughout the summer of 1998 including two in July with Cherry Keen / Cherry Keane (later, simply called Keane). Their manager, Adam Tudhope, remembers the summer gigs. "The Guttridge's Yard shows were great. In my pretentiousness I had named the two-day festival 'Okaziya', which is a word I nabbed from a Nabokov short story. Keane headlined one night with Coldplay as support, and we switched the other. The audience was small but passionate."

Tim Rice-Oxley recalls the gigs: "Chris somewhat generously claimed that we upstaged them on the first night. So, on the second night, he decided to steal the show by taking his trousers off mid-performance to reveal some excellent height-of-Britpop Union Jack boxer shorts."

At one early Keane gig at the Dublin Castle, Camden, the band were ready to go on stage and the room was empty. Chris arrived and sat in the middle of the floor on his own, carrying a small rucksack. "Chris was really sweet like that," said Rice-Oxley. "He came to lots of our early gigs, and also got us on the bill with them at the 12 Bar Club. He was always massively supportive and fiercely competitive – qualities which have served him and the band well, I would say."

In those early days, while in a pub on Tottenham Court Road, Chris asked Rice-Oxley if he was interested in joining the band as keyboard player.

"I said I would," responded Rice-Oxley. "But when we discussed it again a couple of weeks later he said that the rest of the band

ABOVE LEFT The mixing desk that was used during the recording of the *Safety* EP.

BELOW LEFT Photograph from one of the band's first performances as Coldplay: Guttridge's Yard.

BELOW Flyer for Coldplay and Cherry Keane (later to become Keane).

MHP
presents...
Okaziya
Guttridge's Yard
Stoke Newington Church Street
Evenings of Music and Drama
Saturday 25 July
Cherry Keane
Coldplay
Lewd
8.00 - 9.30pm
Sunday 26 July
Cherry Keane
Coldplay
8.00 - 9.30pm
Tuesday 28 July
Shola and Ellen
8.00 - 9.30pm
Wednesday 29 July
Elektra's Brother
8.00 - 9.30pm
Thursday 30 July
Elektra's Brother
8.00 - 9.30pm
ALL TICKETS £3.50
Available on the door from 7.30pm
Bar open until 10pm. Ask the Barman for one of his famous Sea Breezes.
A call for time will be made 5 minutes before each show in The FOX REFORMED next door.

ABOVE/BELOW John Hilton's shots of Jonny and Chris at the Camden Road flat where they lived and rehearsed.

ABOVE Early performance, circa 1998.

LEFT Jonny sets up his guitar pedals for an early London gig, circa 1998.

BELOW 1998 flyer for a gig at the 12 Bar Club in London.

weren't keen on adding a member, so the idea had been shelved. I was disappointed. So, the story that I refused to abandon Keane and join Coldplay is sadly untrue! Though I only have myself to blame for mentioning it in the first place in an interview!"

IN THE CITY

While Chris and Jonny were working as part-time cleaners, the *Safety* EP really served its purpose, earning them a slot at Manchester's In The City (ITC) music industry convention. Phil said: "I remember our absolute astonishment when we got accepted, we couldn't believe it. It's a good job we did because by that point I was beginning to doubt myself. I'd been managing them for four months and felt I hadn't made any progress in terms of getting A&R people to our shows. It was a huge relief when ITC came through."

This annual event involved the A&R fraternity running around trying to see 54 unsigned bands over three nights in a select six venues across the city. Previous years had seen Placebo and Kula Shaker come to the industry's attention.

Chris recalls the events of September 14, 1998, the day Coldplay performed. "There were 50 bands on the bill and Muse were number one and Elbow were number two. Coldplay were number 50. I'm not joking, we were the last band added."

While it's true Coldplay were submitted quite late into the selection process and the industry were already aware of both Muse and Elbow, ITC was a level playing field and no band were billed higher than others.

The day of their performance, the band left London for Manchester but didn't get off to the best start because Jonny had left his guitar pedals behind. Luckily, a lorry driver friend of Chris' mum transported them as far as he could, with Phil and Kris Foof making the 140-mile round-trip to collect them from him. It was also to be the first time the band stayed in a hotel, sharing one room. This was a big deal for them.

It was a miserable evening. The Coldplay (Phil had added "The" because he preferred it) took to the stage at 8.15 p.m. at The Cuba Cafe in the hipster northern quarter of the city.

For The Coldplay show, Chris wore cords and a wool tank top over a t-shirt. "I normally wear a jumper for the first song so I can take it off," he said. "It's very important to take off a piece of clothing at a gig."

Chris was also sporting a huge mop of curly hair and wearing mouth braces. They all looked like the students they were. "Chris had asked me to tune a few guitars for him that night," Kris Foof said. "This was always the worst job, as he had so many different tunings. Myself and Phil were outside trying to muster up some people, but they played to literally ten people that night. I remember the mood was low in the hotel room after that show."

"We were so excited; we thought this gig would change our lives," said Phil "And then only four people turned up."

Little did the band know that there was one person in

LEFT John Hilton's contact sheet of Chris and Jonny at the Barfly, London, 1998.

BELOW In The City listing in A&R live guide for delegates.

66 MONDAY 14TH SEPT

IN THE CITY LIVE UNSIGNED

Cuba Cafe
Free admission

8.15pm

The Coldplay √

Fresh from holidays in Devon, where they've been writing, recording and boogie-boarding in readiness for this showcase. The foursome met at UCL last January - so besides being a brand new band they're possibly brainy too! Supported bands such as Space during their short life. Now ready to take years out to realise their pop destinies.

Contact: Chris Martin

" Torvill & Dean. Laurel & Hardy. These are some of life's great partnerships. One wouldn't function without the other. In that sense I think we're very lucky to have Phil Harvey, erstwhile school friend of mine, to be our manager. He's like a hosepipe when your flowers are wilting. He's like an oven when your cake's not baked. He's the magic special thing. **"**

Chris

attendance that night who began to fiercely champion the band almost immediately they stepped out on stage. Native northerner Debs Wild, an A&R scout, was the one in ten people present who loved what she heard – a mighty potential.

"The Coldplay didn't have an industry buzz, so weren't on my radar, which made them a must-see band for me. I remember having a wow feeling and knowing this was special. They had me rooted to the spot. When they finished their set, I had to get to the next gig, so I darted for the door. Their manager had left business cards pinned to the notice board by the exit. I grabbed one: 'Phil Harvey, Überbitch Promotions'. I didn't use it until I was back in London but I wanted to call him right there and then."

"If you ask me the precise moment of which I knew that things were going to work out and we were going to get a record deal, and this was going to be our life, it was two days after ITC," recalled Phil. "I slept in the corridor of Jonny and Chris' flat in a sleeping bag. It was about midday because we'd been up all night and Debs called me and woke me up. I just couldn't believe it. That was the moment when we stepped through a portal into another dimension," Phil said. "That was the first domino to fall. It was very exciting... we owe Debs everything. Without her, no Coldplay," he added, recalling the moment the band's fortunes changed.

For a second opinion on her newest discovery, Wild passed a copy of the *Safety* EP to one of her closest friends, Caroline Elleray, who worked at BMG [now Universal] Publishing.

"I didn't listen to it at first," said Elleray. "Debs called, chasing me. When I did, I was knocked out. The butterflies in my stomach, prickly eyes and my throat went weird. I'm generally hopeless at recalling events in sequence, but there's one little

Dear Debs,

Thanks very much for your kind words and inquiry into THE COLDPLAY. Please find enclosed a copy of the band's first recording, the SAFETY E.P. First 'proper' single will be out in about 5 weeks' time on Treasure Island Records.

If you want to come and see us playing live, check out Camden Barfly (Tues. 13 Oct. 9.45) + Cairo Jacks, Beak St, Soho (Thurs. 12 Nov). Just give me a ring beforehand.

I'm looking forward already to sending you the next CD!

Yours,

PHIL HARVEY.

THE JERICHO CAFÉ
112 WALTON STREET
JERICHO
OXFORD OX2 6AJ

Design by HETTY HAXWORTH

Abacus (Colour Printers) Ltd., Cumbria. (01229) 885361

P.S. fantastic Super Foots on the way!

RIGHT Postcard sent from Phil Harvey to Debs Wild with the *Safety* EP after In The City.

BELOW Phil's business card – as left at the Cuba Café, In The City.

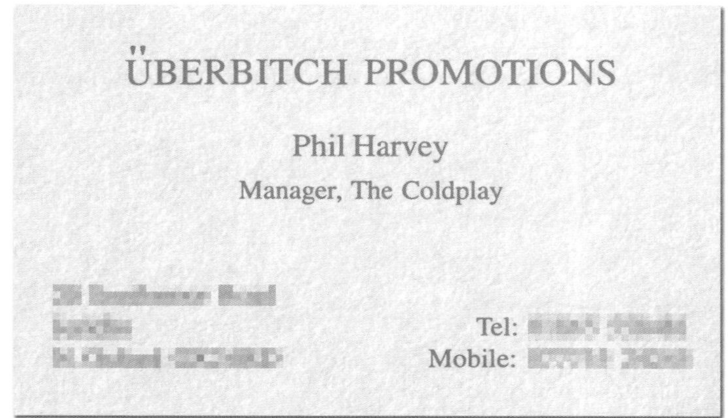

chunk of my personal history during which time I can recall scenes very clearly and visualize moments like snapshots in time, or stills from a film... Maybe it's because that part of my life suddenly had the perfect soundtrack."

The band went back in to Sync Studios with Nikki Rosetti and recorded another two track demo, containing the songs 'Brothers & Sisters' and 'Ode to Deodorant' – the band didn't think much of the latter. "A funky little number with a limited lifespan," according to Guy. Chris simply calls it "shit".

CAIRO JACKS

With the group progressing, it was decided that the band needed legal representation. Wild recommended lawyer Gavin Maude of Russells – who remains the band's counsel to this day. Initially he met Phil "in Bartok, in Camden, on a Saturday morning," said Maude. "I had just had train track braces fitted and was super self-conscious. Phil said the singer had just had his braces removed, so we would have something in common. He gave me a copy of the *Safety* EP and I wrote his mobile number on it. I still have it."

Maude continues: "The band then came to see me and instructed me shortly afterwards. I said that an easy next step was if we could get [independent record label] Fierce Panda, a client of mine, to release a single that would guarantee the press and radio plugging that was missing on the *Safety* EP. I wasn't sure if Fierce Panda would go for the music, as it wasn't really indie enough, but I said I would ask. To my surprise Simon Williams, the label's co-founder, said yes."

THE TALENT SCOUT
BEST OF UNSIGNED - 5 BANDS SHOWCASE PRESENTS
COLDPLAY
THURSDAY 2ND JULY
ON STAGE AT 8.45PM
THE BASEMENT OF CAIRO JACKS, 10 BEAK STREET, LONDON W1
(NEAREST TUBE OXFORD CIRCUS, 3RD LEFT TURN OFF REGENT STREET)
£5 ON DOOR. £4.00 WITH THIS FLYER. DOORS OPEN 7.30PM. BANDS ON 8-12.
DJ + BAR 'TIL 3AM

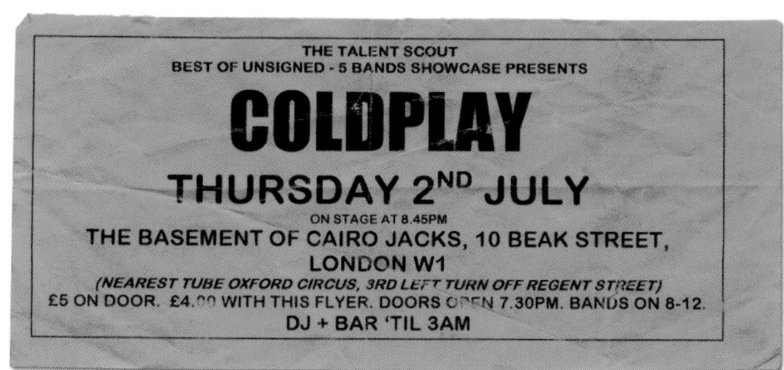

RIGHT Flyer for Coldplay's concert at Cairo Jacks, London, 1998.

BELOW Chris, Jonny and Guy, with Kris Foof at the Wye College Ball, 1998.

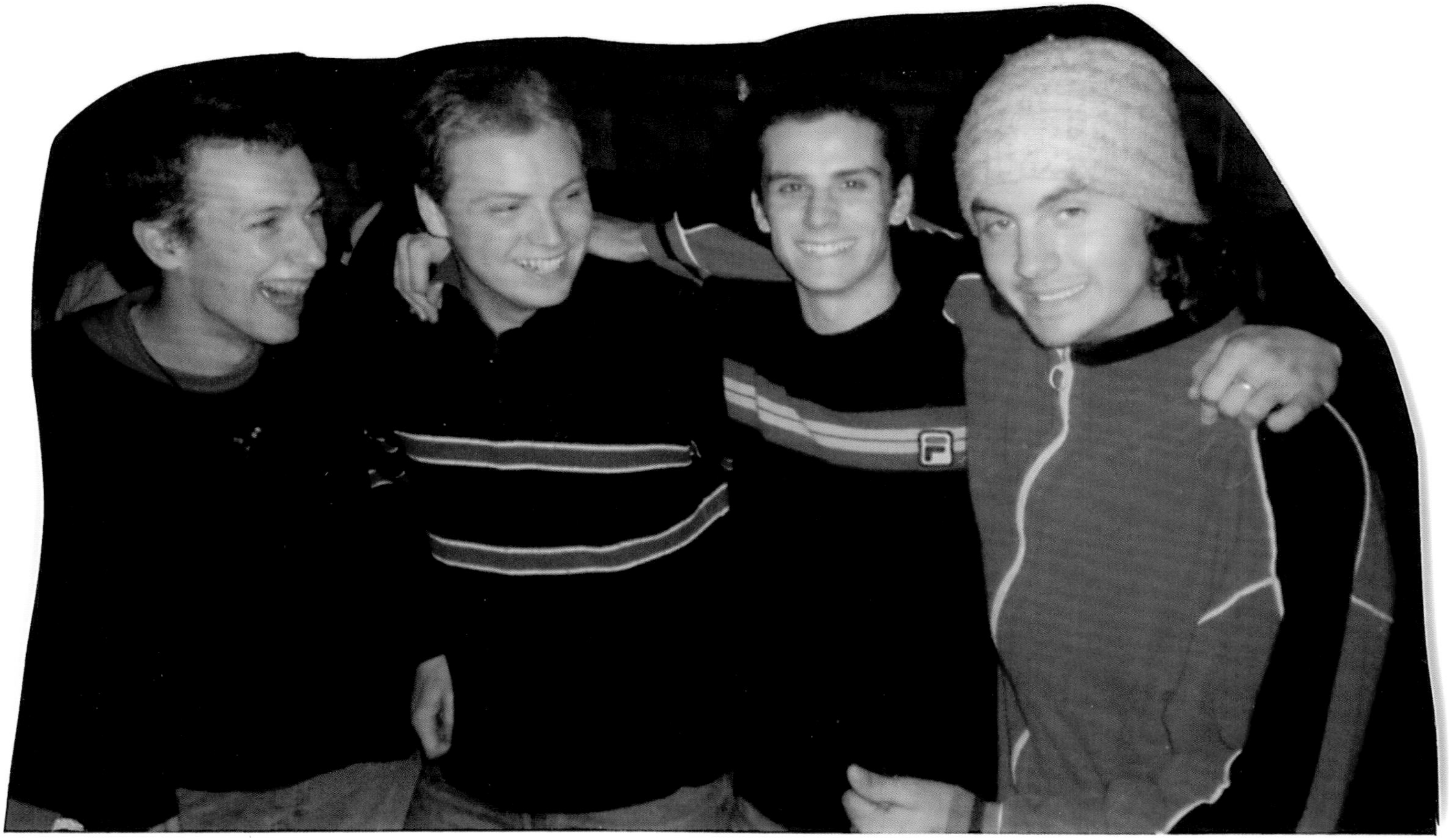

BELOW AND RIGHT Friend and art student John Hilton photographed the band at many of their early gigs in London. The images formed part of his portfolio and led to him being offered a few design jobs.

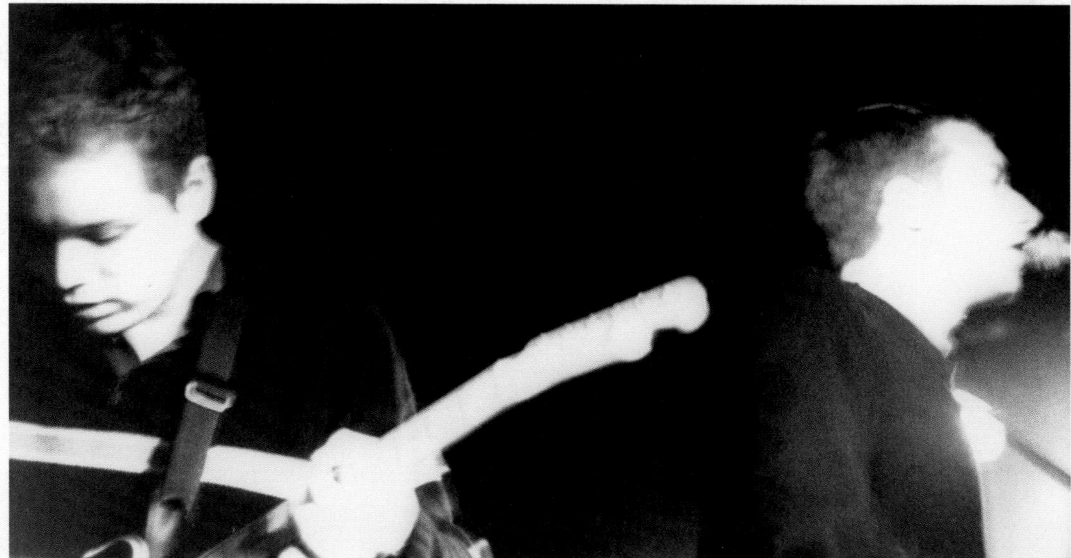

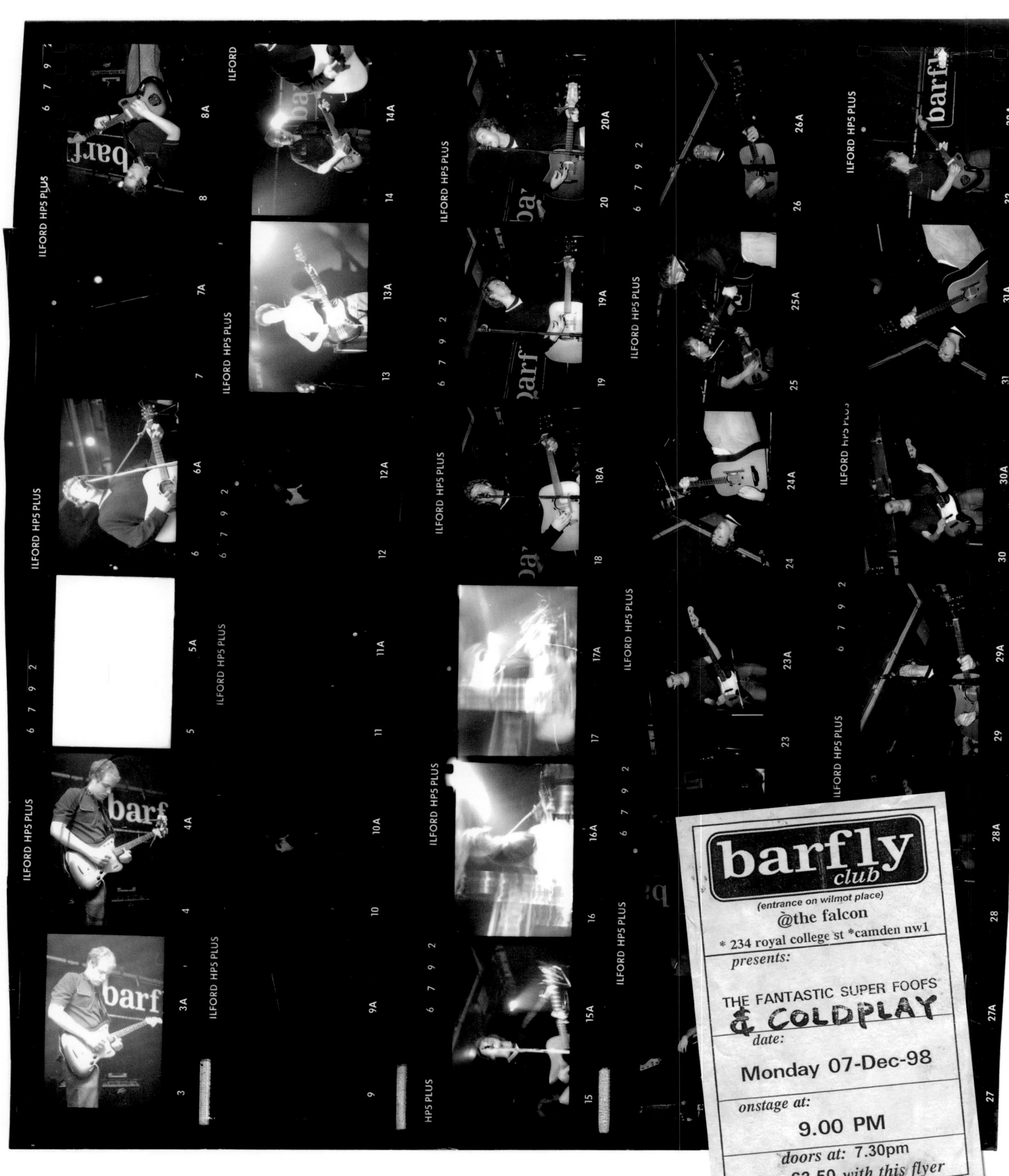
barfly
club
(entrance on wilmot place)
@the falcon
* 234 royal college st *camden nw1
presents:
THE FANTASTIC SUPER FOOFS
& COLDPLAY
date:
Monday 07-Dec-98
onstage at:
9.00 PM
doors at: 7.30pm
£3.50 with this flyer

ronnie scott's Songwriters Festival
24 July - 6 August
www.go2birmingham.co.uk/songfest/
24:7 £5 JAVA SUMATRA + the FOLD + SOULER RHYTHM
25:7 £5 TWIST (UNPLUGGED) + the UNSPEAKABLE TURKS + DAN MOULE
26:7 £10 THE MAGNETIC FIELDS + MATTHEW JAY + JONT
27:7 £7 THE UNBELIEVABLE TRUTH + DAVID POE + CATHERINE TRAN
28:7 £8 BABYBIRD + guests + JACK RUBINACCI
29:7 £15.50 MICHELLE SHOCKED + JO HAMILTON
30:7 £6 COLDPLAY + CARINA ROUND + MICK HART
31:7 £7 MOJAVE 3 + KATHRYN WILLIAMS
1:8 £10 RON SEXSMITH + ANNA EGE + BOOLEY
2:8 £5 NEW ELECTRICS + the ANSWER + SCOTT (BOOHAI)
3:8 £5 COUSTEAU + BEN HUDSON + MUDSKIPPER
4:8 £10 MARK EITZEL + CARINA ROUND + TOM McRAE
5:8 £11 IAN McNABB + MUNDY + BUICK 6
6:8 £6 THE CROCKETTS (UNPLUGGED) + SALT FLAT + LIAM O'CONNELL
BOOKINGS/ENQUIRIES ronnie scott's : 0121-643 4525
FESTIVAL ORGANISERS:
Ticket Details Overleaf

While Phil was working hard behind the scenes, Coldplay focused their energies on the next gig – the Barfly at Camden's Falcon pub, one of London's venues where many up-and-coming bands cut their teeth.

On October 12, 1998, Muse made their first appearance at the Barfly, and Coldplay debuted the following night. "When I think of the humble beginnings of these bands with diverse styles and trajectories that would go on to colour the musical palette of so many people," recalled Be Rozzo, co-founder of the Barfly. "This band seemed to have amassed their own momentum without the usual so-called 'industry buzz'."

Almost from the off, Coldplay were every promoter's dream booking, turning up to gigs with an army of fans. On Thursday November 12, 1998, Coldplay played the bizarre Egyptian-themed venue Cairo Jacks, Soho, for a second time. As expected, their fans turned up in droves. And, this time, so did some of the music industry.

Prior to the gig, Jonny, Chris, Will and Guy met up with Maude to talk shop. "The first recording offer the band received was November 10, 1998, from TVT. It was a six-figure advance inclusive of costs, so it was a pretty big deal for a bunch of final year students living in squalor in Camden. Chris had bought a load of plastic toys to the meeting, explaining that he intended to give them out as free gifts to fans [friends from college] at the Cairo Jacks gig," said Maude.

"We bought a train set and we were going to give that out, but Jonny put a stop to it because it cost £12!" Chris said.

Maude advised the band that if they believed in themselves they should hang on for a better deal than the TVT offer, despite it being a lot of money, and the only offer to date.

Debs Wild and Caroline Elleray were in attendance at Cairo Jacks along with Dan Keeling who, at the time, was Parlophone's A&R scout. As Chris was handing out Curly Wurlys onstage, Keeling told Maude that he was leaving, as it was "too studenty". He thought the band were "OK" and that Chris had stage presence – despite his frequent apologizing – but as far as the songs were concerned, Keeling thought they had a lot of work to do.

"Throughout the whole process they kept asking 'what about Parlophone?' because it was the home of Radiohead and the Beatles," Maude recalled. "In the end I said: You need to forget about Parlophone, they aren't coming to the party."

From a song publishing perspective, BMG general manager Ian Ramage supported Elleray's decision to pursue the band. "Publishing has got a real advantage over records in that regard," said Ramage. "It's easier to be completely clear it's about a talent for writing songs and a camaraderie of spirit in conveying them. If that's not there, you can't fix it."

NO MORE KEEPING FEET ON THE GROUND

Simon Williams was an *NME* journalist who spent much of 1998 trying to secure a worldwide deal for his independent label, Fierce Panda. "At Gavin's invitation I went to see Coldplay at Camden's Falcon towards the end of 1998," Williams said. "Once was all I needed." He knew after just two songs that he wanted to put their single out.

Coldplay returned to play at the Falcon's Barfly night on December 7, 1998, this time with even more representatives of the music industry in tow.

"The story goes like this..." begins Radio 1 DJ Steve Lamacq, "Simon from Fierce Panda, who's my best mate, says, 'Have you heard Coldplay?' 'No,' I say. 'Are they any good?' Simon says they're worth going to see. So, I grab my friend Mark, romp up to the Falcon and honestly, this doesn't happen very often, we stand there, with our jaws hitting the floor as Coldplay play to 40 people, many of whom I suspect are their mates because they appear to know all the words to the songs, and at the end of the set we just gawp at each other. Finally, Mark says

OPPOSITE John Hilton's contact sheet of photos from the Barfly gig alongside an original flyer for the same venue, 1998.

ABOVE Flyer for a show at Ronnie Scott's in Birmingham.

something like 'Excuse me if I'm wrong, but are they the best thing I've seen in months...' I went into work the next day and said we should get them on."

Lamacq's *Evening Session* on January 3, 1999, was the first ever to feature an unsigned band and provided the national exposure Coldplay (and Phil) had been yearning for. Big things were about to happen.

The band were overjoyed to have such an influential figure in their corner playing their music. "I love Lamacq," Chris said. "He's a lovely bastard, that bloke. I think it's so nice to have a few people who were prepared to like something that hasn't got any hype yet."

NME ended 1998 with its 'Ones To Watch' feature for 1999. Among the hotly tipped acts were Coldplay. It's a moment Chris Martin will never forget. "I was in the bathroom at my mum and dad's house, Christmas 1998. I opened the *NME* and there was a page that said new bands for 1999, I was like, maybe I'll know some of these bands through In The City. Muse, Elbow, Bellatrix, Gay Dad... COLDPLAY! I was like, what? I nearly fainted thinking, 'Fucking hell, this really might happen'. That moment was huge and for that I'm forever indebted to Simon Williams."

The piece read: "Mesmerizing foursome in the big-hearted Jeff Buckley mould. Already masters of both the epic chorus and the insular weep-out, they are blessed with many fine virtues, notably the fact that their singer actually demonstrates a sense of humour onstage. 'Bigger Stronger' was their no-key debut release last year on their own label. Expect copies of it to be worth a couple of heavy mortgages come next Christmas."

The dominoes kept on falling. "With each thing that happened it was a sense of disbelief almost," Phil recalls, "We were very wide-eyed and innocent, we had a never ending sense of wonder."

BROTHERS AND SISTERS UNITE

Williams and Andy Macleod, his fellow Club Fandango promoter and business partner, booked the band to play at one of their Pandemonium club nights.

"By the time that gig came around, you could tell there was something in the air," says Macleod of the band's first performance at the Bull & Gate pub, Camden.

Mel Brown, of Impressive PR, was there too. "I had been tipped off about the band," she said. "It was very memorable. Chris tossed Curly Wurlys into the audience. I remember 'Shiver' being a stand out track."

Brown had tipped off her friend, and live booking agent, Steve Strange. He too was blown away. "I thought they were great. You could see all the hallmarks of what they became quite quickly at that early stage. Some of those early songs were just tremendous."

Fierce Panda was the ideal first playground for Coldplay because it let bands decide which songs to release. "All we can do is encourage bands to make sure they choose one of their best," said Williams. "I think if you'd asked me what song I would've really wanted out of all those early demos, I would've said 'Shiver', but really you could have picked anything out of that set back then".

In February 1999, three tracks were recorded on a standard Fierce Panda budget of £400–500 at Station Studios, north London. Engineer Mike Beever had worked a couple of sessions for Fierce Panda, and the label and studio had built up a good relationship.

"When the brief came in for Coldplay, all I was told was this band are going to be big, so do a great job!" Beever said. "It was day two's duty to usher in the recording. First up, 'Brothers & Sisters', followed by 'Only Superstition', and as they had time left, Chris suggested swiftly putting down another track, 'Easy to Please'. To add an ambient element, we set up two microphones at the doorway to the studio to capture the sound of the traffic driving past," explains Beever. "We recorded 'Easy to Please' in one take and managed to capture the studio phone, which just added to the atmosphere. We completed the music by adding the piano. I asked Chris to record his vocals in a corridor with a large cardboard box dangling over his head to try and create an amazing vocal sound."

After completing all three songs on the third day, they headed downtown to see a gig. On the Tube, listening to the tracks on a Walkman, "Chris suggested that we may need to look at remixing, as some levels weren't right. Even at that young age he knew what he wanted," said Beever.

By now, and with the release of 'Brothers & Sisters', every label

RIGHT Artwork for *Brothers & Sisters* EP, released on Fierce Panda records.

OPPOSITE Original artwork designed by John Hilton used to create the *Brothers & Sisters EP* cover. This piece was discovered by a private collector.

Coldplay
Brothers & Sisters

BROTHERS
WAITING
BIGGER STRONGER
CAREFUL

ODE
SHIVER

LEFT Setlist from an early show, circa 1998.

BELOW Letter sent to Debs with demo of 'Brothers & Sisters' and 'Ode to Deodorant', 1998.

BELOW LEFT Early band notes by Chris, including brief member biographies.

RIGHT, CLOCKWISE FROM TOP LEFT London Barfly's October 1998 schedule featuring new bands Muse and Coldplay playing consecutive nights; Artist access pass from The Borderline; Show times for Kentish Town Forum supporting Catatonia, April 13, 1999; The racecard from the BMG Publishing deal celebrations.

18th March. - B+G

The [illegible] to do [illegible]

from the [illegible] 2 ↓ [illegible]

Guy Berryman, 20, brown, Canterbury
Will Champion, 20, blonde, Southampton
Jon Buckland, 21, brown, Mold, N. Wales
Chris A.J. Martin 21, blonde, Devon

Parking at [illegible] Dec 7th

In The City

Hello Debs ?

hope you're very well and new house is delightful. This is new COLDPLAY EP thing which I think you should have a good listen to!

All love.

PHIL

X.

OCTOBER 98

velaria release date of single ..

			1 Replicant Saints / The Samaritans / Monotonic	2 Chi / Pollen 8 / Sugarfree	3 Raindog / the forgotten sons / Mother freedom
5 Coloursound / Velouria / Bouleface	6 Crest / Melatone	7 Sideshow Bob / Feel / Dum Dums	8 NME On Night / Monsoon Bassoon / Crashland / The Junket	9 Guess / Caffeine / Sound Scandal	10 Airfix / Poodlefaker / Coaster
12 Muse / Platform	13 The Cold Play / Ultra Montanes / W.O.M.O.	14 Radar / Panic Button	15 Grifter / Astral / Bootham	16 River / Motorlife Co / Reviver Gene	17 Milltown Brothers / 100+70% / Baptiste / Thermonic
19 Blue Dog Singles / Otis, Ed & Ben / Cookie / Serum	20 17 Stitches / Guiterman / Punch Puppet	21 Dr Martens / Moke / Astronaut / Airborne	22 Brian Jones / Spearmint / Astrid	23 Cartoon / Murry The Hump / Relish	24 Exploding Dragonflies / Riser / April
26 Mucho Macho	27 Vive Finito	28 Salad	29 Kerrang / King Prawn	30 Jolt 70%	31 Snipes

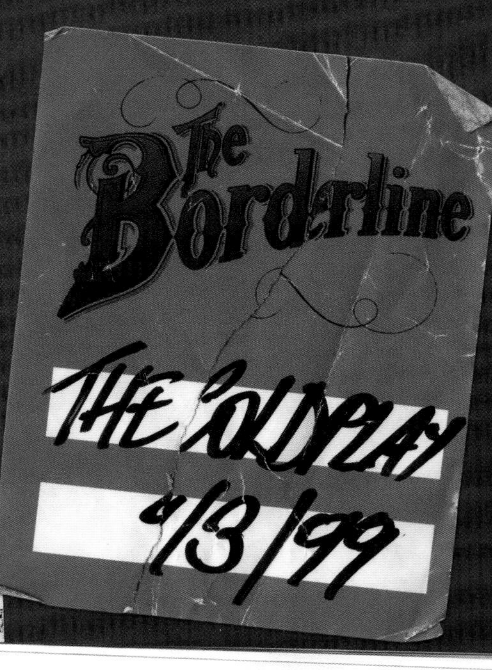

Show Times

Venue LONDON

Doors 7.00

COLD PLAY 8.20 - 8.50

CATATONIA 9.20 - ?

STEVE LAMACQ 10.40 APPROX

Curfew 12.00

Wimbledon Stadium

Featuring Tonight . . . 2nd Trial Stakes Of The

DELL NASH PUPPY DERBY

And The Final Of

THE KEN HARVEY POPULAR RING EARLY BETTING TROPHY

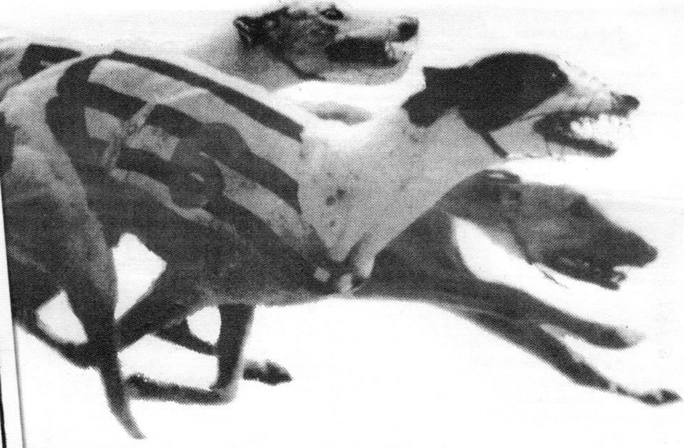

101st MEETING — TUESDAY, 24th AUGUST, 1999

OFFICIAL RACECARD — RIGHT OF ADMISSION RESERVED

boss in the UK was trying to secure a meeting with Coldplay. "As Debs had left her record company position at this point, I was sure that the only home for Coldplay would be at Parlophone with Dan," said Caroline Elleray. Keeling visited Elleray in Manchester.

"I made him sit and listen to the *Safety* EP," Elleray said. "To Dan's massive credit he said, 'Hmm. I think I've got to do some backtracking to win this band over'." Keeling was now excited about the band. "At that point," Gavin Maude remembers, "Dan was asking what he needed to do to get back in with the band. I said think about that scene from *Pretty Woman*, where the lady in the shop is told to show Julia Roberts 'some love'."

Keeling drove to London from Manchester, listening to the *Safety* EP all the way home. "I was listening to it all night. I woke up and was listening, thinking, 'I have to call the band, now'."

It was a Saturday, but Keeling called Phil, who was with Guy. They were about to go to Hoxton, where coincidentally Keeling lived. The three of them met, and from this point, Keeling was dedicated to building a relationship with the band and began "the process of wooing" the members. "Chris was the most difficult in some ways to connect with," Keeling said. "Everyone's complex, but he's an especially complex character. There are so many different sides to him."

"We were mates with Dan almost more than anything else," Phil said. "As soon as we met him, we'd go out and play pool and go out drinking together a lot. It all felt really natural signing to Parlophone, because he was our mate; he was one of the gang."

Miles Leonard, who joined Parlophone in 1996, climbed to Chairman as Coldplay were beginning to burn bright. In March 1999, Leonard was in Miami, where he listened to the Coldplay demo again. "I lay on the bed and 'Bigger Stronger' came on. It took me to another place; it was ethereal and beautiful." Leonard looked at his watch and, working out the time difference, decided to call Phil to tell him, "We get it and we want it." Phil's final domino had fallen – Parlophone were on the hook.

Coldplay returned to the Bull & Gate on April 1, for the Fierce Panda EP's launch. Andy Macleod remembers: "In the venue's 30-year history, this gig ended up holding the record for the biggest bar take in the back room (£3,000) and the biggest queue down Kentish Town Road. By the time Coldplay went on, everyone was packed in like sardines. There were a lot of naysayers, music industry types, who thought they didn't stand a chance."

Dan Green was the sound engineer for the show and recognized their vast improvement. He was impressed and gave his details to Phil.

The Bull & Gate show confirmed what Parlophone had now accepted as fact. Coldplay were good.

Before the band met with Parlophone proper, the group continued with their gigging strategy around London. Their new champion, Steve Lamacq, had secured the band a support slot on April 5, 1999, for the Welsh band Catatonia at Kentish Town's Forum, another legendary north London music venue. It was broadcast live on Radio 1. Catatonia had a national following, and the exposure for Coldplay was to be huge. "Myself and Mat Whitecross were there that night," Kris Foof remembers. "I heard 'Brothers & Sisters' for the first time through a far more substantial PA system. Mat and I just looked at each other... we knew they were really taking off."

Keith Wozencroft, Managing Director of Parlophone, and discoverer of Radiohead, was also in the crowd that night. "Chris came across nervous, but there was something interesting and infectious about him," Wozencroft said.

Phil had called on Dan Green to mix the audio for the show and from that moment, he became their front-of-house engineer. Steve Strange was also there, and soon after he began booking shows for the band. Team Coldplay was growing.

Jo Whiley, the Radio 1 DJ and Steve Lamacq's partner on Radio 1's *The Evening Session* until her departure to the midweek

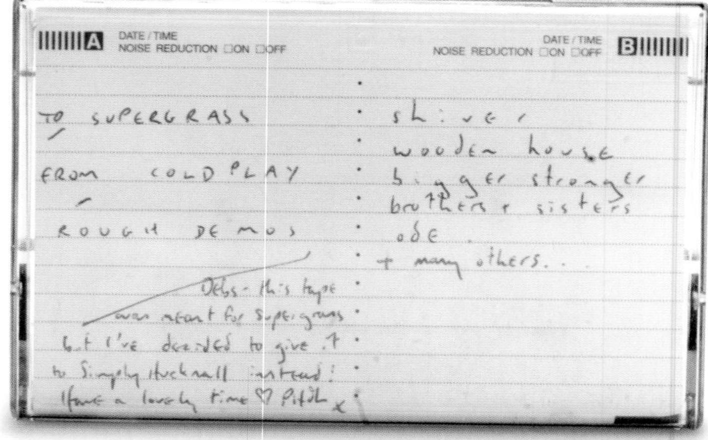

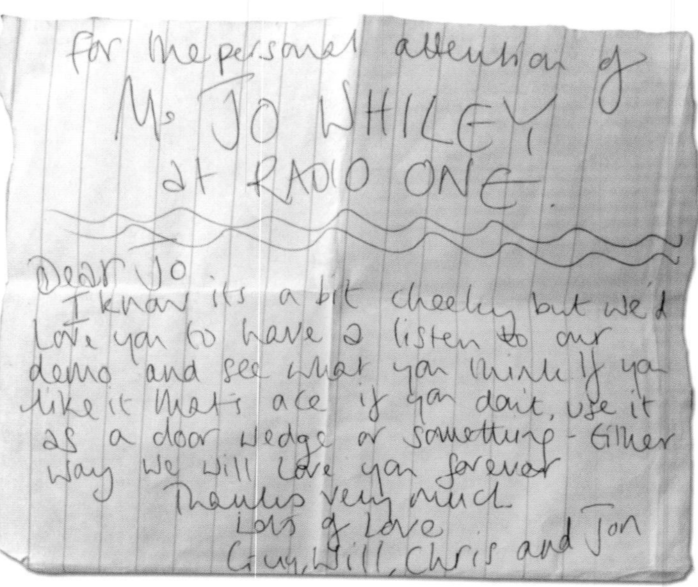
For the personal attention of
Ms JO WHILEY
at RADIO ONE.

Dear Jo,
I know its a bit cheeky but we'd love you to have a listen to our demo and see what you think if you like it that's ace if you don't, use it as a door wedge or something - Either way we will love you forever
Thanks very much
Lots of Love
Guy, Will, Chris and Jon

ABOVE RIGHT Cassette copy of early demos, given to Debs Wild to pass along to Simply Red's management.

RIGHT The note sent to Radio 1 DJ Jo Whiley with a copy of the *Safety* EP, handwritten by Chris.

ABOVE Flyer for a gig in Oxford that took place after the *Brothers & Sisters* recording sessions.

lunchtime slot, was another vital link in the chain that gave Coldplay another leg up on the ladder during this period. Whiley championed the band, and her daytime show opened them up to a broader audience. "We were lucky enough to have people at Radio 1, the main radio station, get behind us," Will said. "There are a lot of people who stuck their necks out for the band. We always got people that gave us amazing amounts of respect. Without those people, we wouldn't be here." To this day, Whiley is often credited as the person who truly broke the band in the UK.

THE DREAM DEAL

Dan Keeling invited the band to come and meet the Parlophone team. "We got very excited," Miles Leonard said. Rather unexpectedly only Jonny, Guy and Will turned up for the meeting. Chris was unable to attend.

"I think that meeting went really well, and we quickly followed it up with another. That's when Chris came in," told Leonard. "At the end of that conversation, it felt like we were really moving forward in progressing the deal." Keith Wozencroft remembers: "Chris was very energetic, nervous and polite. The rest of the band were quieter. They did have a great energy, they were funny and very positive overall."

"In the end, we had seven offers," said Maude. "And while they did sign to the label they always wanted to be on, Parlophone were the last to offer. The deal was signed in Trafalgar Square in April 1999, surrounded by pigeons and pigeon shit."

The moment the band had been waiting for had arrived: inking their record contract with Parlophone.

"Rather than just be in some sweaty lawyer's office, we wanted to do something memorable," said Will. "I went to Homebase and bought a wallpaper pasting table and took it to Trafalgar Square," said Dan Keeling, his wooing of the band now complete. The Sex Pistols famously signed their record deal outside Buckingham Palace – Keeling and Miles Leonard were both fans. "You can only sign the band once and we wanted a unique and different way to try and create a bit of history," Leonard said. "The record company brought some champagne and glasses and we had a little party. Then we went to a pub. It was amazing – we couldn't believe we were signing a record deal." Will added.

WHERE DO WE GO FROM HERE?

It didn't take Coldplay long to realize that they "were suddenly entering a whole new world," said Jonny, "and you realize you've been working towards getting signed, that means nothing, you've really got to write an album."

On Monday April 26, 1999, while the ink of their Parlophone deal was yet to dry, Fierce Panda released the first run of 2,500 copies of Coldplay's first single, 'Brothers & Sisters'. "I believe it got into the charts at No. 99," said Simon Williams. "The band were overjoyed."

moog
SYNTHESIZER

SHOW TIMES

Thursday 1st July

Doors open: 8.00pm

THE UNDECIDED	8.30pm - 9.00pm
FLOE	9.20pm - 9.50pm
COLDPLAY	10.10pm -10.40pm
PENUMBRA DERRY	11.00pm -11.30pm

ADMISSION £3.50
CURFEW: 1am

OPPOSITE TOP Guy, Jonny, Chris and Will backstage after the Manchester Roadhouse show.

OPPOSITE BOTTOM Dan Green, Guy, Chris, Debs, Jonny and Will backstage after the Manchester Roadhouse show.

LEFT AND BOTTOM Showtimes poster for Coldplay's half-hour slot at the Manchester Roadhouse show, and the show itself.

BELOW Will, Chris and Jonny, playing pool pre-gig at a local pub.

LEFT Coldplay's first Glastonbury performance, Sunday June 14, 1999, on the John Peel Stage.

BELOW Reading Festival and Leeds Festival passes, both August 1999.

RIGHT *NME* tour photoshoot, circa March 1999. Other photos from this session show Coldplay with co-tour headliners Terris.

Jonny, Will and Chris spent the days that followed cramming for their final exams: the three members passed their respective courses. To celebrate, they headed off on holiday. The day after they returned, they set off to play a handful of UK dates, driven in a splitter van by their newly appointed Tour Manager, Jeff Dray, with live sound engineer, and future/long term producer, Dan Green. The first date was a summer ball in Oxford. "We were on at silly o'clock in the morning after the main act, the Jools Holland Big Band," remembers Dray. "So, what was left of the audience were very drunk. There was a problem with the power, so the band didn't even play a whole set." Perhaps not the best warm-up gig for their first ever show at Glastonbury, the band's favourite festival.

GLASTONBURY – PART ONE

Coldplay's first Glastonbury appearance almost didn't happen. As a new band, they were scheduled first on the John Peel Stage on Sunday June 24, 1999. They arrived at the wrong entrance. "When we arrived at Glasto, I was directed by the stewards to the wrong gate and the band had to leg it across the site carrying their equipment to make the stage on time," Dray explains. "We had a transit van with all our equipment in it," remembers Guy. "We had about five minutes to get on stage. We had to traverse the entire festival lugging our amps and stuff!"

A few people had turned up to watch them, but it wasn't by any means full. "My first impressions of the band were that they were different from anyone else I had worked with," recalls Dray. "They were all waiting for their degree results and didn't seem to have that jaded worldliness about them. Chris would beat himself up a bit about not having 'paid their dues' travelling around in the back of a transit with the equipment and staying in fleapit B&Bs, but Jonny would whisper in my ear that he liked the way it was."

The band's next milestone came on July 6, 1999. They signed to BMG publishing. "For the publishing deal we took boats, and some booze, out into the middle of the Serpentine, London, and signed it in the middle of the water," said Will. Gavin Maude also remembers the day. "The band insisted that BMG chairman Paul Curran and General Manager Ian Ramage row them to the middle of the Serpentine to sign in a row boat. Chris was so excited he was practising rowing frantically, sitting on the path by the lake, and people were stepping over him and cycling around him. Eventually Will had to ask him to stop."

In October 1999, Chris reflected on the endless summer that saw Coldplay emerge properly into the world. "We've been playing all these festivals, we've been in the studio and we haven't really enjoyed that much of it. The festivals are OK, but it's difficult to get everyone emotionally into it at 11 o'clock on a Sunday morning. We're just learning our trade at the moment and the summer was a real 'what are we trying to achieve?' sort of thing."

As the band galloped toward the end of the millennium, the start of their recording experience under their newly signed contract with Parlophone had begun. Would it be everything the band had dreamed of?

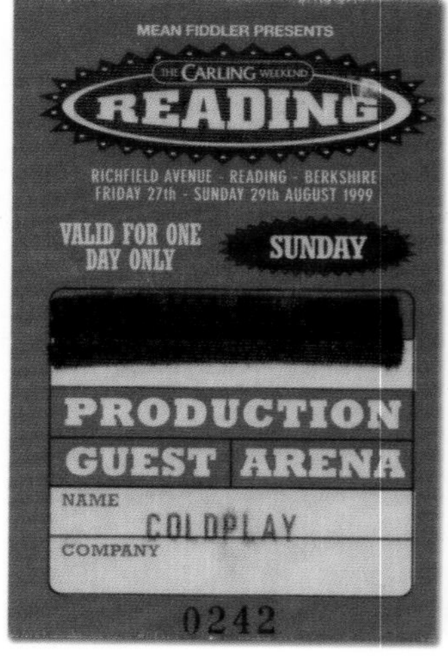

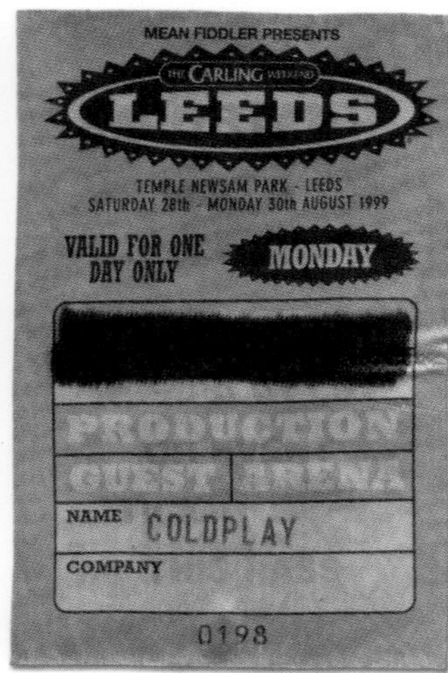

NIKE

C H A P T E R

O N E

WE LIVE IN A BEAUTIFUL WORLD

THE BLUE ROOM EP

Released: October 11, 1999
Producer: Tracks 1, 5 produced by Nikki Rosetti and Coldplay. Tracks 2, 3, 4 produced by Chris Allison.
Tracklisting:
Bigger Stronger
Don't Panic
See You Soon
High Speed
Such a Rush

PARACHUTES

Released: July 10, 2000
Producer: Ken Nelson and Coldplay
Tracklisting:
Don't Panic
Shiver
Spies
Sparks
Yellow
Trouble
Parachutes
High Speed (produced by Chris Allison)
We Never Change
Everything's Not Lost
Life Is for Living (Hidden Track)

It may have debuted at No.1 in the UK charts, becoming an instant classic in the process, but the recording and release of *Parachutes* wasn't all easy. It was a challenging record to make, with the process constantly testing the band. Thankfully, it is an album full of bewitching and urgent melodies, and songs such as 'Yellow', which shone a spotlight on the group as gifted songwriters. And, as Jonny said, "None of this would have happened if it wasn't for 'Yellow'."

JUST YOU TRY AND STOP ME

Parachutes, with its lyrical themes of safety, confidence, self-doubt, and yearning for loving and living life, appears to be a mirror of its creators' emotions. With Chris Allison appointed producer, the band had delayed the start of recording to concentrate on writing more tracks. It soon became clear that not all was as it should be.

"They started up playing in the rehearsal room and they really weren't together at all," said Allison. "I was very honest with them, I said: 'Look, this simply isn't good enough'." The band agreed with Allison to take more time to rehearse before reconvening at a later date. When a new start date to record the album arrived, things were still not quite right.

"I remember going down to the studio with Dan Keeling," explains Miles Leonard. "There was some tension. There was something in the air that didn't feel right."

Chris took Leonard and Keeling aside, on the roof of Orinico

Studios, London, to have a chat. The singer was agitated and nervous. He was feeling pressure that they were spending the label's money, that it was the first thing they had done for the company, and he wanted it to be right. Soon after, a major disruption occurred between band and producer when Allison suggested they weren't technically good enough.

"There was big pressure on the band to replace the drummer with a session musician. Chris had been told if they kept Will on drums they would only ever be 7/10, and he had a big decision to make," recalled Andy Macleod of Club Fandango.

"Things were going wrong in the studio and I told Will it was his fault," said Chris. "He'd be out of time once and I'd be telling him he was shit." As a result, Will was asked to leave the band. "Three days went by and we were doing our thing and playing with a drum machine and stuff. I just felt really miserable. It was an awful time. For a week, Coldplay didn't exist," said Chris. "It was all my fault. I thought to myself: You fucking twat. I was so nervous of us fucking up our one chance."

Replacement drummers were auditioned. "We slept with a few other drummers," Chris would later admit, "but we learned that you can't fuck with the chemistry of our band."

Overcome by guilt and remorse, Chris got blind drunk – something the singer was usually very reluctant to do. Indeed, he claims to have rarely been drunk since. Will was asked to return. "I apologized, but I felt I had to pay," said Chris.

The next day, Will recalls Chris "dribbling red stuff", while lying on the bathroom floor in his and Guy's flat. "All I remember is playing the harmonica on the street, trying to eat his chips and just sleeping on the bathroom floor with all this weird red stuff. What was that red stuff? Vodka and cranberry?" The decision didn't sit well with the rest of the band. Gavin Aherne said, "I remember Jonny, Phil, myself going to O' Neill's pub in Covent Garden and getting wasted when they kicked out Champs. Both were wracked with guilt. It was a very weird time. There is no doubt their bond as a band was cemented after that time, and no one would come between them from then on in."

Following Will's return to the group, the foursome ceased working with Allison. It was a costly experience and left the band feeling vulnerable. "We'd lost a bit of confidence with the Chris Allison sessions," Phil explained. "It wasn't his fault; he just had a different vision of what the sonics would be. We had to rediscover ourselves, what we thought the record was going to sound like. There were tears and fights..."

Eighteen months of non-stop touring to support *Parachutes* took Will's drumming to the next level and no one questioned his ability. "I became more confident, as much as anything else, and I started to hit the drums harder as well," Will said. "I also went and had a few lessons with a teacher to help me with timing, because I

OPPOSITE FAR LEFT *The Blue Room* mailing list card, as sent out to interested parties.

OPPOSITE LEFT *The Blue Room* EP cover.

ABOVE One of the many illuminated globes used on stage during the *Parachutes* tour.

had gotten to the point where I didn't think I could learn any more without learning the basics. My natural ability got me as far as possible without help."

'High Speed' was the only track to remain from those sessions before the album was started from scratch. The idea for the *Blue Room* EP was developed to bridge the gap. "We tried re-recording [some of the songs], but it didn't work out," says Keeling "There are other versions of 'Bigger Stronger' that are well recorded, but they don't have a spark to them." At Keeling's suggestion, original tracks from the *Safety* EP were used. A smart move. "Only two songs on the (*Blue Room*) EP are demos and the reason they're on it is because they're good songs and we want to put them out," said Chris. "Sadly, we couldn't get hold of the masters, so we couldn't remix them, but they've got a really good vibe on them and that's what counts."

The result was a limited 5,000-copy release of a hybrid of five old and new recordings. At this point lyrically Coldplay weren't writing songs about love, as the group had had little experience of it. Chris also believed that "a lot of the best love songs have been written already". Little did he know what was to come. His inexperience may well be why Chris saw his lyrics "more like boy wants to be with girl, but girl would rather play lacrosse." But why was it called *The Blue Room*?

"The studio where we were recording had one of those rooms where you film things on a blue screen and then dub in Hawaii afterwards. We didn't even know what this was, CGI. So, we'd go in there and play cricket and football and what we thought was a tacky set turned out to be really expensive... that's why it's called *The Blue Room*," said Chris.

Before this plan of action was in place, the band enlisted their friend Mat Whitecross to direct a video for a new song they'd recorded, 'Spies'. As 'Bigger Stronger' was the lead track on the band's first release it was decided to shoot a video for that track instead. It was very last minute, so Whitecross was unable to change the video's story, which is why the music video for 'Bigger Stronger' makes absolutely no sense.

Filmed at Durdle Door, Dorset, close to the location for the iconic video for 'Yellow' which was to follow a year later, the video for 'Bigger Stronger' was never officially released, though it was unveiled on the band's website (with group commentary) in 2008.

PARACHUTING

A few months later, on October 11, 1999, the *Blue Room* EP was released. Gig commitments kept them busy, but there was certainly a cloud hanging over Jonny, Guy, Chris and Will – they had yet to decide on a producer for their as yet untitled debut album. What they did have, however, was some working titles that Chris had written in his lyric notebook. 'The Harder You Throw It the Higher It Bounces' was one. "Unless it's an egg," Guy pointed out. "Or a spanner," added Jonny.

Chris also liked 'Maximum Soul' as a title. "That's so cheesy. But that's going to be the feel of it," he said. Chris had doodled the title several times in his notebook. "The common thread is we all want to move people with music and play music that's maximum soul. We're all into music that grabs you by the guts."

The title *Parachutes* didn't come until a few months later, as Chris explained. "We chose *Parachutes* because we had to decide a title. But it works, it fits. Often the things that fit best are the things that have to be decided very quickly, or are a bit of an accident."

In October 1999, during the process of writing and rehearsing songs for *Parachutes*, Chris shed light on the development of the songs. "'Everything's Not Lost' is still sounding a bit cheesy in places," Chris revealed, "and I haven't really written any lyrics for it yet. When we've done that properly it's going to be really good. On this album maybe two songs will be piano-led. I really like playing piano, but you can't do it too much."

In between rehearsals and gigs that Steve Strange had lined up, the band had met several in-demand producers at their rehearsal room in north London. "After about half an hour you forget who they worked with and just concentrate on what they're going to do with us," said Jonny.

The big break for *Parachutes* came in the form of Ken Nelson, a producer who had recently worked with two critically acclaimed artists – Gomez and Badly Drawn Boy.

"Gomez were the first band I ever saw in rehearsal in my first ever A&R job," said Caroline Elleray. "And I thought their production was amazing, so I sought out Ken." Nelson's manager,

ABOVE The band arrive at Abbey Road Studios in London, where The Beatles famously recorded, to master the *The Blue Room* EP.

OPPOSITE Friend James "Pix" Pickering snapped the band at their first – and only – Reading Festival appearance, 1999.

Pete Byrne, recalls how the introduction resulted. "I remember playing Ken 'Bigger Stronger' and he knew he wanted to work with them. Ken's philosophy is 'Good singer, good songs,' and Coldplay certainly fitted that bill even early on."

Nelson's first meeting with the group was in their rehearsal room, but the night Coldplay offered the producer the job, they were playing a gig in Liverpool – with Gomez, strangely enough. The gig gave Ken concerns. "They rushed through the set and I was thinking to myself: 'They just need to calm down.' And in the studio, that's basically what we did. We'd go through each song and get them to learn what tempo to play the song at. I think that's why the album sounds so organic."

SING IT LOUD AND CLEAR

The recording of *Parachutes* took the band to Rockfield Studios in Monmouth, Wales, and Wessex Studios, London, but the bulk of it was recorded at Parr Street Studios in Liverpool.

Recording began in November 1999. "As a lot of the material done at Rockfield didn't make the album, I suppose you could call the Rockfield session the pre-production, and once they started at Parr Street, that was the real start to recording the album," said Pete Byrne. It didn't take long for the band to settle into the rhythm of recording.

"The mood at Rockfield was upbeat and positive," Byrne said. "Chris and myself were fascinated with the fact that the piano in the studio was the one used to record 'Bohemian Rhapsody', so we both spent half an hour trying to learn the Queen track."

"After recording with Chris Allison, the band just seemed eager to get on with making the album," said Nelson. "In hindsight, they must have been very nervous about going back in to the studio at that time. It must have felt like their last chance".

It became clear that Nelson was precisely the producer the band needed at the time. "I knew how I wanted the recordings to sound and they did too. I wanted to record the songs with the band all playing together and this did lead to tensions and arguments," reveals Nelson. "But we worked very hard at getting the great take. We spent a month at Rockfield. We ended up with two great tracks in 'Shiver' and 'Don't Panic'."

Everyone knew that 'Shiver' was the album's lead single – it had to be good – so the label requested a mix to be done by Michael Brauer in New York as soon as possible.

BELOW Sugarmill venue, Stoke, England. Coldplay were joint headliners with Terris, 2000.

OPPOSITE ABOVE Chris, Will, Guy and Jonny at Parr Street Studios during the recording of *Parachutes*.

OPPOSITE Chris at Rockfield Studios during the recording of *Parachutes*.

OPPOSITE INSET Rockfield Studios guest book entry, written during the recording of *Parachutes*.

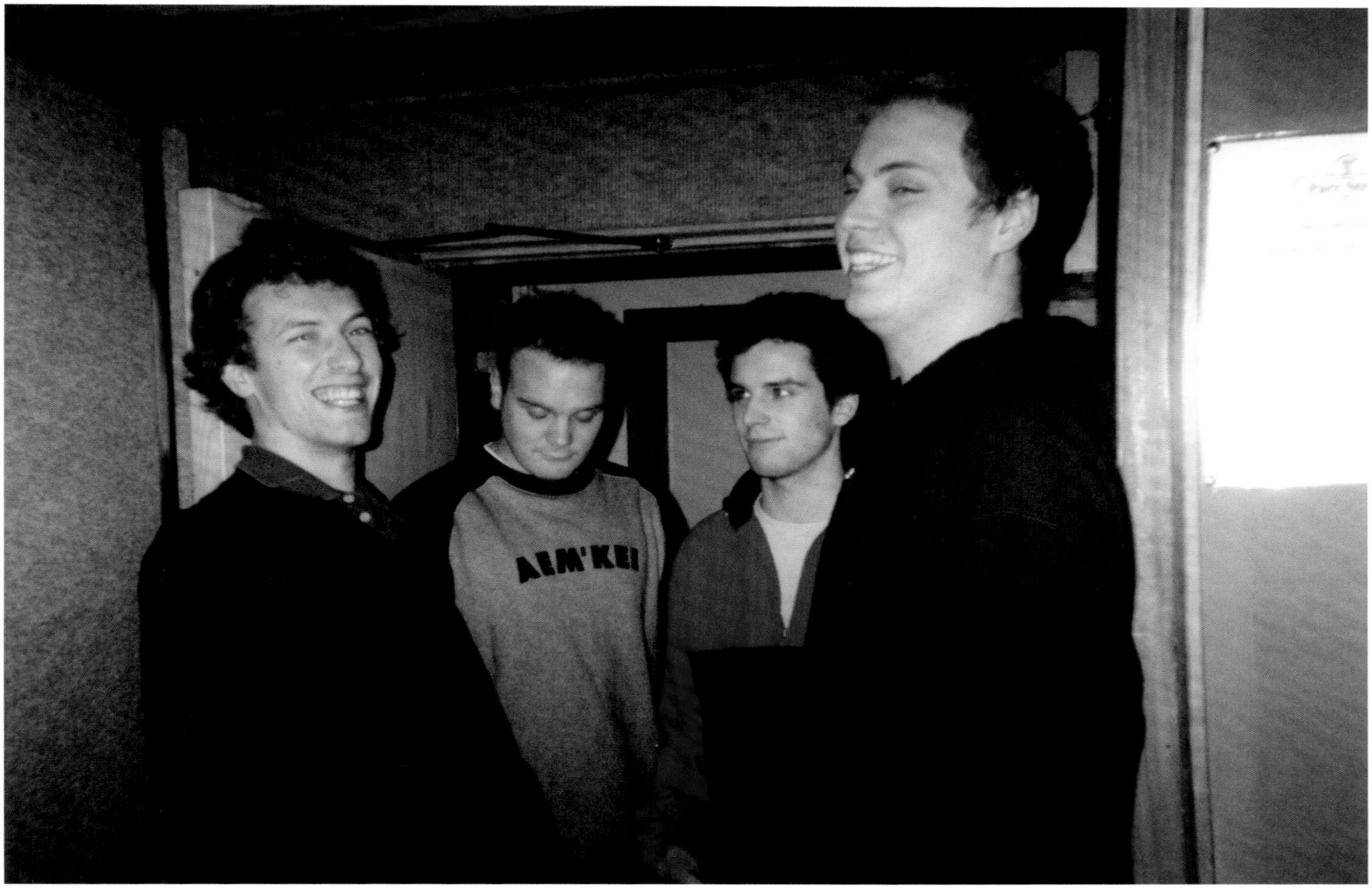
AEM'KEI

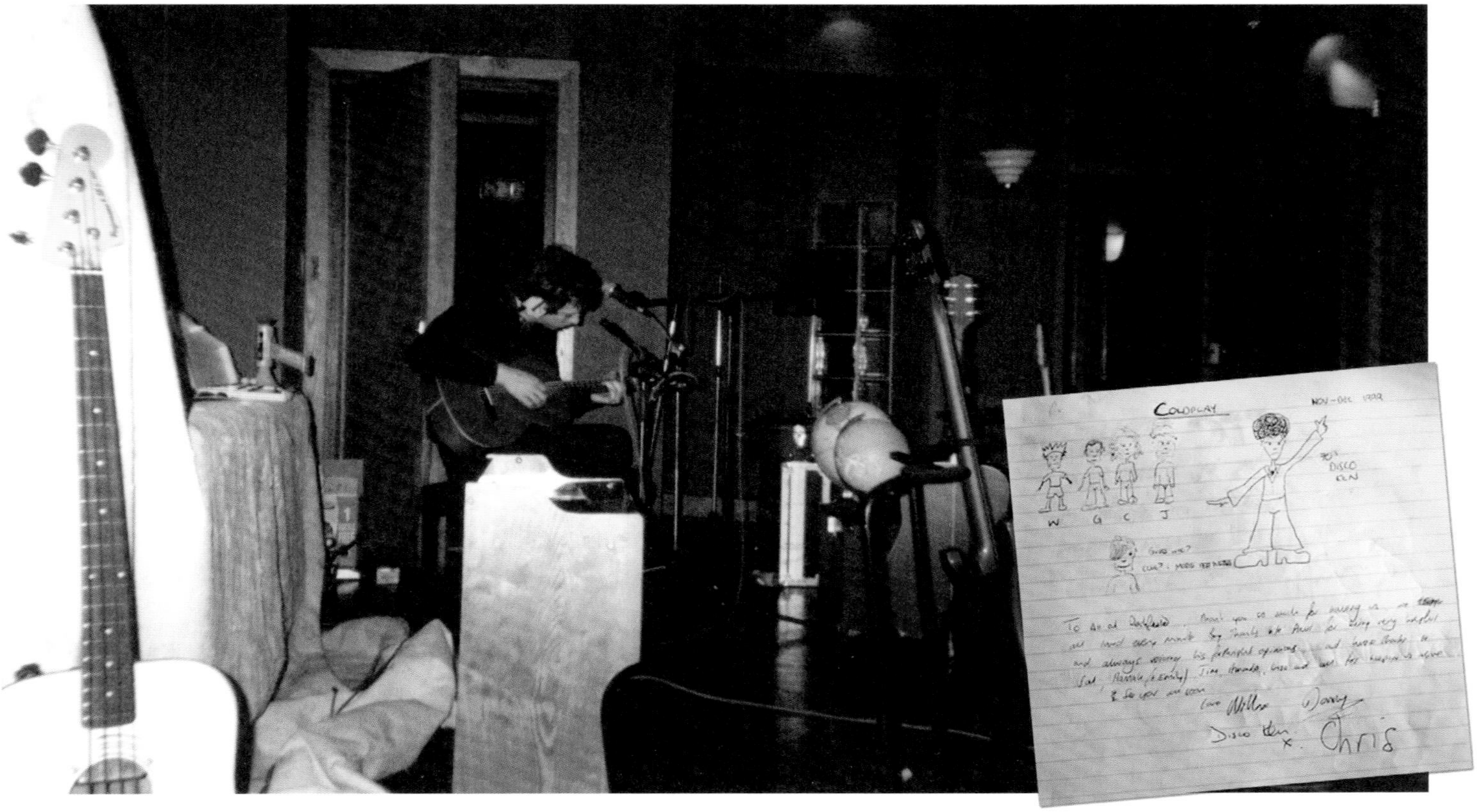
COLDPLAY
NOV–DEC
W G C J
DISCO
KEN
Disco Ken x.
Chris

YAMAHA

INTO SOMETHING BEAUTIFUL

Miles Leonard, Dan Keeling and the rest of the band's label and publishing team knew that Coldplay could write songs. But throughout the recording of *Parachutes* it wasn't guaranteed that singles would arrive. What *Parachutes* lacked, and desperately needed, was that one big hitter. It needed a 'Yellow'.

"It was a really clear, starry night," Guy said of Rockfield Studios. "We all came out in absolute amazement because none of us had seen the sky look that clear. The number of stars was just ridiculous."

"We were all stood outside in the courtyard, Ken had said: 'look at the stars,' you know," Chris recalled. The next day, Nelson remembers, "Chris was singing a new song idea he'd come up with. He made us laugh with a vocal rendition in the guise of Neil Young. There were few lyrics at this point, but the word 'yellow' ended each line." For Jonny's part, the guitarist "stuck some guitars I'd written when I was 16 on it. It fitted really nicely."

Phil, however, wasn't instantly convinced. The lyrics baffled him and he didn't hear a tune. It certainly didn't follow the rule of thumb for song compositions given that it had distorted guitars and no chorus to speak of, but it had a certain magic about it. Fellow songwriters Elbow's Guy Garvey and Noel Gallagher of Oasis would agree. "When I heard 'Yellow' for the first time," Gallagher said, "I immediately picked up the guitar and went, 'Fucking bastards, why didn't I write that?'" Garvey thought "'Yellow' was huge because everybody recognized the spontaneity in it. It was obviously coming from a place of loving music and when that lyric arrived nobody questioned it. It was childlike in its sentiment."

With 'Yellow' in the bank, the band took a break. From recording, at least.

Steve Strange started a dialogue with *NME*'s editor about the opening act on the upcoming *NME* Brats national tour. "I remember telling him he would thank himself if he put Coldplay on," said Strange. "The band and label were very excited when they were confirmed." Along with a musically mixed bag of Shack, Les Rhythm Digitales and Campag Velocet, they played, often, to just one person in the crowd.

LEFT The 'Shiver' video shoot. Note the globe on top of the amplifier, left. The video was directed by Grant Gee.

"I literally can remember on the *NME* tour and the band going on stage with me being the only person in the auditorium. We didn't think anything bad of that, we knew we were at the bottom of the ladder," said Phil. Jeff Dray recalled the same. "On those first tours we sometimes played to just a handful of people."

The tour, however, provided the opportunity to sharpen the new songs, and as Strange pointed out, "It helped knock down a lot of fence-sitters along the way."

'Shiver' was released March 6, 2000, and gave the band their first Top 40 chart position, entering the UK charts at No.35. The video was a simple affair filmed in a rehearsal room.

'Yellow' was released on June 26, 2000. The song's B-side, 'Help Is Round the Corner' is an accurate reflection of how the band felt at this point, recording at Parr Street Studios.

LOST AND FOUND

When the band took the first set of completed mixes to Parlophone (except 'Everything's Not Lost', the last song to be recorded), they didn't receive the reaction they were hoping for. "Keith Wozencroft and Miles Leonard were like headmasters we needed to work extra hard to impress," explained Phil. "I don't know what had gone wrong, but we had a listening meeting and it didn't go well. I remember a feeling of great despondency and thinking maybe we'd get dropped before our record even came out." Leonard's review of the mixes was blunt. "They took it hard when it didn't quite deliver," he said.

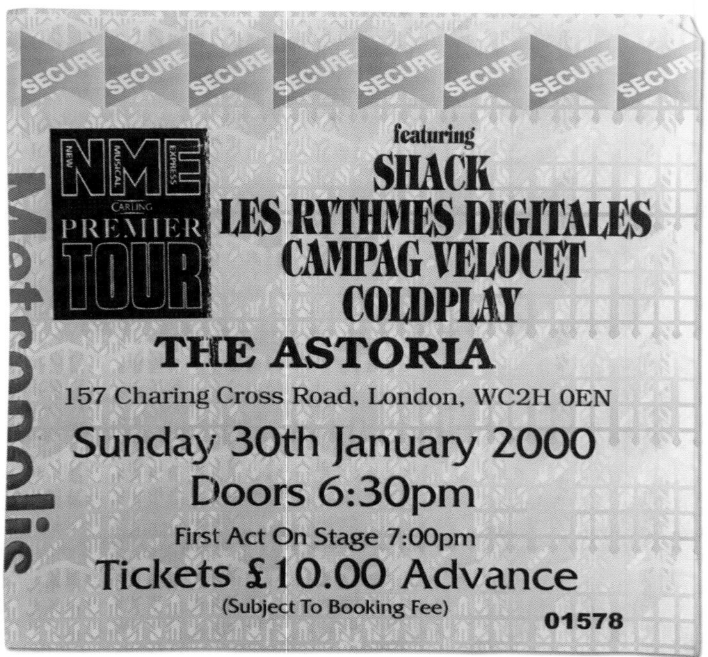

ABOVE Ticket from the *NME* tour at London's Astoria.

BELOW LEFT Chris' studio notes for 'Everything's Not Lost'.

BELOW Soundcheck at King Tuts, Glasgow, in 2000 – the venue where Oasis were discovered.

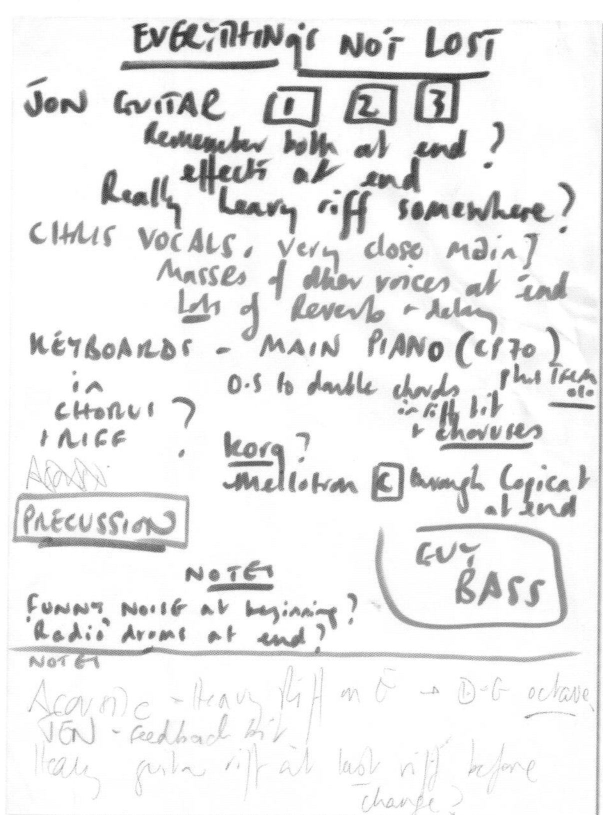

> “Some people are saying that the single will go Top 5, but personally I think we'll be lucky if it goes Top 20.”
>
> Guy

"The criticism was good because it made us work a bit harder," said Phil. The band went back and worked on the songs that weren't right. They flew to New York to meet Michael Brauer and sit down with him as he mixed.

"It was at that point that we became a cohesive entity," Phil said. "Up to that point it had just been an album with a collection of songs. It crystallized. Chris came up with the title, we came up with the track listing, and it became something with a bit more form."

With a finished copy of the album in his hands, Phil remembers "walking through Battersea Park in London, listening to the first copy of *Parachutes* on my Discman. Even though I hadn't contributed a note it was still an amazing feeling of pride and fulfilment." Chris too, was happy in what they had all created together. "We worked incredibly hard, and we believed that it was the greatest record that we could ever make," the singer said. "But you have to approach every record like that – you've got to believe what you're doing is the best, otherwise there's no point in doing it."

The album was complete, but so much had yet to be organized to coincide with the July release: gigs, promotion, videos and album art.

ABOVE HMV, Oxford Street, London. In-store appearance to celebrate the release of *Parachutes*, July 10, 2000.

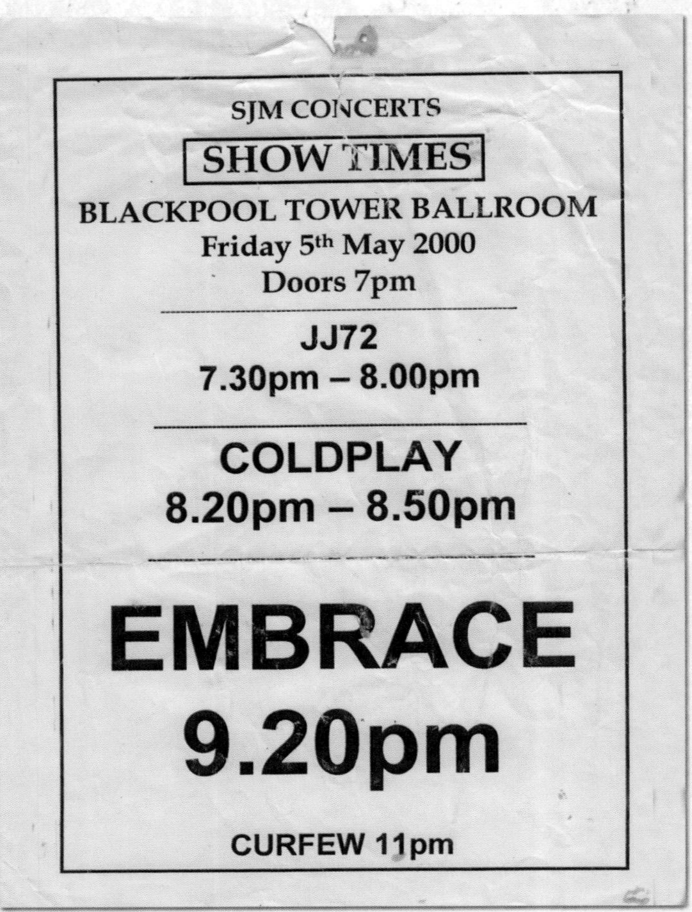
SJM CONCERTS
SHOW TIMES
BLACKPOOL TOWER BALLROOM
Friday 5th May 2000
Doors 7pm

JJ72
7.30pm – 8.00pm

COLDPLAY
8.20pm – 8.50pm

EMBRACE
9.20pm

CURFEW 11pm

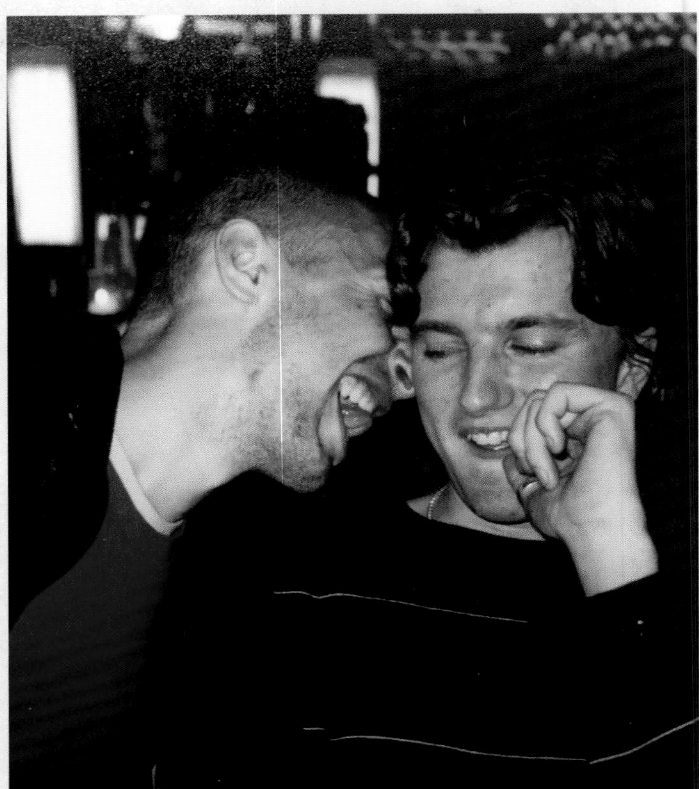

ABOVE Chris with Embrace's frontman Danny McNamara.

LEFT The show times for Coldplay supporting Embrace at the Blackpool Tower ballroom, May 2000.

The frontman of British band Embrace, Danny McNamara, personally invited Coldplay to open for them on a UK tour date. "The late Sean Hughes had them on his radio show and loved them," McNamara said. "Me and Sean were good mates back then and he thought I'd like them. He was right. I think it was the *Blue Room* EP, a radio copy of it. I loved it straight away. We had a big show coming up at Blackpool Ballroom. We asked them if they wanted to support and they said 'yes'."

The gig, one of their biggest to date, was a success. "I don't usually watch the supports," said McNamara, "but I had to see them. I remember thinking 'Trouble' was the standout track. I loved the way Chris waltzed around the stage in a really uncool carefree way. I thought it was really cool, as of course most uncool things are."

Debs Wild remembers, "That was such a great night. A fantastic line-up in an amazing venue. There was a lot of attention after the gig and the band hung around to chat. I recall saving Chris from the advances of a couple of amorous fans."

A photograph taken the day after this show features on the back of *Parachutes* (a shot which also graced the band's first *NME* cover), but the front cover image was proving elusive.

As with the title, it came about at the eleventh hour after a group photoshoot in Harlow, Essex, produced nothing usable.

A few weeks later, on June 15, 2000, while backstage at The Charlotte, Leicester, it was suggested the band take a photo of their stage prop, an illuminated WH Smith globe that Phil had bought for £10. Chris took the photo with a disposable Kodak camera. It is now an iconic image. Although several globes were purchased to go on that tour, the original raised £8,230 in the band's "End of Decade" charity auction in 2009.

The band were busy touring, notably two nights supporting Muse at the (now defunct) Astoria on June 6 and 7, and a headline show at London's Scala, on June 20, as a run-up to Glastonbury, where the band were scheduled to play.

GLASTONBURY – PART TWO

The day of their performance – second stage Saturday afternoon – arrived and with it came some nerves too. Especially for Will, who paced the side of the stage like a caged tiger before they went on. Dan Green looks back at the moment: "It was nervewracking… but it was brilliant. Not quite as terrifying as the Glastonbury after!"

Steve Lamacq remembers this momentous show: "In-between songs Chris was a) a bit cheeky; b) a bit cocky and c) the most self-effacing singer on the planet. It was a perfect Glastonbury appearance, which basically said: 'We're good, and that's why we're here on this stage, but actually we're no different to you lot watching us'."

BMG boss Ian Ramage was there: "This gig felt like a defining moment. One of those, 'Oh God, the whole world gets this now.' They were connecting."

IT WAS ALL YELLOW

The original concept for the video for the second single 'Yellow' featured all four members of the band. Tragically Will's mother passed away, and her funeral was the same day as the shoot. It was decided to go ahead with just Chris appearing. Alex and James, the video's directors, had to change how they planned on filming it, although the location remained the same: Studland Bay, Swanage.

"We initially tried to carry out our original concept, but the weather got so bad we had to completely rethink how best to approach it," said James. It was a 12-hour day, but in reality it probably took less than an hour to shoot. They ran through the song five times.

"We had this elaborate treatment for the video with all sorts of extras and interesting things going on; but the rain just never stopped, so we couldn't shoot any of it," said Phil. "After eight hours sitting in the trailer, Chris just grabbed the directors and said, 'Come with me.' He walked down the beach and a classic video was born."

In the editing suite, the directors wanted it to look natural, as if it was a dark, wet day suddenly becoming brighter. "We started in the blue colour spectrum and gradually brought in reds to warm it up. We did what is called a gradual grade, where the camera operator literally has his hand on a dial and turns the dial slowly throughout the duration, making it become lighter," explains James. "It was supposed to be a bright sunny day, but when you are faced with this type of problem it's always best to make it work to your advantage. Ultimately it became a blessing, as it made the video more powerful," said James.

Dan Keeling sums it up: "The video made it. That was the moment that Chris became famous."

ABOVE Mailing list card for the single 'Yellow'.

ABOVE Promotional button badges for *Parachutes*.

BELOW View from the V Festival second stage, August 2000, and laminate for the same festival a year later when the band performed on the main stage.

RIGHT Flyers for Belgian *Parachutes* tour show.

'Yellow' was released just two days after their second Glastonbury performance and charted at No.4, securing them their first *Top of the Pops* appearance (July 6), which coincided with their first *NME* cover. Following this chart victory, Jo Whiley interviewed Chris on the phone during her lunchtime radio show; he was at the dentist. The rest of the band were taking time off. Jonny heard the news of the single's success on holiday while floating on a lilo in a pool. Will was in the shower. The band had a hit on their hands.

"We all thought 'Yellow' was a great song, we loved it," recalled Miles Leonard. "There was no question of it not being a single, but no one could say they knew this was going to go stratospheric and global."

SPARKS FLY

When Parlophone signed Coldplay, the label anticipated building the band's career over a few years. They had estimated modest total first album sales. "100,000 would have been good," Keeling suggested. "To be honest, we just wanted a hit of any sort."

Coldplay's debut record surpassed expectations by achieving 75,000 sales in its first week, debuting at No.1 in the UK. "We were playing this rock festival in Sicily sandwiched in between all these local heavy rock bands," said Will. "We were No.1 in the UK, but nobody there had heard of us!"

At the time, only two other British bands, Oasis and Embrace, had their debut album go in at the top of the UK charts. "We always hoped and knew we could get somewhere but we didn't think it would happen this quickly," said Will. "The pace that it's happened has surprised everyone."

Music journalist (and the band's future website editor) Chris Salmon said, "There's a theory that any band has one amazing song in them – and 'Yellow' could've been Coldplay's – but it was very clear from hearing that album that they were anything but one-hit wonders."

COLDPLAY

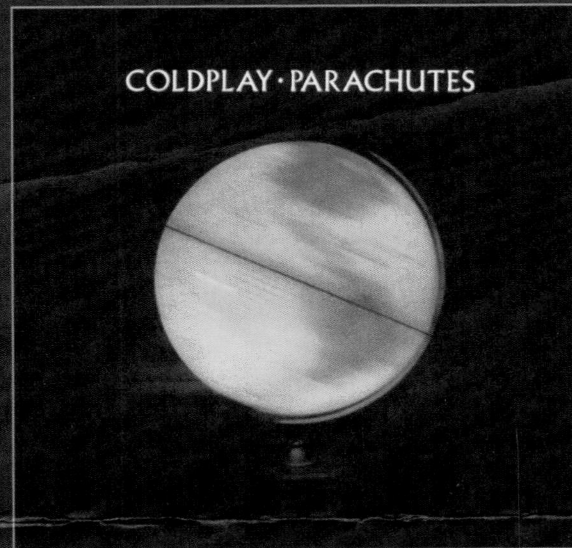

CD: PARACHUTES

INCLUDES: "SHIVER"
"YELLOW"
"TROUBLE"

IN CONCERT
ANCIENNE BELGIQUE
03/11/2000
TICKETS INFOS: 02/548 24 24
WWW.ABCONCERTS.BE

COLDPLA

+ special guest: JJ72

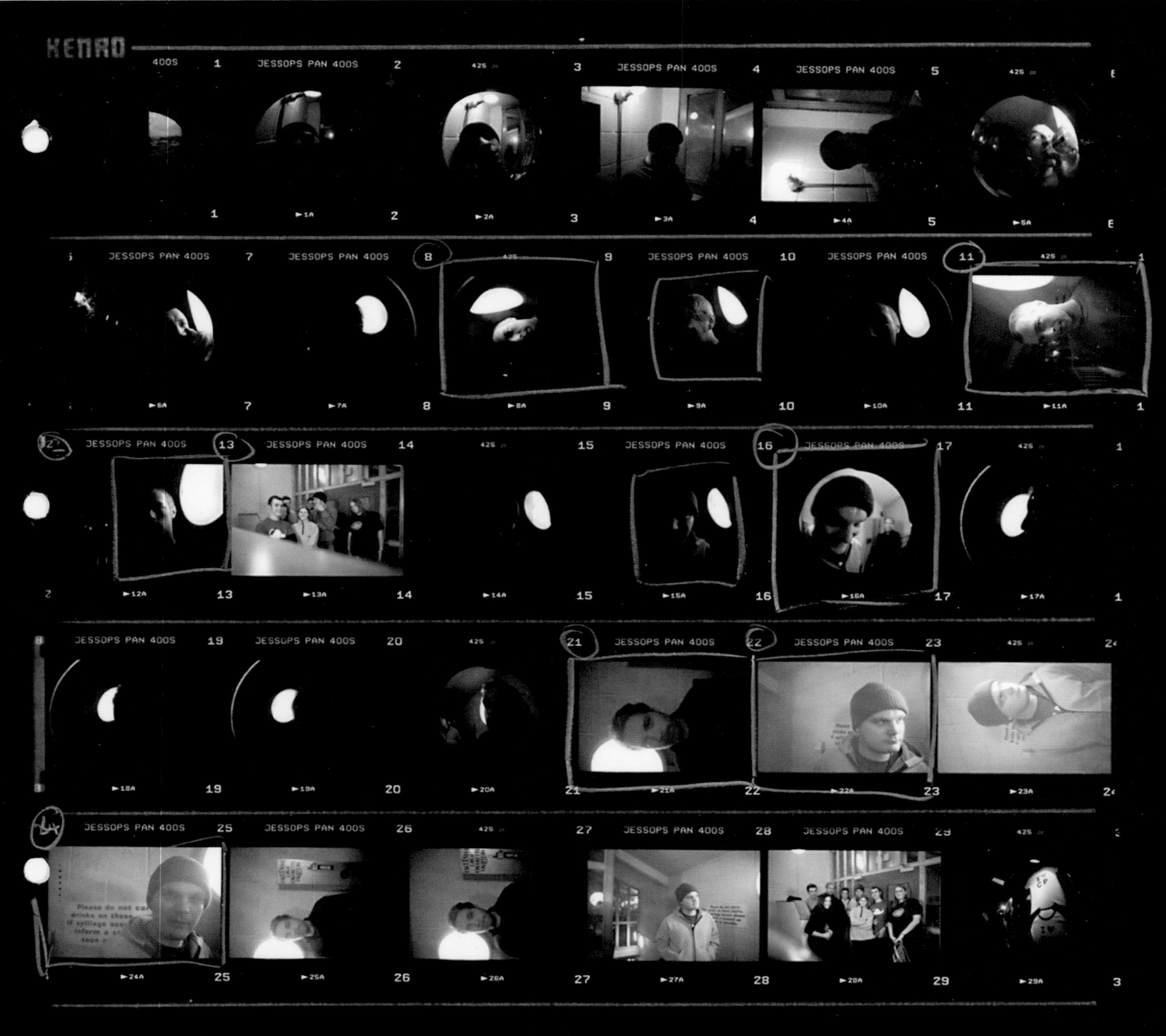
KENRO
JESSOPS PAN 400S
Coldplay @ Cambridge Junction
Oct. 2000

Steve Lamacq was in America when *Parachutes* went to No.1, "For a couple of days I genuinely thought that I should resign from Radio 1 there and then," the DJ said. "In my own head I thought, 'Here's a band we've championed from nothing to No.1 in the album charts and nothing will ever be this good again'."

Debs Wild joined key team players to celebrate, "Even though we already knew the midweek chart position, a little gang of us took a bottle of champagne and a portable radio to Primrose Hill so we could listen to the chart show. We actually missed it, but still, that feeling of *Parachutes* going straight in at No.1 made me giddy."

A CHANGE IS COMING

With overwhelming success, something had to give. Phil Harvey was now in charge of the UK's biggest band.

A typical gig day for Phil before *Parachutes* came out would have involved "booking a couple of taxis to take the equipment from the Camden Road flat to the venue; buying batteries for Jonny's pedals; going around the bar greeting all our fans by name; desperately looking for music industry types; arguing for hours with the promoter over £10."

It became clear quite quickly after the release of *Parachutes* that Phil felt he was in over his head. "The album went straight in at No.1 and all of a sudden I was working 16 hours a day with three phone lines ringing constantly," he said. "I didn't have an assistant, so there was no one to take any of the load off my shoulders. For nearly a year I got through on sheer adrenaline. It was only later that I discovered most international bands have huge teams and organizations supporting them... not just one bloke in a shithole office".

To keep things afloat, Phil hired assistant Estelle Wilkinson, recommended by Caroline Elleray, who released Phil from many of his basic duties.

"Even at that initial stage, Estelle was so much more than an assistant," said Phil. "She was the business brain and logistical organizer that I needed." Eventually she would graduate to co-manager.

Wilkinson became involved with touring and discussing budgets and coordinating between Phil, the label and Jeff Dray. Wilkinson was a saving grace, but not enough to bring Phil back from the brink.

"I remember this all as being an isolating experience," said Phil. "I normally think of myself as an upbeat kind of person – it was all quite a shock. Regardless of how the world might perceive it, [a mental health problem] can strike any person."

OPPOSITE Contact sheet of photographs from Cambridge Junction show, October 2000.

BELOW Chris with Danny McNamara (far right) and members of Travis and Starsailor. Taken in the US.

BOTTOM *Mince Spies*, cover of the rare fan club CD that was given to fans at Christmas.

MINCE SPIES

The band have never been that keen on having a fan club. They've always felt that fans already pay enough buying music, tickets and merchandise without charging anything else on top, which is why at the end of 2001, the short-lived fan club, Coldplayground – operated and lovingly maintained by fans – was closed. While recording their second album, the band pressed 1,000 copies of a limited-edition CD, titled *Mince Spies*, as a parting Christmas gift. It featured two tracks: 'Have Yourself A Merry Little Christmas' and a remix of 'Yellow'.

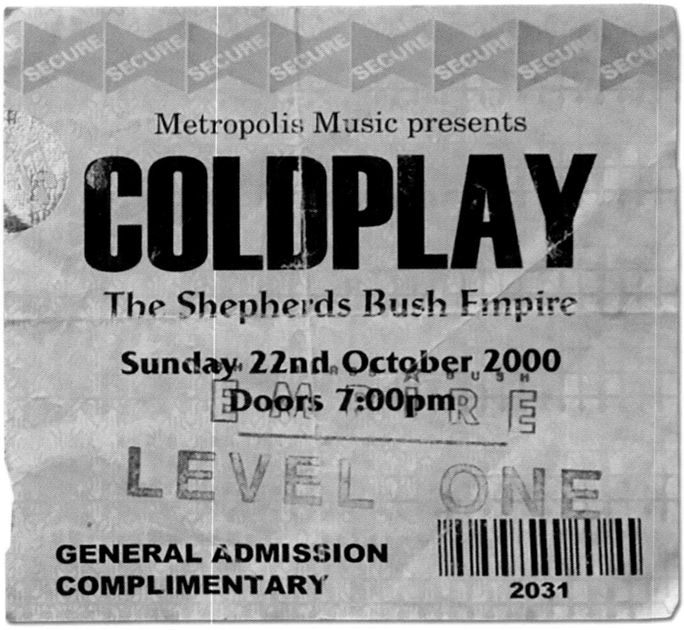

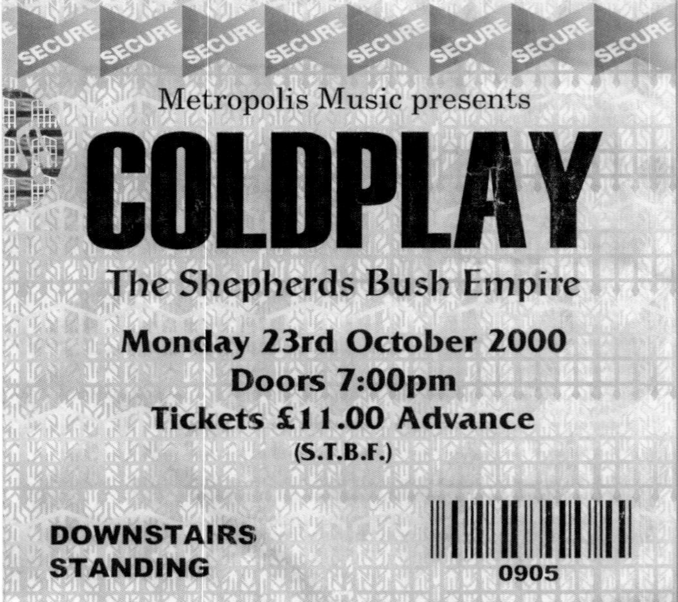

BREAKING THE STATES

KROQ, a highly influential American radio station that reaches a wide audience, got behind the band very early on. "We got very lucky with KROQ," said Phil. "They started playing it out of the blue, that was the first domino to fall in North America."

"'Yellow' was a song made for American radio," KROQ DJ Nic Harcourt said. "That's really what it takes to crack America, that one special song and 'Yellow' was it." Harcourt wasn't the only US radio DJ to have picked up on the band. Before long, tracks from *Parachutes* were on heavy rotation on US radio.

One snag: the band didn't have a US record deal.

The North American subsidiary of Parlophone, Capitol Records, hadn't shown a great deal of interest in the group. In fact, when Parlophone spoke on a conference call to Capitol to say how brilliantly the album was performing and how excited all territories around the globe were about Coldplay, they actually turned the band down. "We were concerned and slightly devastated," said Leonard, who had to have a difficult conversation with the band.

THE STARS SHINE ON MERCURY

Despite a setback in the States, *Parachutes* roared on in the UK and Europe, culminating in a shortlisting for the 2000 Mercury Music Prize Award. They didn't win (Badly Drawn Boy did), but to be nominated gave recognition of how far they had come. Two weeks later, on September 26, 2000, Coldplay were one of three surprise acts to join the bill at a series of gigs in a small 2,000-capacity venue within the Millennium Dome, London (now the O2 Arena).

Actor/comedian Simon Pegg was in attendance with his wife, Maureen, who worked with Toploader, one of the other performers. Chris approached Pegg to tell him that he was a fan of Pegg's BBC sketch show, *Big Train*. "I told him I had watched the video for 'Yellow' at Steve Coogan's house and thought it was really good," said Pegg. "We sort of flirted a bit and he invited me and Maureen to a gig at the Shepherds Bush Empire."

Edith Bowman, friend and BBC DJ and presenter, also remembers Coldplay's rise to popularity during this period. "My first memory of the band was hearing 'Shiver' and it just blew my mind. I remember taking my friend and boss from MTV, to see them at Shepherds Bush Empire. The music just immediately connected with me; it was emotive, exciting and so beautifully heartbreaking. Seeing them live was confirmation to me of how brilliant they were and are."

Accepting the invitation, Pegg was at the Empire gig too. "At the after party, Chris said he needed to get some cash out of the machine and I went with him. It turned out he just wanted to get away from the party because he was a bit overwhelmed by it all, their growing popularity, the size of the rooms they were playing to. The Shepherds Bush Empire has a capacity of 2,000. I talked him down and made him feel better. I think we ended up going back to mine and Maureen's place and watched *Withnail and I*. It was the first of many nights spent at that flat." Pegg and Chris, and indeed the rest of the band, have remained close friends since.

Parlophone were looking how to release *Parachutes* in America. Capitol's affiliate company, Nettwerk, seemed like a great opportunity to ensure the album's US release.

In retrospect, Capitol's initial passing on the band may have been the best thing that could have happened. Nettwerk CEO Terry McBride had absolute passion and belief in the band. Nothing was going to stop him. "It felt like the right home," agreed Wozencroft.

In the US, Nettwerk offered the micro-attention the band needed. It would also introduce the band to Dave Holmes, who has been by their side ever since, as manager. On October 3, 2000,

Holmes flew from the US to meet the band backstage after a gig at Oxford Brookes University. He was their first contact with the American music industry. There was an instant connection. "What probably helped them was having someone in the mix who understood how the North American marketplace worked," said Holmes. "I invited Nettwerk to become co-US managers with me and I started working very closely with Dave. He was our man at Nettwerk with all things America," said Phil. Dave added: "The first five years of us working together was me bringing my experience at the time – which was limited in the big picture – to weigh in and provide some level of guidance amongst Phil and Estelle and everyone. The band were in a learning phase then and how it all works. Now they know how it all works. There's less convincing and more 'We're going to do it this way this time.' They're more seasoned."

Now that the band were guaranteed a chance to be heard in America (*Parachutes* was released in the US on November 7, 2000), Holmes felt instinctively that they were destined for greatness. "From the first album I felt it was happening right away. There was electricity, a buzz about them. It started in the UK… but it spread quickly."

NEVER MEANT TO CAUSE YOU TROUBLE

'Trouble' (originally called 'Spiderwebs'), the third single to be taken from *Parachutes*, was released on October 26, 2000. The accompanying music video directed by Sophie Muller, who became a regular early director for the band, was dark in both tone and concept. It was considered an album track, and a different feel and tone from the previous singles.

This was particularly true for the American market, where a single's job is to sell an album. "They had radio support, but they didn't have hit singles so to speak," Holmes said. "If you look at the chart positions from all the singles, it's not like they had a string of No.1s."

'Trouble' got a US release, but the video was deemed too grisly for American audiences, so a second, much lighter video, directed by Tim Hope, was made. Combining animation with real life footage, the video went on to win the MTV Video Music Award 2002 for Best Art Direction.

In November, the band appeared again on *Top of the Pops* – an unforgettable experience for Phil.

"The best day as a whole was when we played with U2 on *Top of the Pops*. I remember U2's manager, Paul McGuinness, whom I had idolized since I got into music, introducing me to the Edge. I was

ABOVE Bookies' favourites perform at the Mercury Music Prize, London, 2000. Badly Drawn Boy won the award.

OPPOSITE Tickets from two consecutive shows at The Shepherds Bush Empire.

> “We’re the biggest band in the world, apparently. That’s what we get told. No, we’re not. We’re tiny. No one knows who we are. Not even in England.”
>
> Chris

BELOW Tickets, flyers and passes from shows in 2000 and 2001.

trying to think of something suitably reverential to say but before I had a chance to speak, Edge said: 'Oh, so you're Phil Harvey. I was reading about you in the paper at the weekend...' Very weird."

Towards the end of 2000, Chris Salmon spent time with the band for an interview for the London culture magazine *Time Out*. He remembers: "The band were clearly trying to get their heads around the media attention that came with all this success. That thing where suddenly anything you say can be (and was being) taken out of context and made into sensational news to sell papers and magazines. I remember saying to them they should try to be less guarded and worried in interviews – as they had been in a few recent ones – because the only way all their fans could hear from them was via those interviews. Of course, social media has changed that completely. Overnight success is not an easy thing for young musicians to acclimatize to. Nobody expected Coldplay to become as huge in 2000 as they did."

At the conclusion of the year 2000, UK sales of *Parachutes* totalled 877,449, just 23 weeks after its release, achieving an end-of-year chart position of 11.

BELOW One of the band's earliest professional photoshoots, circa 1999.

"I was feeling like death when I should have been on top of the world." Phil

LEFT The band dominated the BRIT Awards at Earls Court, where they also performed 'Trouble'. February 26, 2001.

RIGHT US. tour poster, Seattle and Portland.

HIGHS AND LOWS

At the start of 2001, Coldplay received two nominations for that year's BRIT Awards – the biggest in UK music. At the awards night in February they won both. But while they were on top of the world their friend, and manager, Phil had descended further towards collapse. "I was feeling like death. The band picked up awards for Best British Band and Album, and all I could think about was how much I wanted to be in bed."

Debs Wild sat with BMG Publishing at the ceremony, "The second I saw the presenter's mouth start to form C for Coldplay, I was up on my feet! It was one of the best moments. I was so proud, but had no idea the hell that Phil was going through."

Estelle Wilkinson became aware that Phil's health was failing, "He called to say he had to stop working. The doctor said they hadn't seen results like this of anyone not already in a coma."

Phil had to cease work and no one knew for how long. "My mind and body finally decided enough was enough in early 2001," said Phil. "I got really ill and had to take several months off. I certainly thought about giving up then. It crossed my mind that I simply wasn't tough enough."

Business was not as usual, but with Wilkinson deputizing for Phil in the UK, and Holmes taking control in the US, the band went back on the road. Touring was about to change completely too. It was time to break America.

"I was able to say, if you want to break America you have to tour like an American act. I think they got that," Dave Holmes said. "They were young enough that they didn't have those commitments, that would have made it more difficult to commit to those long stretches of time that they put in."

"We'd all done tours in vans," Jonny's long-serving guitar tech Matt McGinn said. "Me and the crew (most of whom are still around) hadn't done stuff any bigger. But then when Coldplay took off we were just as fucking surprised as they were. And everybody was like 'Here we go!' The boys could have easily turned around and said, 'We better get some proper roadies who've done this before,' but they didn't. They said: 'No, you lot are coming too!' It was brilliant... but terrifying as well."

Touring the States changed the band very specifically. In early 2001, they began playing clubs, acoustic sessions and US Radio Festivals but still had a reputation for being quite stage shy. "The band always seemed to be on in between heavy rock acts, and would frequently be pelted with whatever came to hand – a lot of shoes I seem to remember," said Jeff Dray. Chris said, "There were metal heads in the audience going for us. It was terrible."

On tour in the US, the stamina and commitment of Coldplay was tested. One such moment was when Chris got back on the tour bus after a particularly grim and exhausting show and thought he had two choices. Either pack up and go home or, "just admit to other people – other than myself – that I think we're the greatest band in the history of man and every performance we have to try and change people's lives and make music that makes people feel things and unashamedly so. If people don't believe us when we're on stage, how can we expect them to enjoy the music?"

At their next headline show at Atlanta's Tabernacle, they tried a new approach of losing themselves in performance, totally immersing themselves in the music they believed in. It was a pinnacle moment. "We're desperate to make every single person in the room have the best evening's entertainment they've ever had," said Chris.

COLDPLAY

THE end 107.7

the Stranger

SEATTLE

FEBRUARY 9

SHOWBOX

7PM/21 AND OVER/TIX AT TICKETMASTER 206-628-0888

94.7 NRK

PORTLAND MERCURY

PORTLAND

FEBRUARY 10

ROSELAND

8PM/ALL AGES/TIX AT FASTIXX 503-224-TIXX

MONQUI PRESENTS
monqui.com

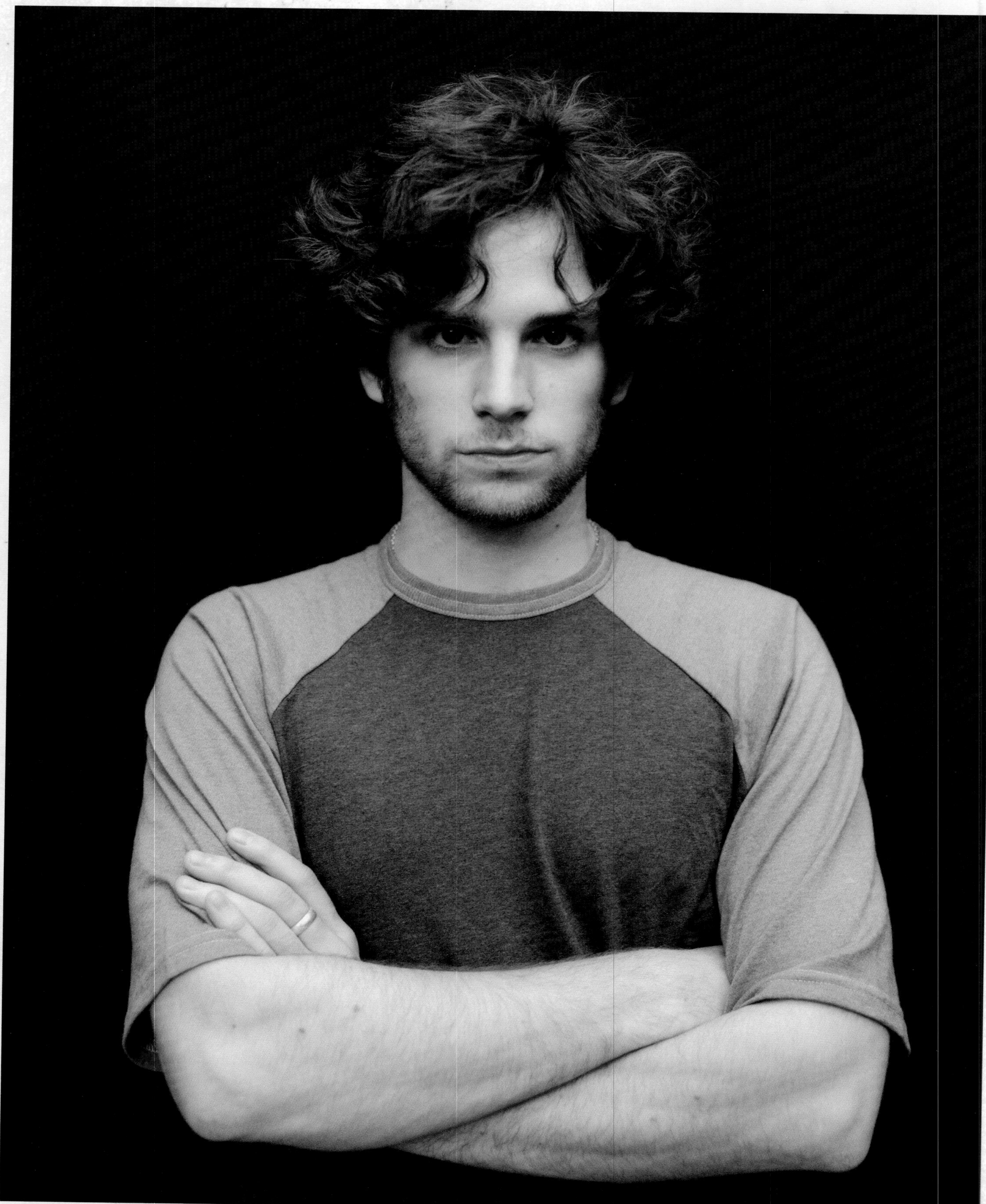

GUY BERRYMAN

Guy Berryman is the proprietor of Coldplay's soul, a bassist and songwriter forever on the hunt for a groove and armed with an almost limitless knowledge and passion for music and creativity in all its forms. Guy has the looks which have been a constant source of fascination, mainly by Chris: "My entire life is spent trying to push Guy forward at photoshoots," said the singer. "He's our packaging… responsible for all our calendar sales." But there's much more to him than that…

MAXIMUM SOUL

"I started playing bass when I was 12 years old," Guy recalled of his formative years growing up in Scotland, "from the songs of Motown, James Brown and some funk, soul or anything where the bassline is really accentuated. I got into those groups after seeing a band at school when I was a kid. I wanted to be a part of that scene." Naturally, Guy's earliest influences were more groove-led than the other members of the group's influence. Guy spent much of his teenage years listening to James Brown, Kool & The Gang, Pink Floyd, Lynn Collins, Maceo Parker and the J.B.'s. Guy's passion for soul and funk music is well known, as is his increasingly bulging rare record collection at home. "I haven't found my favourite song yet," he has said.

Born April 12, 1978, and raised (until the age of 12) in Kirkcaldy, Fife, Guy began his musical education by playing the trumpet and drums in the school band. It was then that he discovered he was a leftie who plays bass right-handed. He formed his first group, Time Out, when his love for playing and learning music became the most important thing in his young life. "I've always been interested in music. I was in my first school band when I was 13." But Guy never felt satisfied with playing the same sort of songs as other local teenage cover bands. He sought out a larger musical education. "Everyone was into bands like the Smiths and the Stone Roses, but I wanted to find a music that I could call my own. That was my form of rebellion." Time Out became Guy's first musical outlet; surrounding himself with other musicians was paramount to Guy expressing his creativity. "There were four of us in Time Out, playing pretty bad Genesis covers and renditions. It was guitar and keyboards, we played terrible, terrible stuff. The best musician in the group was really into Genesis. We would agonize for hours trying to work out horrible prog rock stuff with ridiculous solos. We never got anywhere near it – we'd muck about and make a noise." Since he was an accomplished drummer, Guy played his first gig as a musician performing 'Another Day in Paradise' by Phil Collins. "Nobody sang it, we had a saxophonist who played the melody."

ABOVE Debs' photo of Guy performing at Manchester Roadhouse, 1999.

BELOW Debs' photo of Guy relaxing backstage, the afternoon before the band's first Glastonbury headline: June 28, 2002.

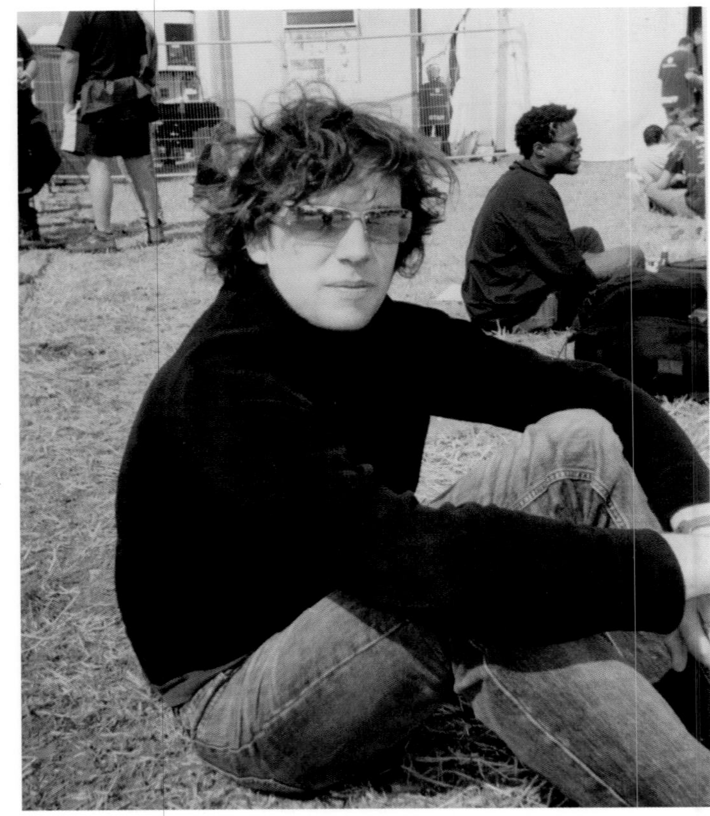

LEARNING CURVE

All four members of Coldplay left their homes in smaller towns to study in the big city at UCL in 1996. In truth, the boys all wanted to form a band – getting an education was just a bonus. Guy chose Engineering as a way to funnel his creativity. "I gave up my course because I hated it and started a degree in architecture. I gave that up as well." While the rest of the band completed their degrees, Guy paid his rent by working as a bartender in a local pub. It was clearly music that Guy was most interested in, and university quickly fell by the wayside with the introduction of Jonny, Will and Chris.

Kris Foof remembers Guy at UCL. "Guy was a quiet young man who had been put in 'Paris Block', the less populated block of rooms in Ramsay Hall. The rest of the band had been placed in 'New York Block', but not Guy – he was the outsider. But he was the outsider that the insiders all knew about, namely from his stockpile of rad musical instruments in his room, not to mention his record collection. He was a man of few, but meaningful, words."

A friendship between the four had started to form in their first year of studies, but it took a bit more time for Guy and Chris to gel. "We have very similar brains, but they come out in different personalities," Chris has said. "He's someone I got the wrong impression of when we first met. He's not as scary as he looks – he's a lot nicer. Guy's the dark member of the band. Everyone thinks he's moody. Soft-spoken is better."

> "We were more capable of producing shit. But the longer we went on, you could tell Chris had the magic."
> Guy

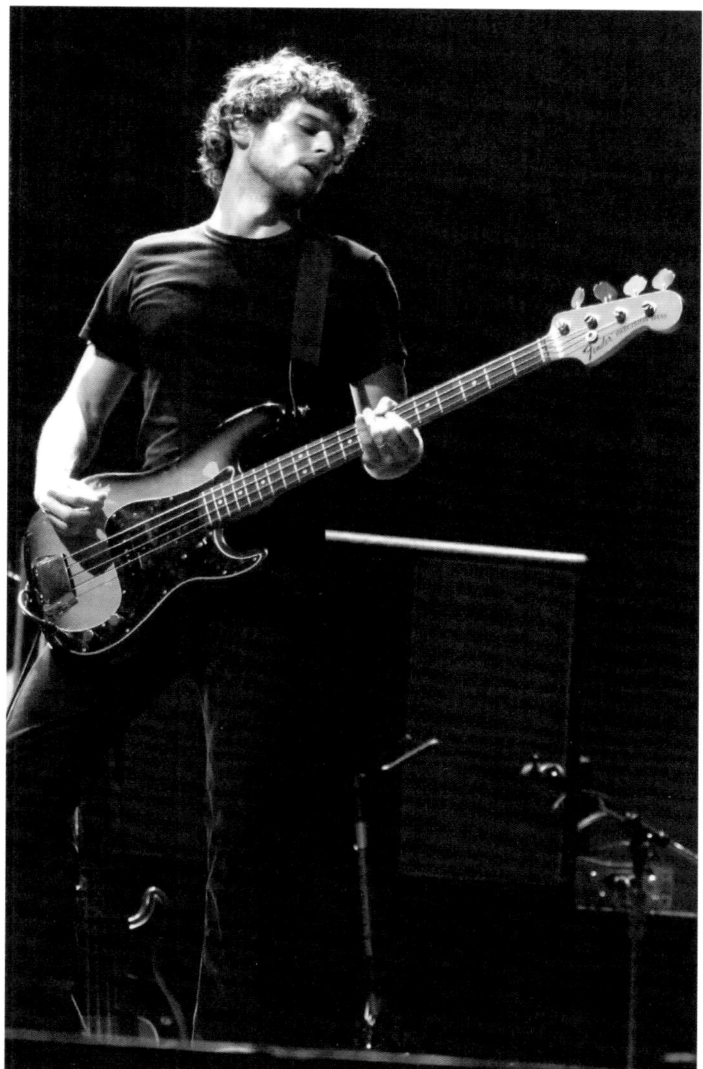

ABOVE Guy at Lancashire County Cricket Club, September 12, 2009, on the *Viva la Vida* tour.

LEFT Guy on stage at the Nippon Budokan, Tokyo, Japan, July 18, 2006, during the Twisted Logic tour.

Coldplay's sudden, almost instant, rise to success impacted the band. "There was no learning curve. It was a vertical gradient," Guy said. Out of the band, he has been the most persistent at staying out of the limelight. "At first, when Chris got all the attention, I was jealous," he has said, "but when you realize how much hassle it is, the appeal wears off."

Regardless of all the side effects of stardom, Guy is grateful for the band's success ... a fact that, to this day, still inspires him. "It's been an incredible journey. I have to pinch myself and appreciate the fact that it's not really a job, it's a passion. We don't have to put on a shirt and tie every day and go to work. We just have to travel around and be in a band."

Guy now chooses to spend his time outside of the band diving deep into his other creative outlets. "The most important thing in life is to be passionate. Even worse than losing all your money, it's losing the feeling of waking up and feeling excited by what you love."

> “If there was one goal we had when we were getting together back in 1998, it was to make music and achieve something. And regardless of the success we've already had, we're still trying to achieve something.”
>
> Guy

ABOVE Guy performing during the *Mylo Xyloto* tour, November 10, 2012, in Auckland, New Zealand.

OPPOSITE Guy signing the *Ghost Stories* artwork.

SPEED OF SOUND

Guy is a deeply passionate individual whose creativity is not solely bound to music, and the success of the band has allowed him to become an avid collector of classic cars, a lover of photography and design, music production, art and fashion, and most recently antiques. He runs marathons too. Guy hopes, sometime in the future, to release a book of his photographs into the wild. “I learned photography when I was studying architecture at college. It was on the X&Y tour that I have really been very active. I have taken lots of pictures. I take a camera wherever I go.”

Guy's “fundamental love of music” has helped the bassist to discover a life not only behind a lens, but also behind the control board, as a producer. “I'm never happier than when I'm being creative, whether that's with Coldplay or other artists. I just love being in the studio.”

Indeed, in 2011, Guy (as The Darktones along with Rik Simpson) produced the Pierces' album *You & I*. Captaining the Pierces' project in the studio allowed Guy to expand his repertoire of talent, this time with production. "Myself, Rik Simpson and the girls formed a little gang of four and we just beavered away in the Coldplay studio and Electric Lady Studios in New York. I haven't really made records with anyone on this level before. I had to learn a whole bunch of new skill sets – about how to speak as a producer, rather than speaking to one of my band members. I definitely feel that the process has made me better at what I do and what I know." Aside from the Pierces, Guy also formed Apparatjik, with Magne Furuholmen from A-ha, singer/guitarist Jonas Bjerre and drummer/producer Martin Terefe, and released the albums *We Are Here* in 2010 and *Square Peg in a Round Hole* in 2012.

Debs Wild on Guy: *"Guy is so much more than the 'handsome one' who plays bass guitar. People assume he's quiet and shy but he's an observer with a quick wit. Despite his rock 'n' roll antics of yesteryear, he still knows how to have a good time and get the best out of his life's opportunities.*

Even though I have always encouraged every artist I've ever worked with since to complete their education, I remember back when Guy stepped out of study at UCL thinking: 'There's really no point, he won't need a degree where he's going!'

Guy and soul are often mentioned in the same breath because of his love of that particular music genre, but to me, Guy's soul lies in his kind-heartedness and generosity – something all Coldplay's members have."

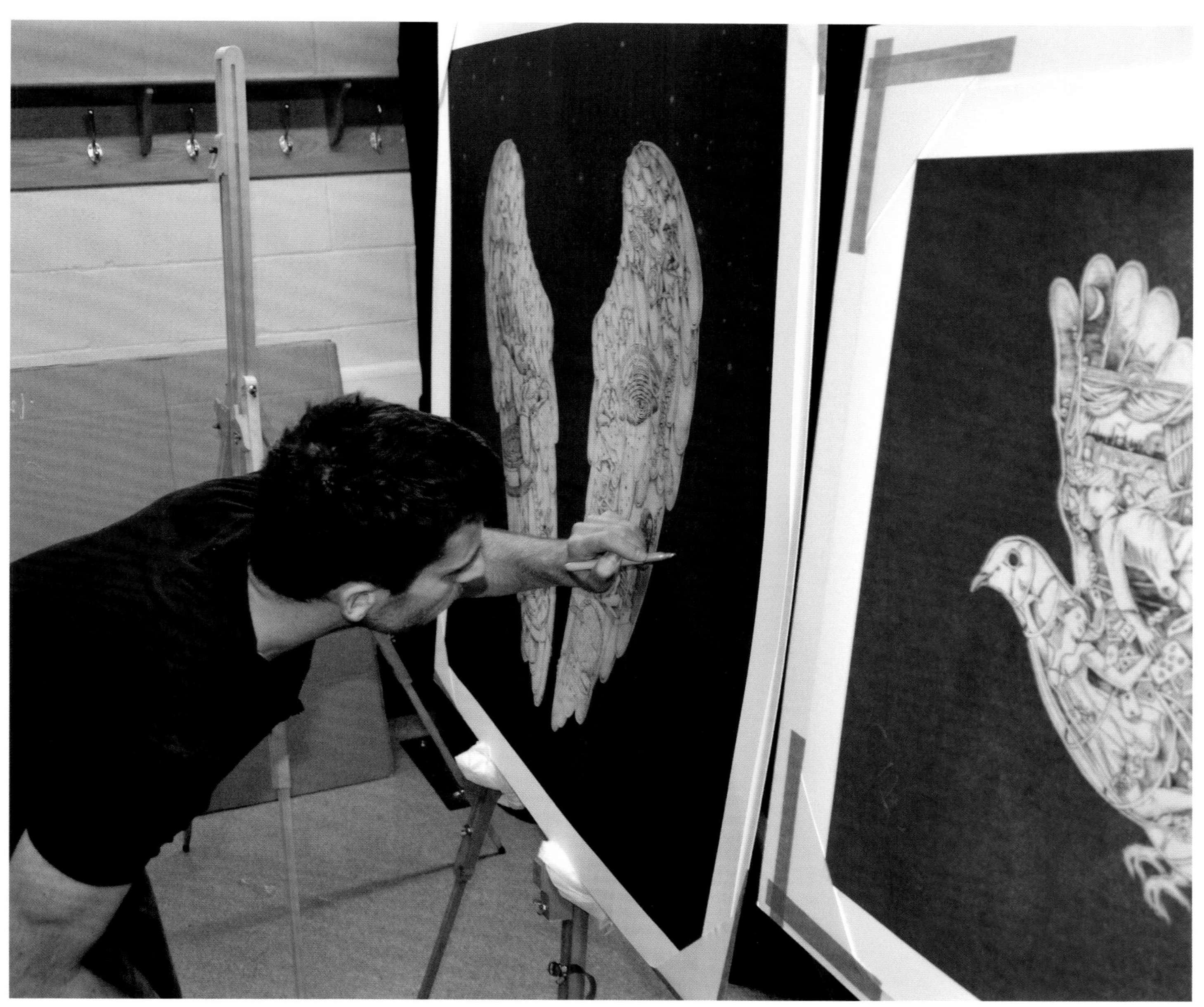

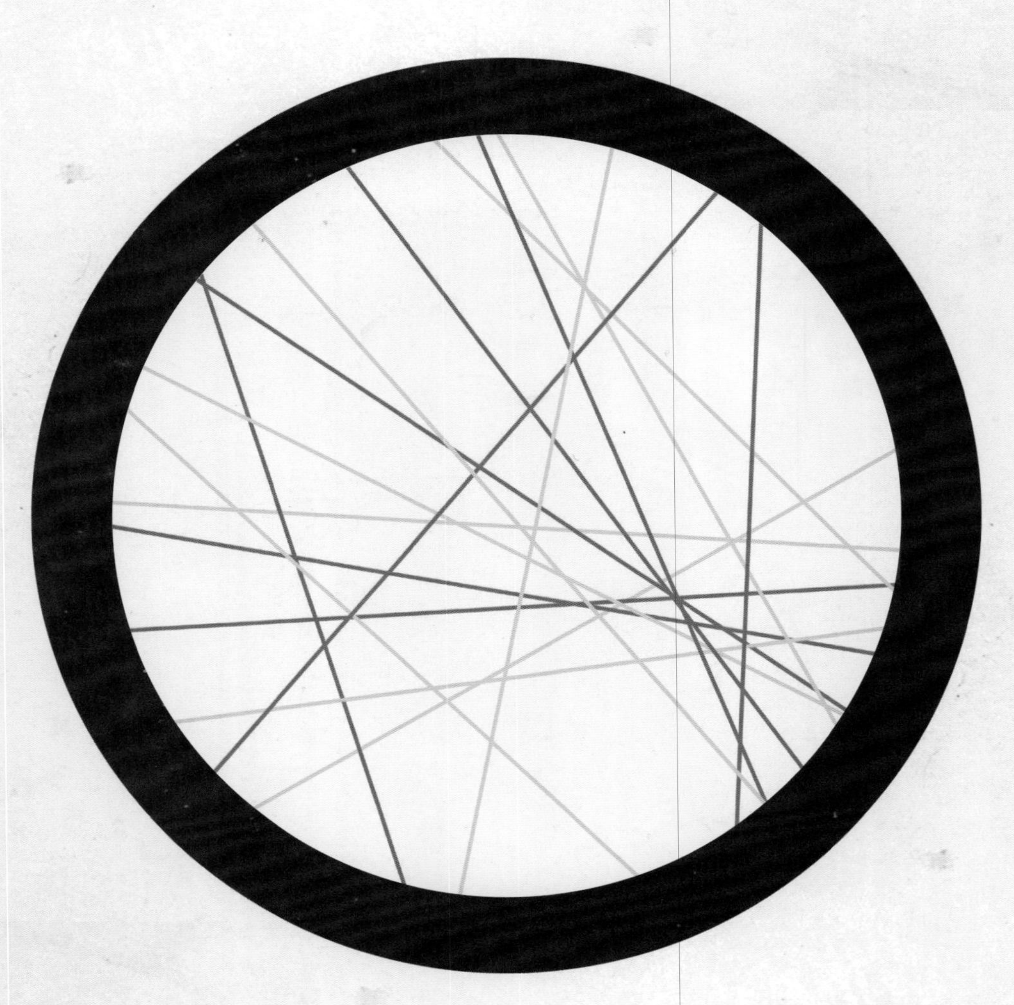

CHAPTER

TWO

SCIENCE AND PROGRESS

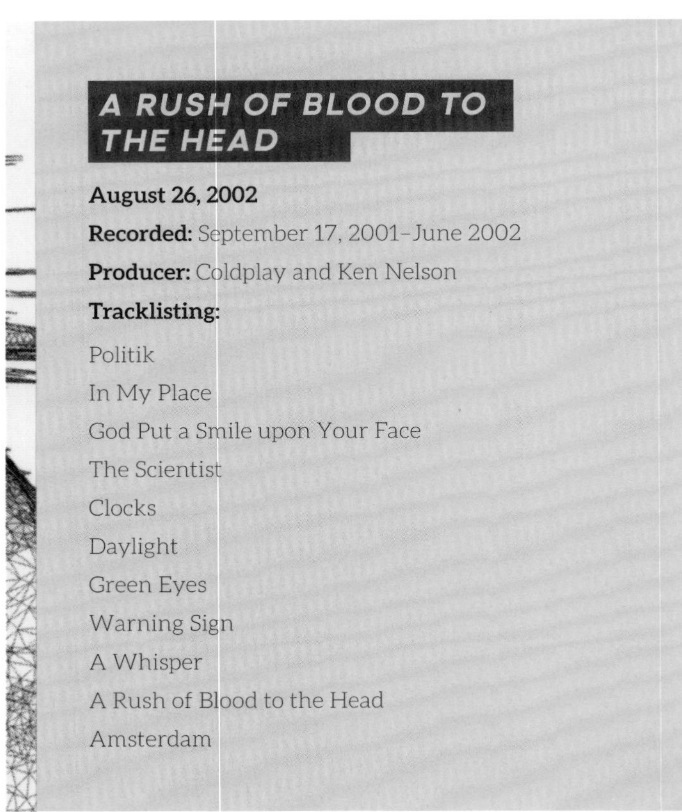

A RUSH OF BLOOD TO THE HEAD

August 26, 2002

Recorded: September 17, 2001–June 2002

Producer: Coldplay and Ken Nelson

Tracklisting:

Politik
In My Place
God Put a Smile upon Your Face
The Scientist
Clocks
Daylight
Green Eyes
Warning Sign
A Whisper
A Rush of Blood to the Head
Amsterdam

ABOVE Postcard promoting Oxfam's Make Trade Fair campaign.

> "I have to step aside now to give the band a proper shot; they need a real manager."
>
> Phil

A Rush of Blood to the Head delivered on the promises made by _Parachutes_, and then some. It sent the band hurtling even further down the rabbit hole of fame, fortune and world-touring.

EVERYONE MUST FIND A PLACE

Coldplay were freshly flushed with confidence from BRIT Award success for Best Album and Best Band in February 2001 (and, a year later, their Grammy for Best Alternative Album, of which Chris would say, "Of course we're absolutely delighted to get this Grammy thing even though it's total nonsense, it's still good nonsense to win."). However, the road to the release of their 'difficult second album' was paved with much hyper-critical analysis between the four members. They were the biggest band in the UK but they felt they "had to decide whether we were a bunch of students who got lucky or we were going to admit that we are really fucking good," exclaimed Chris. One thing they knew for certain: they weren't going to just cut and paste what they had done before.

> “Not a single night goes past where I don’t wake up sweating and thinking no one will like this record. We poured every ounce of soul, emotion and love into it, and now we can only wait and see.”

Chris

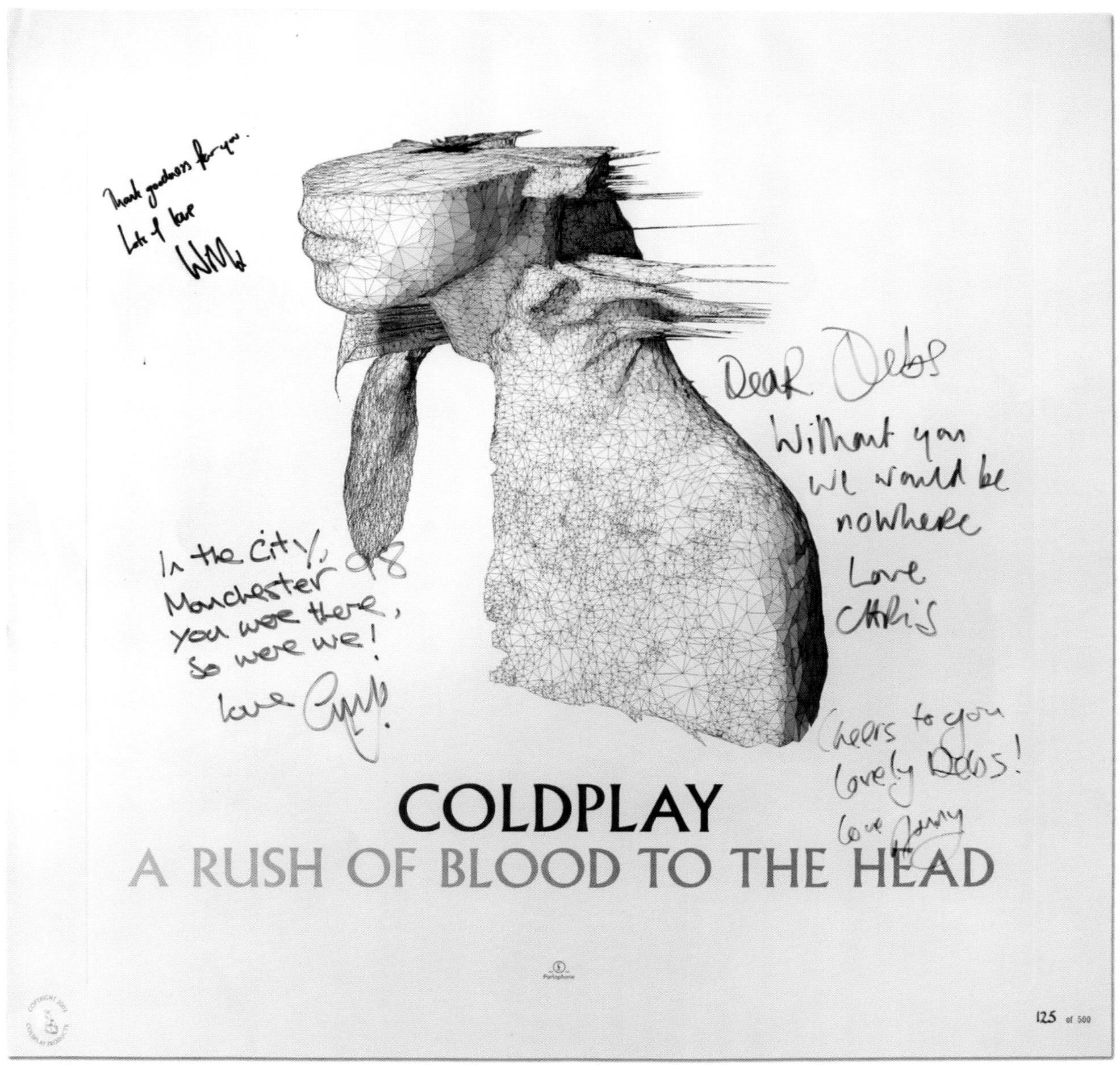

LEFT Chris remained in the studio in the UK, leaving Will, Guy and Jonny to collect the 2002 GRAMMY award for *Parachutes*, which won Best Alternative Music Album, February 27, 2002.

ABOVE Debs' personalized, signed *A Rush of Blood to the Head* lithograph to commemorate the album's success.

"It's no good for anyone if we make *Parachutes* MK II because it's not interesting for us," Chris continued. "For us it was important to progress and try to improve upon our abilities as musicians."

Between the release of *Parachutes* and the recording of *A Rush of Blood...* the world had changed dramatically. With the events of 9/11, everything changed overnight. The fallout affected and impacted everything – news, culture, politics, economics, music, art.

But, Coldplay being Coldplay, they put all the negative world energy to effective use.

"Of course, the album is affected by September 11," said Chris. "Will says songs come out of the way you're feeling at that time or they just arrive and we don't really know where they come from. On September 13, I was feeling a bit angry and upset because of the state of the world, and so this song just came out and it also came out of the idea where we all just bashed our instruments with no fragility or niceness," said Chris. That song was 'Politik'.

They booked Mayfair Studios, Primrose Hill, London, to begin preparations for a new album. However, Ken Nelson and Mark Phythian (on additional production duties) were detained elsewhere for a short while, so the studio asked freelance engineer Rik Simpson to come in and record the band until their arrival.

On his first day, Simpson walked into the studio where, oblivious to his entrance, Chris was sitting at a grand piano running through 'Politik'.

"He was giving it loads and performing even though he didn't know I was there." Rik Simpson dipped in and out of the studio for the remainder of the recording, and has remained a long-serving collaborator ever since.

"Phil said to me: 'Oh, you should have a song called Politik," said Chris. "It's as simple as that. We imagined 'Politik' to be your beliefs about something, your own politic," Chris continued.

"All I said was: 'How could anyone not be affected by something big like 9/11? The song comes out of us thinking, 'Fuck! We're all going to die!' That's what most of the album's about. There's a theme running through the album which is: 'This could be your last meal – so make it a nice meal,'" exclaimed Chris. Guy agreed completely: "We could not have put this song in any better position than No.1 on the album, and there is no better song than this to open our show."

RIGHT Debs' photo of Jonny backstage before the Bath Pavilion show, during the band's Glastonbury warm-up tour.

BELOW Chris and Jonny wait for *A Rush of Blood...* photo session to begin in London, December 19, 2003, in front of Sølve Sundsbø's artwork.

As with *Parachutes*, writing and the process of recording the album proved difficult.

They had songs. But not *the* songs. "There was lots of material just prior to going in to the studio – a whole album's worth of material. It was rejected by the rest of the band," said Phil.

"After we'd recorded *Parachutes* we had one song left – 'In My Place'," remembered Chris. "When Jonny played me the guitar part I thought, 'Well, we have to record that. It's the best song we've ever written'."

Guy did not remember it as being so easy: "It was hard recording 'In My Place' because we'd been playing it live for a couple of years, so when we actually finally sat down to record it in the studio, we didn't know how it should sound."

Towards the end of the *Parachutes* tour, the band were already road-testing other new tracks, as well as 'In My Place'. 'God Put a Smile upon Your Face', 'Animals', 'Harmless', 'A Rush of Blood to the Head', 'Murder', 'Warning Sign', 'Amsterdam', 'Idiot' and 'A Ghost' also got an airing or two. Some of the songs would get the band's approval, others would be abandoned, leaving Chris to continue writing, full well knowing they had agreed to headline that year's Glastonbury. They had to deliver.

"Absolutely ridiculously," said Phil. "Michael Eavis had invited us to headline Glastonbury. We'd released one album and were still absolute minnows. For him to ask us to headline the biggest festival in the world was insane. So, we knew that was the date we had to have the album out by, otherwise who would be crazy enough to play Glastonbury without even having a second album?"

Suddenly, London didn't feel right. It was home. It was safe. But Coldplay wanted to get out of their bubble. "We got a bit stale in London," said Will. "We kind of listened to all the stuff we recorded there and we were disappointed with a lot of it; I mean some of it was OK, but a lot of it wasn't. We really needed to get out of London where there's no distractions and where we could just focus on recording."

Meaning business, the band decamped to Liverpool. "Parr Street was really important to them early on. They felt really at home there and really comfortable there. It was more that the studio just worked for them," said Miles Leonard. "We were absolutely itching to make it by the time we got in there," said Will.

A Rush of Blood... was pencilled in for a June 2002 release, but the deadline came and went, putting them – and the label – under pressure.

Chris thought the album wasn't good enough, and kept writing. Many of the songs that turned up toward the end of the recording process, went on to change the shape of the album. "'The Scientist', 'Clocks' and 'Daylight' were all written and recorded very fast in Liverpool. I don't know where any of them came from. I just can't believe we got them."

"'The Scientist' reminds me that we were almost finished recording the album and I recall Chris saying that something was missing and we needed a piano-led song," remembers Nelson. "A couple of days later Chris played us 'The Scientist' with Jonny accompanying him on guitar." According to the album's sleeve notes, The Scientist is Dan Keeling. The reason wasn't immediately clear, but Chris announced to Dan that he'd written the song for him about his recent, painful break-up. When Keeling first heard it, he said, "I feel worse now!"

Phil was very insistent that the band also include another new song – 'Clocks'. "Phil asked us to record one more of the demos," said Nelson. "He felt that it would be a good addition to the album."

The release date of the album slipped again so that 'Clocks' could be finished and added. Dan Keeling said that hearing 'Clocks' in Air Studios was "one of the best moments of the whole thing". 'Clocks' would go on to win the Grammy for Record of the Year at the 46th annual Grammy Awards.

Jonny reflected on the recording process of the album just before their Glastonbury headline slot that summer: "It was quite long: it took about seven months and we did it in three studios. It was quite tense especially towards the last month or so when we missed the deadline." The press picked up on the delay and ran the story. "I'm not really concerned about anything media-wise because at the end of the day, we set out to make a good record and that's what I think we've done," said Guy.

WHAT WOULD PHIL DO?

The final day of recording *A Rush of Blood to the Head* arrived when the band were at Air Studios, London. This was also the day Phil decided to break the news of his departure to the band.

"They would have preferred me to stay," said Phil. "That was made quite clear. I think to some extent they felt abandoned and let down – and to some extent they were right. That was not a good conversation. It was pretty dramatic, and not just because I was the manager but because I was Chris' best friend and I was buggering off to the other side of the world. When I left it was a natural fit that Dave Holmes would carry on looking after the band with Estelle." Phil had no hesitation recommending to the band that they co-manage. "She was so brilliant at handling everything." Wilkinson wasn't expecting to be the offered the position and felt overwhelmed. She firmly believed that Phil would come back and thought of herself as an interim co-manager. When strategizing and decision-making, she would often think, "What would Phil do?"

According to Wilkinson, Phil's sabbatical contributed to him missing out on the MMF Manager of the Year award – something that angers her to this day – but despite breaking the band around the world, Phil felt walking away was the right move.

The band could not afford to stop, so began focusing on their fast-approaching third Glastonbury appearance in three years.

"There was a period where we thought we should cancel it because the album wasn't finished," said Will.

It was decided that a mini tour might be the perfect warm-up for Glastonbury, and a chance to practise the new songs live.

Five cities, initially chosen for their proximity to each member's birth city, were booked: Edinburgh, Liverpool, Bath, Portsmouth (cancelled) and Truro. They also played London (the Meltdown Festival, with David Bowie as curator). The new songs finally got an audience – albeit an intimate one – before Glastonbury. "I did not have any sense of 'We're going to be fine to headline the festival', said Phil. "The only sense of any real confidence came later, probably the last day before I left, at the Kentish Town Forum show."

An air of heavy anticipation and excitement surrounding Glastonbury and the record was growing. There was prevalent media attention; 'In My Place' got its first radio play, there was an *NME* cover, and a cover article in *Q* magazine. "We've rehearsed for just over three weeks," said Jonny. "It's the first time we've had a long period of rehearsals since before *Parachutes* came out and so it's actually quite good that we've got everything running." Guy said: "We've put a lot of work into the production, trying to get it just right".

ABOVE Time off in Bangkok, July 2003. Left to right: Matt McGinn, Miller, Guy, Jonny, Dan Green.

'THE SCIENTIST'

On October 4, 2002, 'The Scientist' music video premiered on MTV. Filmed in various locations such as Kentish Town, Camden and Bourne Wood, this was another video to feature only Chris. That was a decision made by the clip's director, Jamie Thraves.

"Originally it was just a story with a character, not featuring the band, but Chris is a really great performer, so it made sense to use Chris," said Thraves. "He was a bit sceptical and was concerned it would come across too cheesy."

Shooting in reverse to appear as if the action in the clip was moving forward was tough for the singer and director. Thraves had to visualize every camera's movement and reverse it.

"It took Chris a month to learn the lyrics backwards, I believe," Thraves recalls.

Though it was stressful, it was a lot of fun and Thraves was very pleased with the end result. He spent a long time making sure that when audiences rewind the story it would make perfect sense.

While it was hard to get the clip substantial airplay (there were obvious concerns about a music video involving a car crash), the video went on to scoop three US video music awards.

BELOW Photo of Chris with actress Elaine Cassidy and director Jamie Thraves, from 'The Scientist' video shoot.

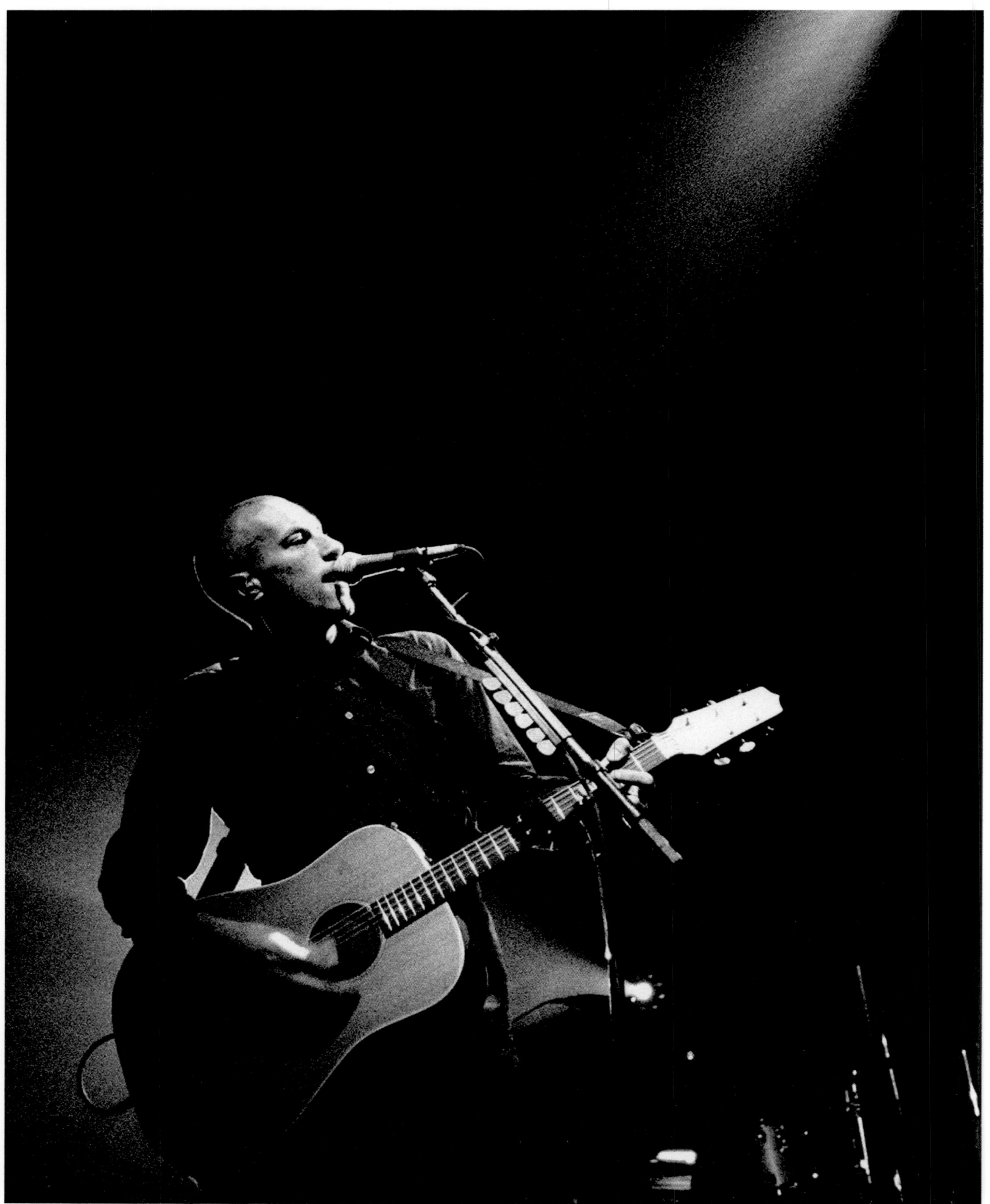

> **"** Very nervous about Glastonbury, I think we all are. It'll be the biggest gig we've ever played, I think – well, hopefully, if anyone turns up! **"**
>
> Jonny

GLASTONBURY – PART THREE: FIRST HEADLINE SHOW

Performing on the Pyramid Stage at Glastonbury is a big deal for any band. On June 30, 2002 – a mere three years after the band made their inaugural Glasto appearance – the day of the big gig arrived. Everyone wanted to get to the site early, except Chris, because he was having a session with his vocal coach, Mary Hammond. Even then, he knew the importance of protecting his voice, and the training was part of a ritual that also included a personal trainer who soon began to travel with the band. They all wanted to be match fit for touring, but Glastonbury was an extra-momentous occasion.

Speaking to Chris Salmon, Will also remembered, "It was kind of do or die. We were either going to fail miserably or come out of it the other side a much better band. Thankfully it was the latter."

Indeed, it was a triumphant set, featuring a green laser that could be seen for miles.

Will admitted he couldn't really see anything beyond his drums apart from the laser. Jonny reflects: "When I saw the laser during 'Clocks', I remember thinking we might have pulled it off."

"I remember getting to Glastonbury in 2002 just as the band took to the stage," recounts Edith Bowman. "I arrived and ran towards the stage so I could catch the set, and ended up sleeping in my car that night."

The band's tour manager, Jeff Dray, felt the pressure of the performance. "The crew were all shitting it," he exclaimed. "None of us had ever done anything that big. When Chris hit the final chord of the acoustic number ('Life Is for Living') that Phil insisted should stay in the set and the crowd, who had been silent for the song, roared, everyone felt that we had cracked it."

"It was a bold move to headline with only *Parachutes* under their belts and having to showcase songs off a new album. I watched the show out front and was really nervous for them, but as soon as they kicked off with 'Politik' it felt special. 'The Scientist' was a highlight for me and I think the whole crowd," added Keith Wozencroft.

RIGHT Personal assistant Vicki Taylor's tour laminate, with things to remember during the show. It was her first tour.

LEFT Chris bathes in the spotlight during a concert at Enmore Theater, Sydney, Australia, August 7, 2001.

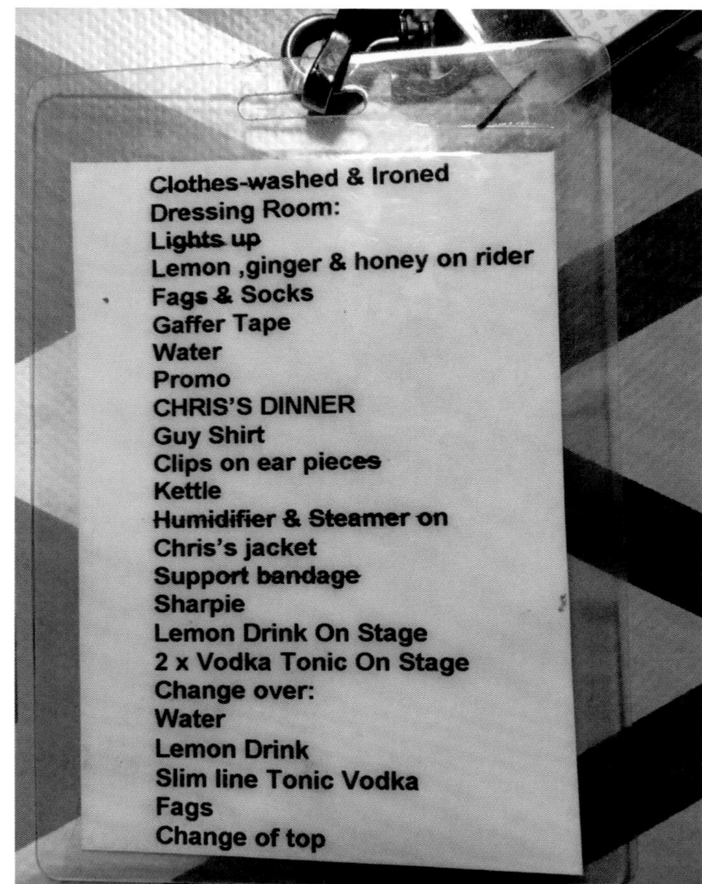

Dan Green remembers the show too. "Once 'Politik' was out of the way, it felt very big. It gave us the confidence to say we can do this and we can do that."

THE ALBUM SEES DAYLIGHT

"I can remember listening to an early promo copy of *A Rush of Blood...* lying on the sofa in my flat, and being absolutely blown away by it," remembers Chris Salmon of June 2002. "It's very tough to follow up a great, successful album with an even better and more successful one – but it was clear that Coldplay had done that, and that they were on a path to the stratosphere. Those songs, man. Those songs."

A Rush of Blood... was still two months away from official release, but the band started touring the album right after

MAKE TRADE FAIR

Although this was a stressful period designated to finishing the album, it was the start of the group's first public acts of altruism, and something the band cherish to the present day. On April 11, 2002, Oxfam launched their Make Trade Fair campaign around the world. London's Trafalgar Square hosted a free show where Chris performed 'Many Rivers To Cross'. There was a mixture of music and speeches from politicians. Coldplay were approached to be involved and agreed to crusade for the cause for a two-year period. They continued past that date because of their strong belief in the changes that would be achieved. Chris took to writing maketradefair.com on his hand and on the side of his piano to promote awareness for much of the period that surrounded the recording and release of *A Rush of Blood to the Head*. It was also through Make Trade Fair that the band struck a friendship with Emily Eavis, the daughter of Glastonbury founder Michael. 2002 was also the year in which Chris Martin went to Haiti with Emily to help raise awareness and funds for Oxfam.

ABOVE Roddy Woomble, Lou Rhodes of Lamb, Simon Pegg, Chris and Jonny at the Make Trade Fair show in aid of Oxfam, London Astoria, October 29, 2002.

LEFT Chris & Noel Gallagher at the Astoria, Make Trade Fair show.

Glastonbury, playing shows in Europe and across the US.

Now the record was finished, the band asked Rik Simpson to help out with backing tracks for the live shows.

As Dan Green points out, "*Parachutes* was just the four guys playing, there was no backing tracks. *A Rush of Blood...* was a different direction in production, so there was a lot of synthesizers, additional parts that are really key to the sound. I put together this system with Rik and we took all the stuff from the album and put it on these early digital machines." After setting them up, Simpson joined the band on tour for a few months.

'In My Place' was released on August 5, 2002, and gave Coldplay their highest single chart entry to date, debuting at No.2 in the official UK charts.

August 26, 2002 rolled around and *A Rush of Blood to the Head* was released. With the relief of release, came anxiety. Even more than usual. "Not a single night goes past where I don't wake up sweating and thinking no one will like this record," exclaimed Chris. "We poured every ounce of soul, emotion and love into it, and now we can only wait and see."

Co-manager Estelle Wilkinson remembers the time too. "One of the saddest things is I actually didn't often have a sense of euphoria at these amazing things that were happening. My general sense was more relief: Thank God it's as big as it is. The band's desire and level of expectation was already so high, as they knew what they wanted to achieve."

Coldplay were always striving to be the best they could. ("What's the point, otherwise?" Will would say.) The initial seconds of happiness about being No.1 in so many countries would be swiftly followed by wondering where they were not No.1.

Reflecting on the album's release, Will wrote in his journal: "I stopped listening to the album when I knew there was no way of changing it anymore. The period of waiting was like waiting for exam results, knowing that we felt confident (sort of) in our own

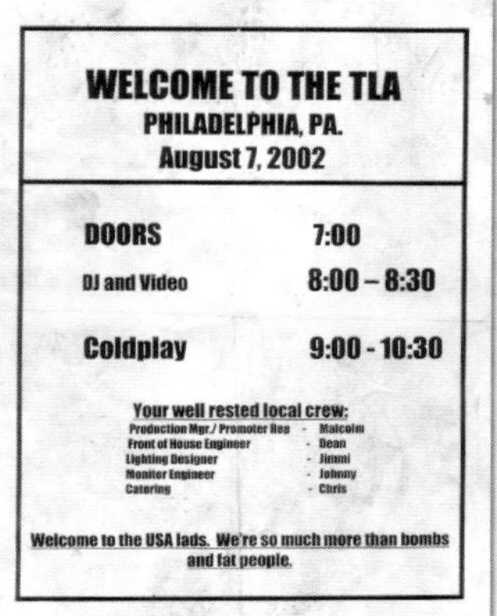

WELCOME TO THE TLA
PHILADELPHIA, PA.
August 7, 2002

DOORS	7:00
DJ and Video	8:00 – 8:30
Coldplay	9:00 - 10:30

Your well rested local crew:

Production Mgr./ Promoter Rep	- Malcolm
Front of House Engineer	- Dean
Lighting Designer	- Jimmi
Monitor Engineer	- Johnny
Catering	- Chris

Welcome to the USA lads. We're so much more than bombs and fat people.

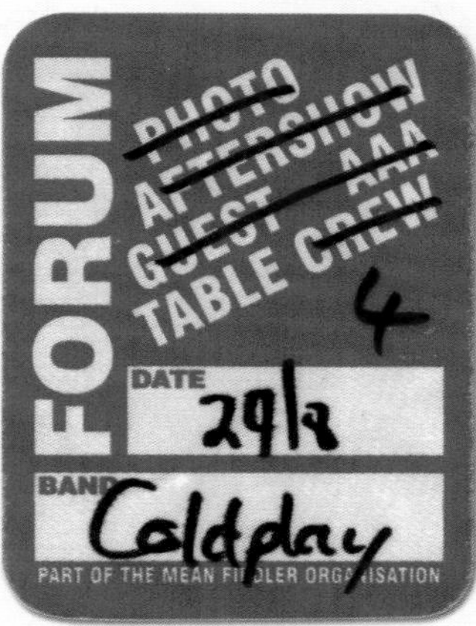

ABOVE Show times for Philadelphia show, 2002.

ABOVE RIGHT VIP seating pass for the Forum.

BELOW Contact sheet from the Make Trade Fair concert at the Astoria. Also featuring Simon Pegg, Chris, Jonny and Ms Dynamite.

heads about what we'd done, but not having a clue whether our best was good enough. Knowing that people seem to be into what we are doing even if it is different to what we did before is really amazing for us because for a long time, we really didn't know."

On Phil's birthday, August 29, the band were in the UK after a small tour of the States and performed a gig at the Forum in Kentish Town, London – attended by family, friends, fans and celebrities.

"Playing at the Kentish Town Forum was a real relief; for the first time we didn't have to apologize for playing lots of new songs, and we certainly felt more relaxed and played the best we had for ages," Will remarked.

The show was Phil's last day with the band. "It was an emotional day for sure," the manager remembers. "Tears were shed. I said goodbye to the band and went travelling round the world, with no plan whatsoever. I ended up at university in Melbourne, Australia."

On Sunday September 1, 2002, the second album from Coldplay stormed to the top of the UK chart. *A Rush of Blood to the Head* achieved the same number of sales on its first day as *Parachutes* had in its first week – 75,000 – and more than 274,000 copies in its first week, making it the highest sales in the first week of a release that year, beating both Eminem and Oasis.

The record hit the top of the charts in 27 countries, including Canada, Germany and Norway, and a significant chart position – No.5 – in the United States.

Chris was pretty speechless, but Jonny wasn't – "Tottenham are top of the league and we're No.1, this is the best day of my life!"

The band celebrated the news in London with key people from the team. Debs Wild was there once again. "Me, Caroline and Ramage felt it was only fitting to repeat history on Primrose Hill, but this time Estelle and the band – except Will, who was at home cooking a Sunday Roast – and Vicki (Taylor, the band's assistant) were able to come along. It was quite surreal, looking back. I doubt we could do that now. We ended up in a pub where Chris quietly asked me to tell the bar manager – discreetly – that all drinks were on him for the next round. It was anything but discreet when the manager rang the bell and loudly announced who was buying. I actually stepped in when I heard one guy make his order of two bottles of wine!"

The album's dramatic artwork turned many heads: Norwegian-born artist Sølve Sundsbø had created an image for the magazine *Dazed & Confused* which Chris saw some time later. He approached Sundsbø about using the image for the cover. Chris wanted something iconic and also asked for singles artwork ideas. "I suggested scanning the four members of the band for the four different releases," Sundsbø said. "The album was hugely successful, which was nice. I can think of a lot worse images to be associated with. It is unique."

LIVE 2003

The band's *A Rush of Blood...* tour was due to end in September 2003. It made perfect sense to document it with a Live DVD filmed in one of their smaller tour venues, Sydney's Hordern Pavilion. "The reason we didn't film a big gig was, we had to leave ourselves somewhere to go," said Chris. "There are lots of people that don't want to see us in a massive place and so the DVD we're releasing is like a medium-sized place which we really wanted to do as our first one."

The DVD also featured a tour documentary with footage from behind the scenes that included a historical anniversary. On June 5, 2003, 20 years after U2 recorded their live album *Under a Blood Red Sky* at the iconic Red Rocks amphitheatre, Coldplay performed there.

Coldplay Live 2003 was released on November 10, 2003 [November 3 in the US].

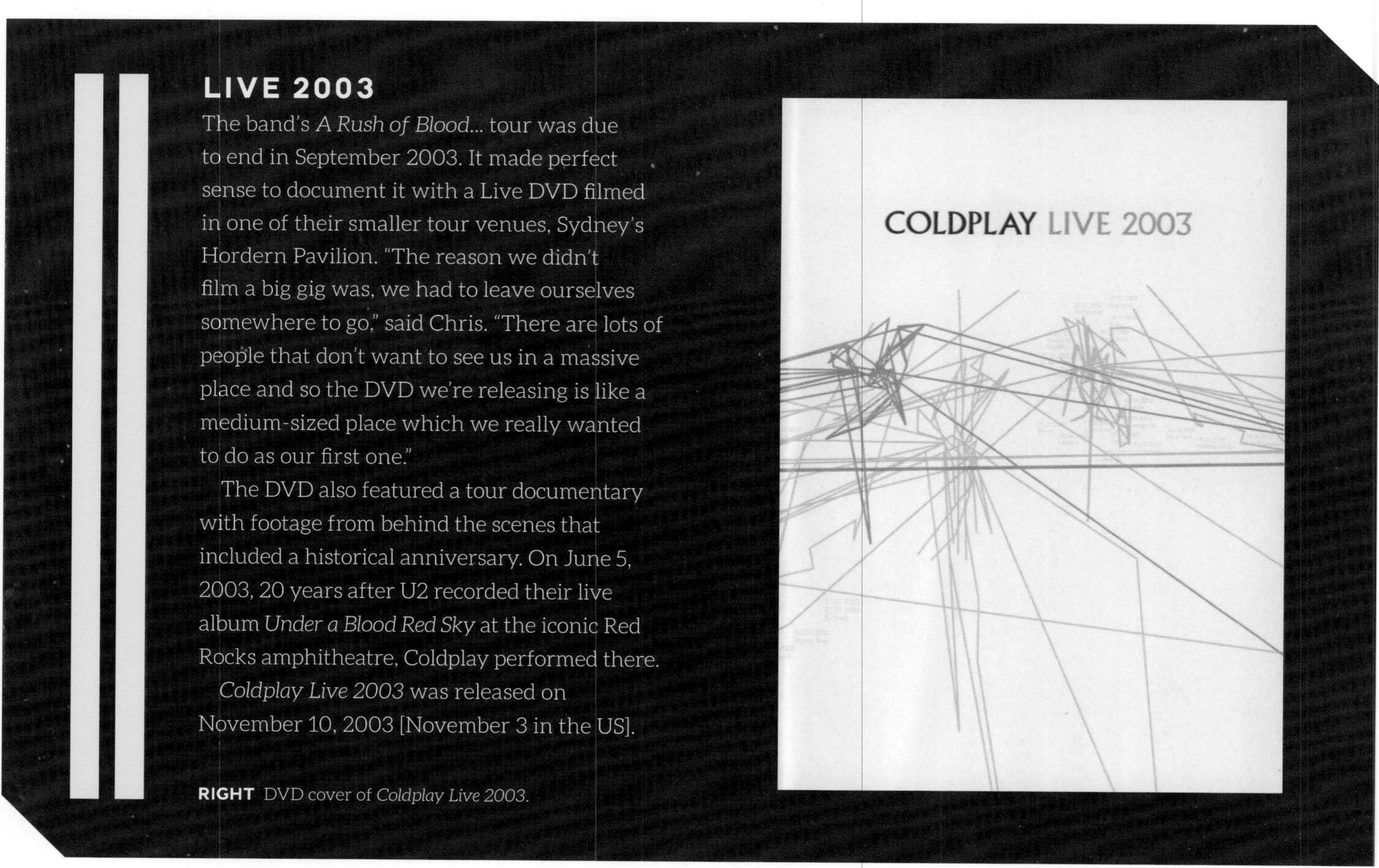

RIGHT DVD cover of *Coldplay Live 2003*.

CONQUERING THE US

The new year, 2003, ushered in a period of intense touring of the US, as well as Canada, Europe and Japan. "They were bona fide rock stars after the second album," said Nic Harcourt. Their rock star status saw them get a leg-up to arena-playing. In April, 2003, the album tour brought them back to the UK and Earls Court, one of the country's largest arena venues. It felt like a really big leap.

With a much larger stage set-up, Coldplay began their back-breaking tour of America. This period would come to highlight just how much of a hard-working band they are. "One of the things that Coldplay realized right from the start is that in America you've really got to spend the time here and log in those road hours," said Harcourt.

The world tour, and in particular shows across the States, would take the band up to the edge of the new year. It was around this time that they began to assess how they acted on stage... and how they could put on the best show possible.

"I think we were confident when we were playing in Jonny's bedroom, even when we first started out," said Will. "Chris always had great stage presence. But it wasn't until the second album that we started to get really confident in front of bigger audiences."

America was a challenge Coldplay knew they had to work for, but the rewards would be worth it. It would open the door to global exposure.

ABOVE RIGHT Jonny in a Mexico City karaoke bar with personal assistant Vicki Taylor, 2003.

RIGHT Left to right: Vicki Taylor, Ian Ramage, Caroline Elleray, Debs Wild and Estelle Wilkinson celebrating *A Rush of Blood to the Head* debuting at No.1 in August 2002.

BELOW Backstage antics, Mexico City, 2003.

BELOW RIGHT Aftershow pass for Earls Court, 2003.

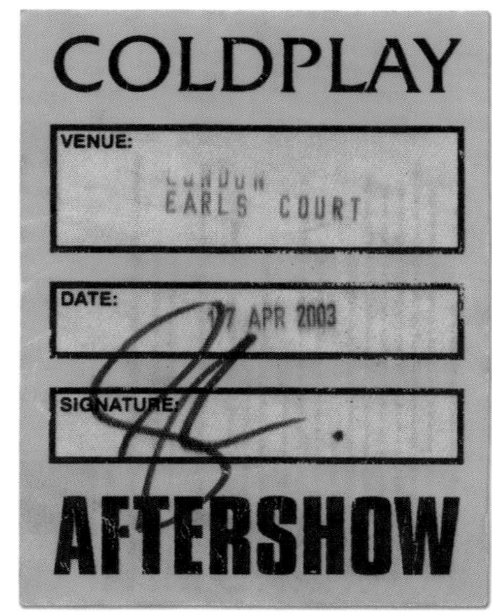

COLDPLAY
VENUE:
LONDON
EARLS COURT
DATE:
APR 2003
SIGNATURE:
AFTERSHOW

“The name of the album means doing something on impulse. I’ve realized that time is not infinite, and all my friends aren’t going to be around forever and maybe I’m only going to get to do certain things once. My grandfather always used to tell me to do things right now because whatever you have, it’s not going to last forever.”

Chris

BELOW In London, the band pose for a portrait shoot in 2002.

RIGHT Coldplay watching the England vs Argentina football match in July 2002. England won 1–0.

Coca-Cola

"Coldplay toured America so much and they did put the hard work in," said Dan Keeling. "One thing they realized is, no matter how good your record is, if you don't go over and play all these places in middle America, then you're not going to sell any records. It doesn't work like that."

"They always loved playing Europe, but America was always the dream and something they had to do. They put the time in and they went back, they understood why they needed to work it and to go for long periods of time, but it was really hard work and hard on everyone. There were tours where it was a struggle internally within the band when they were all finding their own dynamic," Wilkinson continued, "You can do Europe in a month, but after multiple tours in America it became too much. Everyone knows it's hard slog, but it brings you to breaking point."

Touring continuously indeed took its toll. It was decided in the future, as a result of the pressure-cooker flyover of the US, that they would – where possible – not spend more than three weeks away from home in one leg.

Steve Strange introduced US booking agent Marty Diamond to the band at an early show. To elevate the band to a greater

ABOVE Promotional sew-on patch.

LEFT New York's Madison Square Garden ticket, June 13, 2003.

BELOW Radio promo show for WPLJ in New York, June 12, 2003.

RIGHT Ticket to David Bowie's Meltdown 2002 at London's Royal Festival Hall.

BELOW London's Wembley Arena ticket for October 20, 2002. Coldplay also played October 21.

BOTTOM Promotional drinks coasters for *A Rush of Blood to the Head.*

ROYAL FESTIVAL HALL
David Bowie's Meltdown 2002
COLDPLAY
PETE YORN
Media Partners Time Out & Radio 3
SATURDAY 22 JUNE 2002 at 8:00 PM
LEVEL 4
TERRACE A7 £18.50 CHEQ STAN
50 Royal Festival Hall

Block Row Seat
001 17 M 194
Enter by: RED SIDE
METROPOLIS MUSIC
presents
COLDPLAY
plus special guests
REAR SIDE VIEW
Sunday 20 October 2002 7.30pm
£19.50 Ticket Presented to Guest
1 1075 181002 163251A
0123745794909000

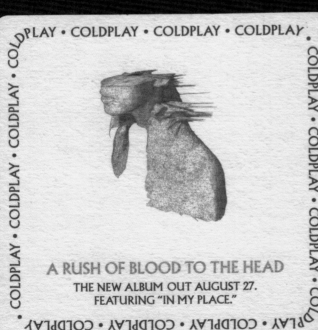

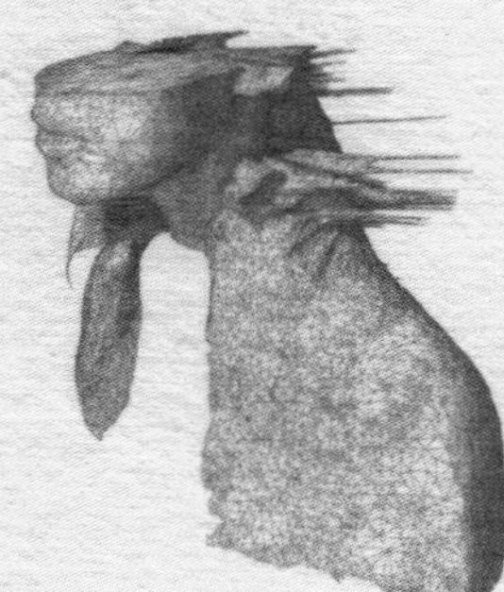

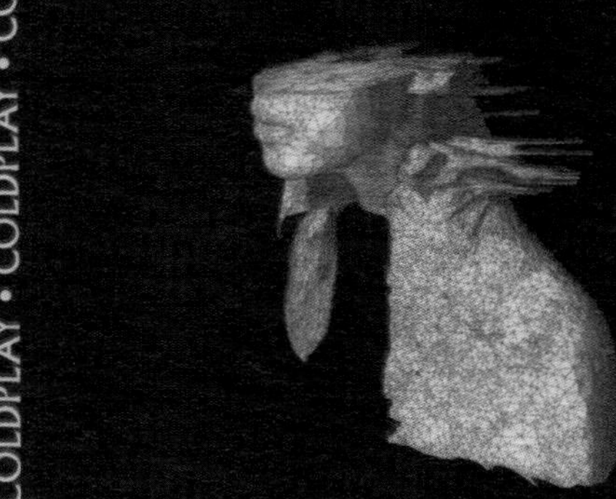

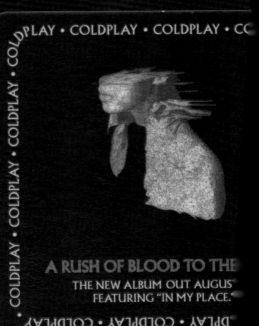

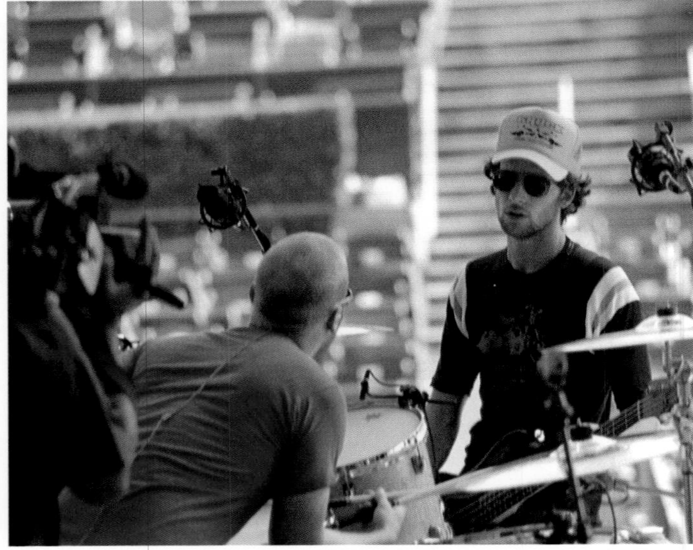

height, and with *A Rush of Blood…* blowing up, Diamond booked two nights at the prestigious Hollywood Bowl, California – a gig that would elevate Coldplay to serious contenders. The band also announced that they were to play New York's Madison Square Garden. Tickets sold out in under an hour.

Radio 1's Lamacq interviewed the band for a radio documentary, *Ticking of Clocks*, about the band's meteoric rise. When he asked Chris if the success meant he didn't worry as much – as had become the norm – the singer replied no: "the bigger a balloon gets, it doesn't take a bigger pin to pop it."

Around this time, as they were upsizing to international arenas, one of the crew members began to capture the band behind the scenes. "I started making short daft films of me and the rest of the crew," he said. "Slowly, I started to point the camera at the band a little more often. I thought to myself: 'Wouldn't it be great if the band did a service where they sent all this kind of stuff, in good quality, from right inside the tour?' I can send back some great photos, and video clips of the band going about their day – like little postcards from the frontline." He became Roadie 42, whose exploits have now become a great source of connection between the band and fans.

With the band on tour all over the world, Phil on hiatus in Australia, and *A Rush of Blood…* accelerating towards "modern classic" status, Chris began work on the album that he boasted would "reinvent the wheel". It proved to be their toughest adventure so far…

ABOVE Hollywood Bowl soundcheck, June/July 2003. Coldplay played twice at the venue.

RIGHT Publicity shot, circa 2003.

OVERLEAF The band take a well-deserved break from recording *A Rush of Blood to the Head*.

MAE
TRADE
FAI

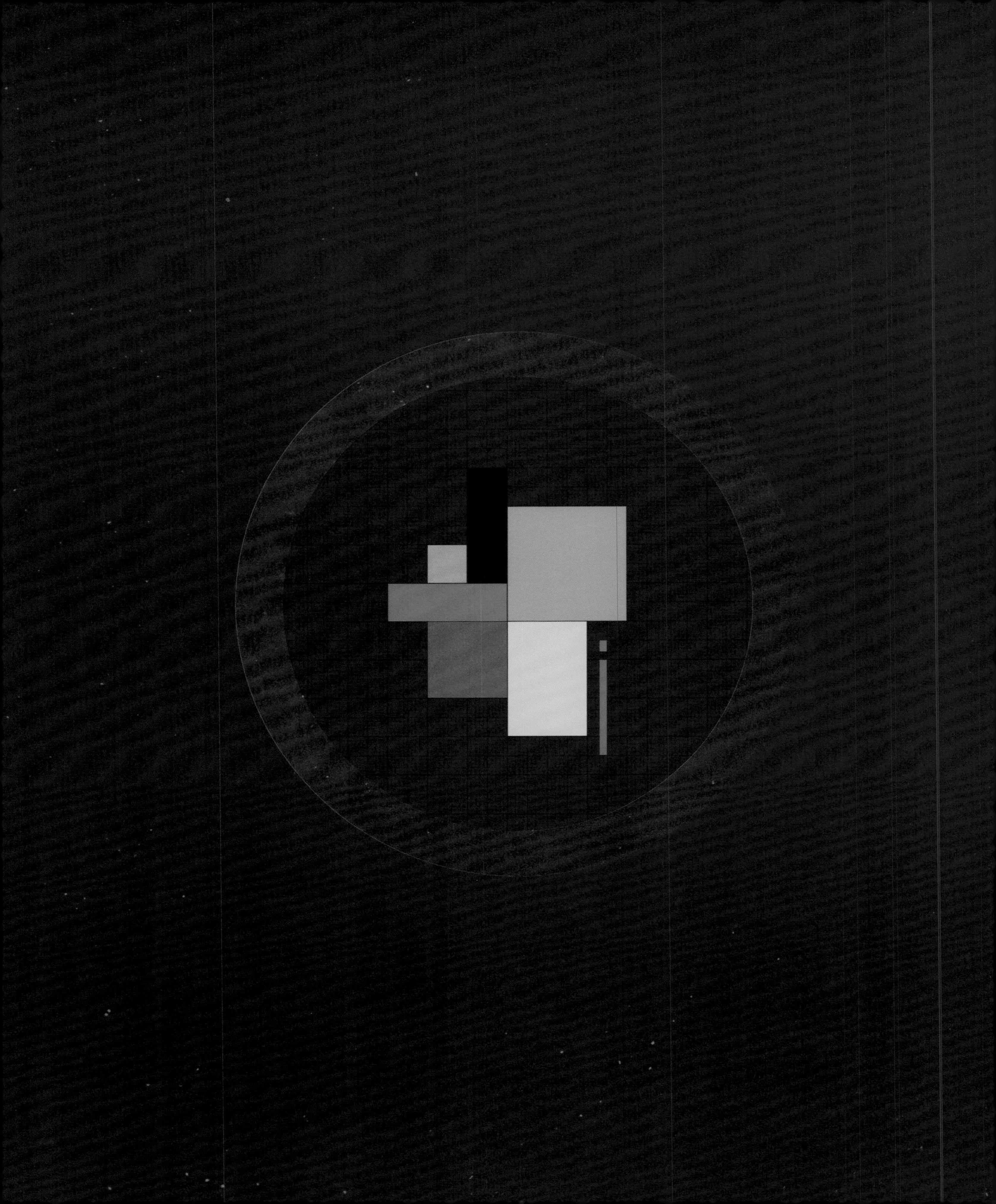

CHAPTER THREE

STUCK IN REVERSE

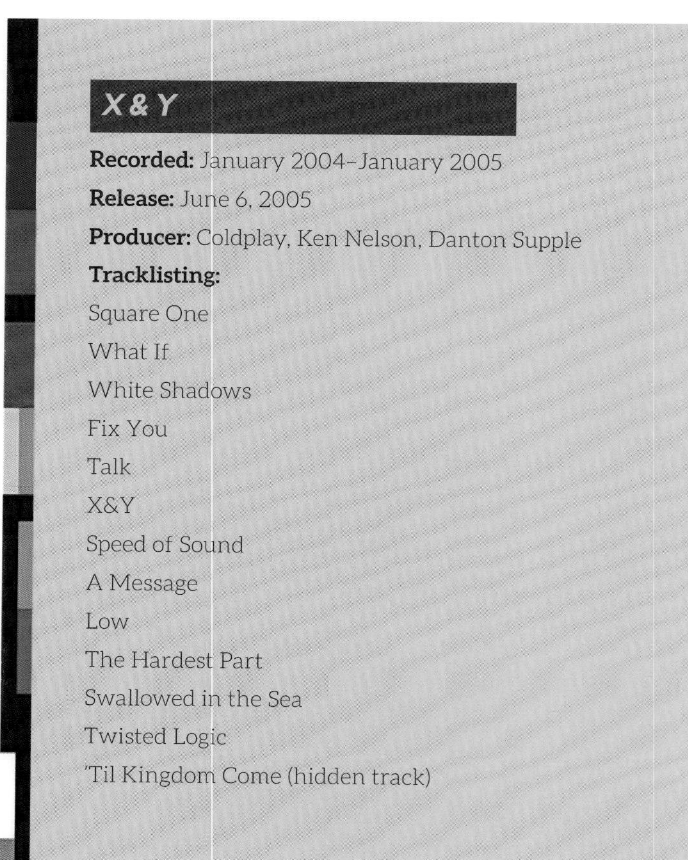

X&Y

Recorded: January 2004–January 2005
Release: June 6, 2005
Producer: Coldplay, Ken Nelson, Danton Supple
Tracklisting:
Square One
What If
White Shadows
Fix You
Talk
X&Y
Speed of Sound
A Message
Low
The Hardest Part
Swallowed in the Sea
Twisted Logic
'Til Kingdom Come (hidden track)

Follow-ups to debut records are commonly referred to as the 'difficult second album'. Released three years after *A Rush of Blood to the Head, X&Y* became the band's very difficult third album. Like the laborious recording process from which it was born, *X&Y* was long: at over 62 minutes it ushered in a rule that any further albums must come in under 42 minutes, and missed deadlines were adding more stress. "Somehow we got to the end of this intact," Chris said, "despite all sorts of confusion and nonsense." One thing was made evident throughout all the noise: they were missing their fifth member.

DRIVEN TO DISTRACTION

Chris' head was bursting with ideas that he was itching to get down in the studio (he knew that Guy, on the other hand, was happy to "not to see an instrument for a few months").

The exhausting *A Rush of Blood...* tour had changed them, that much was plain to see. "We needed to see our families, our friends – just be normal," said Will. "It's not like we hated each other –we just weren't talking much, and things started to fall apart a bit."

> "We were bigger than we were better. So, we wanted to try and go back to exactly the way it was when we got together in 1998."
>
> Will

RIGHT The CD cover of *X&Y*.

Speaking in October 2003, three months before recording for *X&Y* was scheduled to begin, Chris said: "After the last album was finished, I went through about three months of thinking there wouldn't be another album". Songs came and went but after 18 months of writing, the band felt they were going around in circles. The foundations for the album began when Chris and Jonny started recording demos in a studio in Chicago in early 2004. "I don't think we were ready," the guitarist said. "It took us a while to get used to not having that adrenaline rush of playing live every day. Some of the songs made it on the record, so it wasn't a waste of time by any means."

"There's a difference between burying a song because it's not right and burying something because it's shit. We probably ditched 30 songs in Chicago and the reason is they'd been usurped by other things," said Chris.

"We don't scrap them that easily," Guy agreed. "We work on them and work on them and they eventually get scrapped. Well, they never really get scrapped, they just sort of get put on a shelf." "The first album has a naive beauty to it," said Keeling. "The second album was more finessed and quite dark but came together easily compared to the third, which was really not easy for them to put together."

With such great success comes an enormous pressure to repeat that success but there was a problem: they were missing each other.

TIME TO TALK

During the *X&Y* period Chris became an A-list celebrity through his high-profile marriage. The four members had spent ten months trying to record songs, but the dynamic between the band had become flat, with parts being laid down separately, the members often alone and in different countries. It was clear they were disjointed. They weren't a "strong unit", to quote Chris. Even though it was difficult, Jonny was mindful to keep some perspective, "If we complained about how hard it is, we'd look pretty foolish. A lot of people would cut off their right arms to be as stressed as we get," he said.

As Chris admitted in 2015 during an interview with Zane Lowe, "We had lost our way a bit." It was a time where even the softly spoken guitarist Jonny was pushed to his limits. "Jonny's only lost his temper with me once, in 2004. He said: 'I'm sick of your shit!'" It was decided that in order to move forward they needed to come back together. "It's been turbulent," said Chris. "We've been through a lot of songs and a lot of sounds, a lot of studios. It took us a long time to realize the four of us should go into a rehearsal room again and play together rather than rely on technological assistance."

BELOW Chris playing drums during a soundcheck for the concert at the *Manchester Evening News* Arena.

"The feeling we got when we went back into the studio and decided that we needed to be a band again, is exactly the same feeling as when we first got together. It's the feeling we always try and capture in our live performances, which we realized was the essence of our band," said Will. "It just felt like we were not quite what we had set out to be. We were bigger than we were better. So we wanted to try and go back to exactly the way it was in 1998."

The band also felt the need to breathe new life into the recording process so they introduced Danton Supple, the album's co-producer, the mix engineer of many songs on *A Rush of Blood...* "We worked with Danton towards the end of making the second album," said Guy. "So we already had a relationship with him. It was important to not take a risk of going with someone completely strange to us. Danton's a really nice guy and he's got the most ridiculous amount of energy. It just made us feel like it was a fresh start. We were feeling a bit stale before."

Recording at Sarm West Studios in Notting Hill, London began with the band and Danton dissecting and analyzing the songs they had recorded.

There were lots of great songs to choose from. It was just finding the right skin to dress them in. "On one song I played the pump organ and we all sat in a room together recording live takes," said Will. "On others I would play the drums to a guide piano or guitar and singing, and then we'd layer it up from there". One day, said Jonny, the producer, musician, and artist extraordinaire Brian Eno "just came in with plastic bags with all this weird equipment in, and he said, 'Can you feed me some of these keyboards?' and he sort of danced around the room making them sound weird! And then left."

Coldplay had connected with Eno previously, and used 'An Ending (Ascent)' from his 1983 *Apollo: Atmospheres and Soundtracks* album as their intro music on the Rush of Blood tour. Eno's arrival gave the band the confidence to experiment – for example, using crystal wine glasses as percussion on 'Low'.

RIGHT Photo from the video shoot for 'Talk'.

BELOW Photograph from 'The Hardest Part' video shoot.

ABOVE Time out from the video shoot for 'The Hardest Part'.

RIGHT Ticket for the *X&Y* album launch gig at KoKo, Camden Town, London, 2005.

"What we really care about is having great songs and making them different than what we've done before. We came up with a couple of new songs we were happy with," Will said. "So we dragged the older numbers up to the standard of the new ones until we found the ultimate versions."

There were three versions of 'Talk' or rather, as Will said, "There are three different verses. The chorus has pretty much always been the same and the music and the melody." The song was almost left off the album, but they pulled it apart and put it back together. "Some songs went through about ten different versions," explained Jonny.

It was with 'Speed of Sound' that the band found their footing again. It was the obvious track for the first single. "The song came out very naturally and very organically," unlike many of the others, said Chris.

And, of course, there was 'Fix You'. "It's the most important song we've ever written," says Chris. "My father-in-law, Bruce Paltrow, bought this big keyboard just before he died. No one had ever plugged it in. I plugged it in, and there was this incredible sound I'd never heard before," he explained, "All these songs poured out from this one sound." Chris cites Elbow's 'Grace Under Pressure', written around the same time, as the direct influence for 'Fix You'. It is Coldplay's attempt to write a gospel song. Elbow's frontman Guy Garvey doesn't quite believe the story. "If you listen to those two songs they have absolutely nothing in common. I know what's going on there, that's Chris trying to find a way to big up Elbow. He was just being a gentleman."

While the band were upstairs in the big room preparing rehearsals for the impending tour, they ended up working on a new idea, 'Square One'. "I think it started from a drumbeat and a riff Jonny was playing," Guy said. "We liked what we were doing on my laptop and it ended up staying on the record."

As soon as the song arrived, all the band members agreed it had to be the all-important opener. "You can't have a song called 'Square One' and put it as track seven," said Chris.

One song not originally intended for the album was 'Til Kingdom Come', a track Chris had written for Johnny Cash and recorded with Rick Rubin. "All that was missing was his vocals," said Chris. Cash was due to fly out to Los Angeles to record them, but sadly he died the week before. The track was reworked, and Chris' vocals added.

> "We could have released an album ten months ago with enough hit singles on it, but it wouldn't have done anything for us."
>
> Chris

LOVE UNKNOWN

Over the Christmas break of 2004, Chris handed an unfinished copy of the album to Danny McNamara and Ash frontman Tim Wheeler. They both came back with the same analysis: this album is almost there, but it's missing something. Just a really simple song. Chris was frustrated and despondent. "I've broken my back over this record!" he said. In January, he went back to the drawing board, and taking inspiration from a hymn called 'My Song Is Love Unknown' Chris wrote 'A Message' at 2 a.m. "I sat with the guitar, and in five minutes it came. It's brilliant. It was the first song I've ever written without any clothes on," he said. "'A Message' was the last song written for the album," Jonny confirmed. "It came pretty much while we were trying to mix. Once we got that song, suddenly it all started to feel complete finally – it felt like we had the right ingredients."

From a song perspective, the album was finished. "It's a natural progression from the last record," Will said at the end. "The difference between 'In My Place' and 'Clocks' on *A Rush of Blood To The Head* represented the change between the oldest and newest songs of that album and there are songs on the new album that kind of pick up where 'Clocks' left off, but also ones that have moved on a bit".

SOME THINGS YOU CAN'T INVENT

For the title of the album, the band looked internally and externally. "We believe that we're a great band – but sometimes we don't believe anyone else thinks that," Will said. "The reason the record is called *X&Y* is partly because it looks cool and partly because we felt like everything we were singing about had two sides to it," said Chris. "A lot of the songs are about love and loss or they're about the great things in the world versus the terrible things in the world." To reflect this underlying tension between two sides, the album was also split into two parts.

"We're always looking for answers to our questions," said Jonny. "*X&Y* represents the answers that we can't find," said Guy. "There's a running theme through the album, a sense of duality – the idea that you can't have light without dark, or yin without yang. Black and white, or hope and despair, or optimism and pessimism. Everywhere you look there's a tension of opposites."

Throughout the final recording sessions for the album, the potential track listing was pinned to the studio's control room wall along with some curious-looking artwork – blocks of colour. Based on Émile Baudot's code – an early telegraph communication system – those translate into X and Y.

THE WHEELS JUST KEEP ON TURNING

Advance copies of the album were sent out to the media, under the secretive moniker The Fir Trees. Chris went on record saying, "We'll never top this."

Steve Strange set about booking a promotional tour. "The launch shows were to create the heat for the album coming out. It was good to do some really exciting in your face underplays – as they were at that point – and then announce arenas on the back of that. The launch of the album had more of an impact because of the reviews."

The promotional campaign for *X&Y* was in full swing throughout April and May 2005. "One thing we did learn on this tour is the balance between albums," said Chris. "We didn't really play anything from *Parachutes* on that buzz tour, we all kind of thought it'd be nice to."

The first single, 'Speed of Sound', was released on April 18, 2005, and charted at No.8 in the *Billboard* Hot 100 in the States in its first week – the highest first-week debut achievement by a UK artist since The Beatles' 'Hey Jude'.

DEBS IS THE BEST AND
SHE DISCOVERED US
MANY YEARS AGO Signed Coldplay Sept 2005
COLDPLAY
european tour june/july 2005
AAAA
159
June Mon 13 Travel
Tue 14 Load in Day
Wed 15 Hamburg Volks Park
Thur 16 Load in Day
Fri 17 Koln Fuelinger
Sat 18 DAY OFF
Sun 19 Berlin Wuhlheide
Mon 20 DAY OFF
Tues 21 Load in Day
Wed 22 Dublin Marlay P
Thur 23 DAY OFF
Fri 24 DAY OFF
Sat 25 Glastonbury Festival
Sun 26 Load in Day
Mon 27 London Crysta
Tues 28 London Cryst
Wed 29 DAY OFF
Thur 30 Load in Day
July Fri 1 Glasgow Bell
Sat 2 Glasgow Be
Sun 3 Load in day
Mon 4 Bolton Reebok
Tue 5 Bolton Reebok Stad
Wed 6 Load in day
Thur 7 Arnhem Gelredrom
Fri 8 Load in day
Sat 9 Munich Kulturwie
Sun 10 Vienna St Polten
Mon 11 Verona Open Ai
Tue 12 DAY OFF
Wed 13 Locarno Piazza
Thur 14 France Six Fou
Fri 15 Arrive Home
COLDPLAY
EUROPE
TWISTED LOGIC
AAA
128
COLDPLAY
VIP
COLDPLAY
TWISTED LOGIC TOUR 2005
CRYSTAL PALACE TUESDAY JUNE 28th
COLDPLAY
Twisted Logic Tour 2005
Sportpaleis Antwerpen
woensdag 26/10/2005 - 20.30
R1413004/C1791927
Zone

ABOVE Various tickets and passes from the Twisted Logic Tour.

ABOVE The band pick up the award for Best Song ('Speed of Sound') at the Europe Music Awards, Lisbon, Portugal, November 3, 2005.

Just before the album's release, rehearsals were underway. "We've all got new roles," said Guy. "I'm playing piano in a couple of songs and harmonica and singing. We've got a whole bunch of new songs, which is always exciting. Even though we've learned how to play them, I think we still see it as a challenge to try and improve on our performances of the newer songs every night. I think that's always something that makes you push that little bit harder. And also we've got a whole new production; new lights and new visuals and stuff like that, so it's going to be exciting for us to see what the reaction of people is to it."

On June 6, 2005, five years since Coldplay's inception, *X&Y* sold an astounding 151,000 copies on its first day of release in the UK, and debuted at No.1 in 32 countries. "When the numbers started rolling in, it was brilliant," said Will. In the US, it was the year's fastest-selling rock record, notching up more than 737,000 sales in its first week.

GLASTONBURY – PART FOUR AND MORE

Three weeks after the release of *X&Y*, the band headlined Glastonbury for the second time, on Saturday night, with a tried-and-tested set list. The band had not intended to play the festival in 2005, due to other touring commitments, but when Michael Eavis informed Chris there would be no Glastonbury in 2006, he changed his mind in "40 seconds".

Coldplay were much better prepared this time than their first headline show. "I don't expect it to be seen as some revolutionary concert, but I do expect it to be fucking good," said Chris. This gig will always go down as the gig where they came to another level.

At home, watching on television, inventor and West Country

> **"** In some respect it was a quick record to make. It just took us a long time to figure out how to do it. **"**
>
> Guy

native Jason Regler was experiencing a very dark time. During opener 'Square One', a lyric grabbed him:

"Is there anybody out there who is lost and hurt and lonely too/
Are they bleeding all your colours into one?"

"That song is the reason the Xylobands happened," said Regler, who sat and watched the rest of Coldplay's set. During 'Fix You' and some years before Chris penned the lyric "glowing in the dark" for 'Charlie Brown', Regler envisaged LED wristbands that light up. Held aloft, they would be a lot like lighters in the air – and Regler felt that Coldplay would be the perfect band. But not quite yet.

This Glastonbury was a muddy affair. Even though the rain eventually stopped, the sun wasn't enough to dry out the festival. Spirits remained high, and Chris changed the lyrics of 'Politik' to suit the moment: "Give me weather that does no harm, Michael

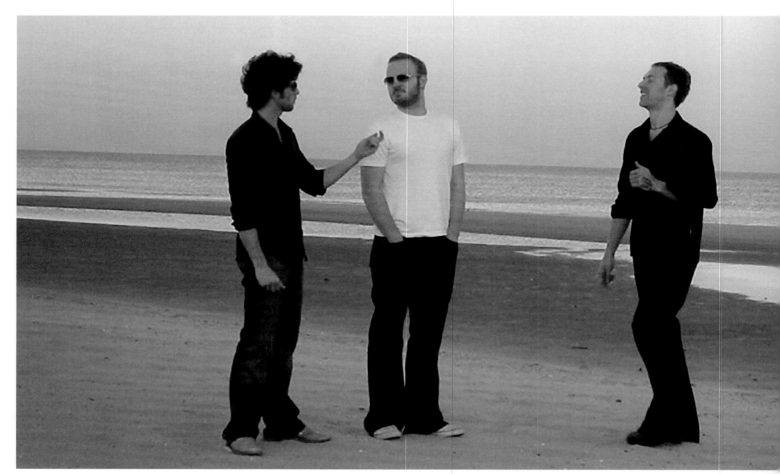

Eavis and Worthy Farm. Give me mud up to my knees, the best festival in history."

During the encore, the band played a fitting tribute to their friend Kylie Minogue, who had to pull out of her Sunday headline slot due to illness. The band covered her hit 'Can't Get You Out Of My Head'.

Their second single 'Fix You' was released, and its accompanying music video premiered on August 3, 2005, a month after the Glastonbury gig. The video carried certain emotion in light of a series of co-ordinated bombings across London on July 7, as the first part of the video shows Chris walking through the streets of the capital. It seems to pay homage although it was actually recorded on June 29, before those tragic events.

By the end of 2005, *X&Y* was the world's best-selling album, achieving sales of 8.3 million copies. The accompanying Twisted Logic tour took Coldplay to over 23 countries, selling out arenas across the US, Canada, Europe, UK, Australia, China and Japan. In a chart announced at the end of 2005, Coldplay had become the second biggest selling UK artists since 2000, with combined sales of more than 28 million albums.

With *X&Y* released, and the Twisted Logic tour winding down, it would be another three years before the band would start recording the next album properly. Other than collaborations, there were no new Coldplay releases from this period, except for 'Gravity'. The band had played it during the tour, but as yet hadn't recorded it (eventually their version would appear on the B Side to 'Talk'). "I remember Chris ringing me up and asking if Embrace wanted to have 'Gravity' as a song," said the band's singer Danny

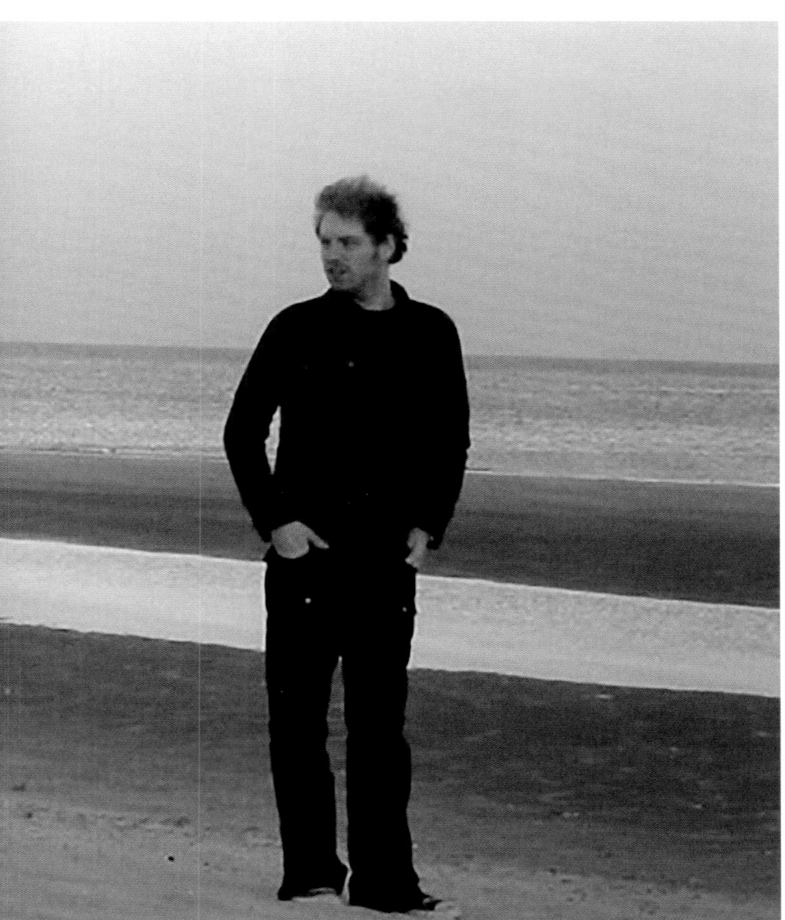

LEFT, OPPOSITE, ABOVE The band taking time out, post Coachella, 2005.

BELOW Hard Rock Hotel and Casino chips given to the band when they played in The Joint – the casino's venue – on the hotel's tenth anniversary weekend, April 29, 2005.

McNamara. "He wasn't sure how to ask. I don't think he'd given a song to anyone else before. I have to say initially I wasn't sure. We'd never done a song by anyone else, and we'd worked for three years on the album we were just finishing. We talked about it as a band and decided to record it and then decide. The version we did with Youth (producer) came together really quickly. I went around to Chris' house and played it. It's very different from the Coldplay version. We've sung it together but never in public; he does a great harmony over the top."

At February's BRIT Awards, 2006, the band picked up two trophies: for 'Speed of Sound', Best British Single, and for *X&Y* MasterCard British Album. During Chris' speech he happened to mention that the band would be disappearing for a while, which led to the tabloid front page headline, "Coldplay Quit". Despite the large critical acclaim and commercial success that *X&Y* enjoyed, and the fact that it featured 'Fix You', it remains the album the band cite as their least favourite.

In 2014, Chris told Zane Lowe that he felt they only achieved 60 per cent of the record they set out to make. "The next record will hopefully validate us a bit more," said Chris in 2006, in preparation for the next record. "We've taken the piano ballad and the falsetto as far as it can go, and that's very freeing for us. Now we can try some different things. We're only on our third record… we're still getting to the point where we want to get to."

LEFT Ticket to Radio 2 show at Abbey Road Studios.

BELOW Chris leaning back on his piano stool at Madison Square Garden, New York, September 6, 2005.

OVERLEAF Chris in Leipzig, Germany, November 18, 2005.

LIVE 8

As well as Make Trade Fair, and other charity campaigns, Live 8's global poverty-relief agenda was a cause close to the band's heart. On Saturday July 2, 2005, mere weeks after the album dropped, Coldplay performed at Live 8 in Hyde Park, the gig put together by Sir Bob Geldof. An audience of 150,000 and 25 artists united to promote awareness of the Make Poverty History campaign, alongside the G8 summit that was being held the same weekend in Gleneagles, Scotland. The show was more than just a concert, it was history. And it began with Paul McCartney performing 'Sgt Pepper's Lonely Hearts Club Band' with its poignant opening line "It was 20 years ago today" referencing the 20 years since the original Live Aid.

"We're very excited to be playing Live 8. We're not sure how we're gonna feel following the Beatles and U2!" exclaimed Chris. "I think we'll do great for the drinks vendors. You always notice on TV when there's an ad break cos there's an electricity surge, I think we can expect the same sort of thing." The band performed a small set early in the afternoon, as they had another performance scheduled for that evening. They played 'In My Place', the Verve cover 'Bitter Sweet Symphony' (with Verve's Richard Ashcroft), and 'Fix You'.

BELOW Clockwise from top left: Elton John, Chris, Paul McCartney; Elton John and Chris; Chris, Will and Guy watching from the wings before they perform; Chris on stage.

“As a group, we're a strange mixture of arrogance and self-doubt. We believe that we're a great band, but sometimes we don't believe anyone else thinks that.”

Will

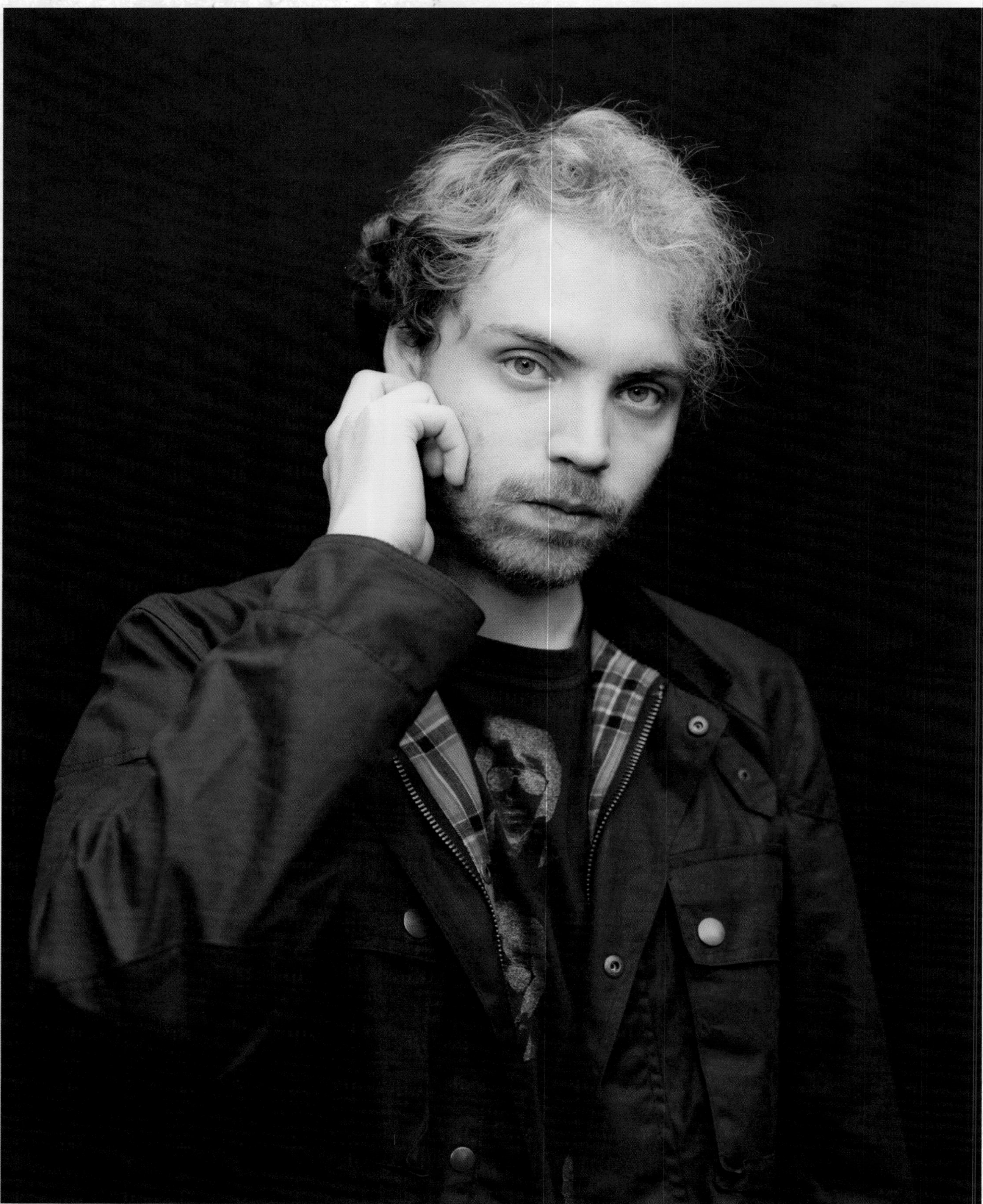

JONNY BUCKLAND

Jonny Buckland's "talent for calmness" is the vital ingredient that completes Coldplay's chemistry. He may be known as the friendly, quieter member of the group, but that's only because the guitarist is happy to let his guitar playing do all the talking. "Jonny just has a way of writing melodies," says Chris. "There would be no Coldplay music without Jonny. They'd be Chris Martin songs, which would be a travesty."

Jonny Buckland was born in the London borough of Islington on September 11, 1977, but relocated to the town of Pantymwyn in Flintshire, North Wales, when he was four years old. He began learning the notes and chords on a guitar when he was 11, as a pupil at Ysgol y Waun primary school, Gwernaffield, and continued at Mold Alun High. His music teacher, Margaret Parr, remembers Jonny fondly: "He was always extremely interested in music and had immense talent for the guitar. When he studied A-level music his strength was in his composition, and I always felt that he would do well."

Jonny was raised on a musical diet of Jimi Hendrix and Eric Clapton records owned by his mum Joy and dad John, a former teacher at Holywell High School. When he hit his teens, Jonny's older brother Tim (who also encouraged him to play the guitar and whose band Domino State once supported Coldplay at the O2, London) allowed him access to his record collection, which included LPs from seminal bands such as My Bloody Valentine, Sonic Youth, Stone Roses, Ride, George Harrison and U2. Inspiration took hold of the young guitarist, who by now made sure his guitar never left his side. These early musical influences also left an indelible mark on the guitarist's technique. "I've never gone in much for the solos," Jonny said. "I was always more interested in atmospherics. Listening to bands like Mercury Rev or My Bloody Valentine or even the Verve, the way those guitarists played. There's no Van Halen in me!" As a guitarist, Jonny has now entered the pantheon of rock 'n' roll greats, one who inspires other guitarists. "Jonny is an inspiration to guitar players everywhere," said U2's guitarist, the Edge. "I am proud to know that I was one of his main influences. It makes me feel like a real rock star."

THE QUIET LIFE

Growing up in the quiet and unassuming town of Pantymwyn gave the quiet and unassuming Jonny a desire to pursue his academic education while surrounded by the urgency and vibrancy of a big city. "I really think we came to university with the same idea that we would try and form a band with some people," Jonny recounted in 2008. Those earliest days of studying at UCL, while residing at Ramsay Hall, connected Jonny to other music lovers and players, even if he still felt compelled to keep his burgeoning guitar-playing skills a secret – much to the astonishment of his future bandmates. "It soon became apparent that [at Ramsay Hall] there were a lot of musicians, a lot of show-offs and a lot of people playing 'Redemption Song' on their acoustic guitars," said Will. Jonny was not one of those show-offs. While Jonny did take his guitar to university, he chose to hide his acoustic behind his dorm room door. "When the door closed," Will said, "you'd hear these amazing sounds coming from inside."

> "As we go along, we enjoy ourselves even more. The older you get, you realize how lucky you are."
>
> Jonny

ABOVE Friend James "Pix" Pickering's photo of Jonny backstage at the Reading Festival, 1999.

LEFT John Hilton's photo of Jonny at London's Barfly, 1999.

Chris too would hunt for these sounds. "We were living in the same building at college in London. I'm not a very big sleeper. So, I'd always be awake through the night anyway, working or writing stuff. Jonny was sitting at 3 in the morning, playing some piece on guitar in a room nearby. And I was like, 'I didn't know you played guitar.' And he was like, 'Well, I don't really tell anybody.' And something in my brain was like, 'OK, let's meet tomorrow.' And we did. And then we spent every day together since."

Jonny's resistance to simply trotting out bad cover versions of 'Redemption Song' was in part due to his daily concern that he would "end up in some shit band", but also because his quietness always got the better of him. Will noticed: "The bloke who turned out to be the best guitarist out of all of us was the bloke who had his guitar hidden in his cupboard and who never got it out or was pushy about his guitaring. He was really quiet and timid; it was great because a lot of people were too pushy and too cool, and the people it turns out who were in the band were those who were just really passionate and not pushy."

As is the way in most rock and roll bands, there is a duality to everything. Light and dark. Black and white. Loud and calm. For Coldplay, Jonny was the calmness to Chris' intensity. "If you sit with us for half an hour," Chris freely admits, "I'm the only one you'll get an impression of because I'm a loudmouth idiot." With

> "We love playing music. It's the best job in the world. We want to work all the time. It's hard to make us take a holiday."
>
> Jonny

Jonny, Chris had finally found the Yin to his Yang.

Their meeting was to change the two young men's lives forever. While the band have gone on to change the world, to his bandmates Jonny has cheerfully remained the same guy he was at university. "He still doesn't like to tell people he plays guitar," Chris said. "Even on a stage, he tries to hide as much as possible. My entire life is spent trying to drag him out of the shadows, because I know that he's a guitar hero – to me, anyway."

For the remainder of their days at UCL, Jonny and Chris were inseparable. "Meeting Jonny was like falling in love," Chris said. "He is the guy I've been looking for the whole of my life." "When we first met it just seemed perfectly right," Jonny said. "It couldn't possibly be any other way. Plus, I couldn't really say no!" "I got extremely excited," said Chris, "I forced Jonny to write a song with me!"

JONNY AND CHRIS

By the beginning of 1997, Jonny and Chris had begun writing their first songs together, often writing as many as two songs a night. "We practised every night for two years," Jonny said. "There was a long period where we had no drummer, because Will hadn't joined the group yet and there was no original drummer. So we didn't have any gigs or anything. We were just writing and writing and writing. We were so into it that one member of the band – who shall remain nameless – pretended to have broken his

ABOVE Jonny and Chris visit the MuchMusic Studios in Toronto, Canada, May 9, 2005.

ABOVE LEFT Jonny plays his signature guitar, a Fender Telecaster Thinline, live in Australia, at the Hordern Pavilion, July 2003.

ankle and got a month off sick. But when he went back to work, he had to keep a set of keys in his shoe to remember that he was supposed to limp. That's how dedicated we were."

Dedication has remained a key ingredient to the band's success ever since. That and the fact that the band had no Plan B. "We were determined to do it," remembered Jonny.

While his guitar brought the resonance on tracks such as 'Yellow', 'God Put a Smile upon Your Face' and 'Square One', the guitarist himself became known for his sparse delicate melodies.

"The challenge," he said, "is always finding a guitar part that makes the song better without cluttering it up. I probably get that from listening to bands like the Stone Roses, where everything just jangles and rings. I try to bring in a great melody or a new musical idea that doesn't obscure or weaken anything that is already there."

THE GUITAR HERO

Of course, Jonny has always taken his bandmates – and the world's – praise of his playing with a degree of self-deprecation, especially in the band's earliest days, when he was content to stay in the shadows.

"I'm not technically very good at all," Jonny said in 2002.

RIGHT Performing 'Hurts Like Heaven', Jonny takes centre stage at Ahoy, Rotterdam, Netherlands, December 17, 2011.

BELOW Jonny at the Odyssey Arena Belfast, Northern Ireland, December 19, 2008.

"In fact I'm pretty shocking. I've got really awful technique, but I think Joe Strummer said somebody struggling with their instrument was the best thing to see." Though, more recently, "I think I've gotten quite a bit more confident," he says. "A few years ago I had tendonitis in my wrist, so I stuck to playing simple things that I could keep going through. I had an operation, and I can play a bit more now."

But when it comes to taking credit for his guitar parts – lines that, as Chris says, complete the songs – Jonny remains resolutely, well, nice. "Truthfully, I feel ridiculous taking credit for it all. So many of them happen by chance, or because someone in the band stops me when I'm playing and says, 'Hey, that is amazing.'"

"Jonny gives my songs life. I love having a tune ready for Jonny so he can roll up his sleeves and put those unforgettable lines over them. He'll just pounce on it. They come so effortlessly and they turn out so lovely," Chris said. " He can make a hard riff simple and an easy one seem impossible... like how on bloody earth did he come up with that? He's the only person that's ever made anything I've written sound any good."

> **"** We have very different personalities but we do have the same kind of ambition and goals when it comes to the band. **"**
>
> Jonny

Debs Wild on Jonny: *"What can I say about Jonny that won't make me look like I'm making it up? One of the nicest human beings on the planet that I've had the pleasure to meet and he's not changed at all. Rarely seen without a smile on his face – don't be fooled by any broody guitarist poses – his laugh is infectious and he's a joy to be around.*

He's unassuming and although being in Coldplay brings a certain financial privilege, I remember so vividly asking him in the relatively early days if he'd actually spent any money on anything significant yet. 'I bought a boat,' he told me. I was pretty impressed, 'Wow, really?'

'No, of course not!'

And he still hasn't."

C H A P T E R

F O U R

FELL FOR THAT SPELL

VIVA LA VIDA OR DEATH AND ALL HIS FRIENDS

Released: June 12, 2008
Recorded: November 2006–April 2008
Producer: Markus Dravs, Brian Eno, Jon Hopkins, Rik Simpson and Coldplay
Tracklisting:
Life in Technicolor (Instrumental)
Cemeteries of London
Lost!
42
Lovers in Japan / Reign of Love
Yes
Viva la Vida
Violet Hill
Strawberry Swing
Death and All His Friends

PROSPEKT'S MARCH

Released: November 21, 2008
Recorded: November 2006–April 2008
Producer: Markus Dravs, Brian Eno, Jon Hopkins, Rik Simpson and Coldplay
Tracklisting:
Life in Technicolor II
Postcards from Far Away
Glass of Water
Rainy Day
Prospekt's March / Poppyfields
Lost+ (featuring Jay Z)
Lovers in Japan (Osaka Sun Mix)
Now My Feet Won't Touch the Ground

"We don't come in every morning anymore and say, 'Okay, what's today's piano ballad?' You know what I mean?"

Chris

On March 4, 2007, the exhausting Twisted Logic tour came to a spectacular conclusion in Mexico City. As had become a familiar end of tour statement, Chris said, "We really feel that we have to be away for a while, I think people are a bit sick of us." A five-year hiatus was speculated in the press, but unsurprisingly that was nonsense. The itch to record returned rather quickly, and changes to the band's set-up in London came thick and fast, including Phil Harvey's return. Jonny said, "It's just the best time to be in the band."

WELCOME BACK, PHIL

At the end of the tour, Phil returned to the UK after more than three years away. With Chris and Phil both living in north London, they started hanging out again.

During Phil's hiatus, much had changed within the band. "In the time that I was gone, Chris had married and had two kids," he said. "When I came back, I was struck by his change in stature – both physically and his presence. He was walking taller."

At the time, Phil was training to be a clinical psychologist but was happy to pop his head in the studio to give his opinion every now and again. Of course, it didn't take long for this to become a permanent role.

Dave Holmes, the band's sole manager at this point, was – as Phil puts it – "super cool" about Phil's return. "Dave plays more of an authority figure. We need that, we need Dave to be the grown-up in the room."

Holmes' role allows their ex-manager and the frontman's relationship to exist as friends who share creative ideas.

"Dave allows Chris, Will, Guy, Jonny and I to dream up crazy dreams and interact as friends and bandmates rather than anything more formal. My job is to bring those crazy dreams to reality," confirmed Phil.

Phil's return prompted Will to describe Phil, a few years later, as the "reason we've been getting better since 2005" – a remark that highlights just how difficult making *X&Y* was, and just how important Phil is.

"A big part of it is the internal dynamic between Guy, Will, Chris, Jonny and me in that, for whatever reason, the dynamic just works better when there are five of us. It just works, I don't really know why," said Phil.

RIGHT *Viva la Vida or Death and All His Friends* and *Prospekt's March* CD covers. Both feature paintings by Eugène Delacroix.

VIVA LA VIDA

PROSPEKT'S MARCH

"Phil was the biggest difference of all on *Viva la Vida*," noted Jonny. "We missed him so much on the last one. He's our wise man, sounding board, buffer zone, everything. It's amazing how much easier things are when he's around. Phil gave us a sense of security".

It's hard to imagine where Coldplay would be without this guru they all call "the wise, handsome, frightening one who tells us what to do." "The band encourage me to say that I'm the Creative Director, which I fucking hate," said Phil of his vital role. "I'm not particularly creative, but I guess I do try to give them some direction from time to time."

Like everyone in the team, it's about facilitating the vision to make it a reality. It's a collaborative relationship. Aside from the administrative side of his management role, Holmes likes to think about things a little differently, he thinks outside of the box. If everyone is looking right, he will suggest they look left. "I feel really blessed that I get to be involved in everything," Holmes said, though he admitted he's not keen on being present during the early stages of creating music.

"I have to say I've enjoyed the second stint a lot more than the first!" Phil said of being back in the fold. "Essentially I'm just part of the gang and I try and make myself useful wherever I can. That can be from getting videos made to designing a show to being in the studio every day to writing press releases... I'm like a multi-purpose glue that fills in any cracks."

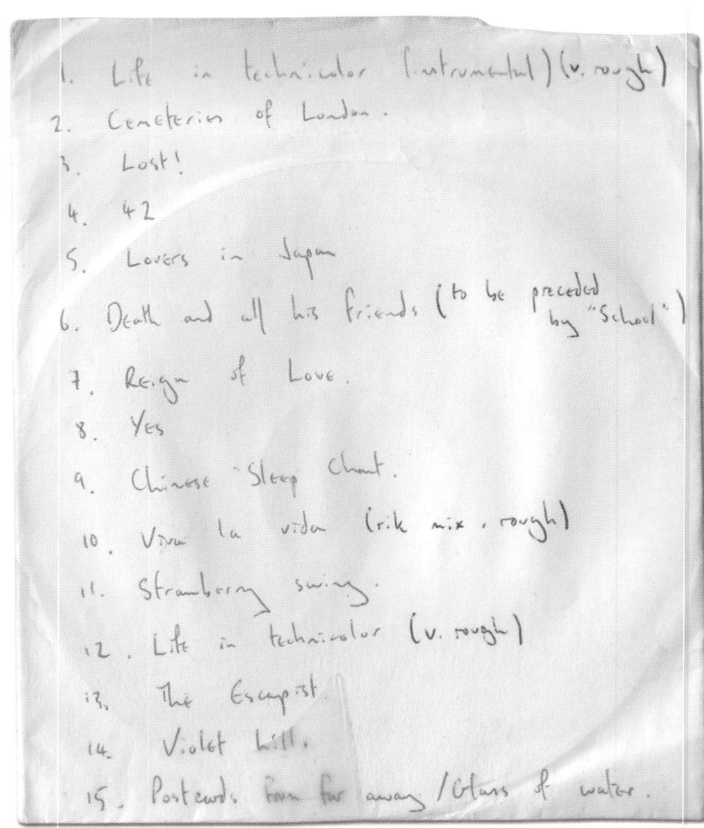

1. Life in technicolor (instrumental) (v. rough)
2. Cemeteries of London.
3. Lost!
4. 42
5. Lovers in Japan
6. Death and all his friends (to be preceded by "School")
7. Reign of Love.
8. Yes
9. Chinese Sleep Chant.
10. Viva la vida (rik mix, rough)
11. Strawberry swing.
12. Life in technicolor (v. rough)
13. The Escapist.
14. Violet Hill.
15. Postcards from far away / Glass of water.

ABOVE Collaborator John Hopkins with Phil Harvey.

ABOVE RIGHT *Viva la Vida* CD with rough tracklisting, handwritten by Phil, for Debs.

FRIENDS REUNITED

X&Y had shifted big numbers. But the whole process had taught the band several lessons. "They had incredible success [with *X&Y*] but I think the weight of that success almost pulled them under," Phil said.

As the band finalized the Latin America leg of the Twisted Logic tour, they began to talk about entering the studio. Recharged, the band set to work on the "big change" album, or, as Will called it, the "fuck it" album. "We were very hungry to improve on a basic level," said Chris.

But this time, everything had to be different. "We had to work through a lot of stuff, there was a lot of talking through those *Viva* sessions," said Phil. "It was very much establishing the second act of the band. There were new dynamics and new rules and new personalities. In some ways, we had all become different people." They also considered the musical changes. "I think we felt after *X&Y*, like we had done that sound as much as we could do, and we don't want people to get tired of our sound, so we have to change it. A bit," said Chris. They wanted to create a record that would not allow people to pigeon-hole them. "We don't want to be thought of as just one-trick ponies," agreed Guy. "We all listen to a broad range of music and I think this album reflects it more than ever, and more than the last three albums."

Chris explained the album's lengthy title: "It is one or the other. Depending on whether you find it uplifting or depressing. We

“I like to think of myself as kind of like Bez from the Happy Mondays, except I can’t dance and I can’t play maracas.”

Phil

thought it was funny that some people would listen to a song of ours and find it really warm and embracing. And other people would listen to the same song and find it really miserable. So, we thought, this time, let’s not tell anyone what they’re supposed to think. If you find it depressing you can call it *Death and All His Friends*. And if you find it uplifting, *Viva la Vida*.”

THE BAKERY

A decision was made to create their own sanctuary, somewhere just to spend time together playing and recording music. “In all of these years working together we haven’t had an HQ, our own studio or anything like that. We want somewhere where we can hole up and see what happens,” said Will.

That somewhere was a former bakery in Hampstead, north London, which is how it got the moniker “The Bakery”. “It’s the first time we’d had a proper band home since we were rehearsing in my student bedroom in 1999,” said Jonny. “And it made a big difference.”

Rik Simpson and Dan Green set up the studio, helping them design and build it in a relatively short space of time. Simpson knew how to run a studio, and Green understood what they needed as a band. The band were jamming within a couple of months. “We wanted somewhere where we could feel free to experiment, somewhere where we felt comfortable and free to do whatever we wanted to do and get everything done under one roof, like photos, artwork and the clothes,” Will said.

There were also more dynamic changes creatively. Composer and violinist Davide Rossi was invited to join them in their new space, in November 2006, to try a few things while they were still working on the demos for the album. Rossi said, “As soon as I came in and tried a few notes on a song they were working on,

ABOVE The band and Phil looking at postcards sent from fans across the world. A project inspired by the band’s song ‘Postcards from Far Away’.

Chris enthusiastically came out of the control room and asked if I was available to work with them. He said: 'This is what we need... Jonny's magic with you on top takes it to another level.'"

Rik Simpson started engineering the project. "Then Brian Eno came on board, and he's a great galvanizer of ideas," said Simpson. "I'd be at the helm and put my oar in where necessary. After about a month or so, we brought in Markus Dravs, an amazing producer. The connection is that Markus used to engineer for Brian."

Dravs was happy to be back working with Eno, "I have a huge amount of respect and love for him. It was great to witness him push the band musically, but also his constant encouragement to look forward and not be analytical but just embrace the moment with all your 'egoless self'. Me and Brian have a very honest relationship. We don't always agree on a particular direction, but we are both quite comfortable with that. It's more tricky for a band, I guess, but it all settled in nicely when people got to know each other better."

Simpsons' involvement became so valued he was elevated to co-producer, and had a lot of input in to the sound.

WE KNOW ENO

Chris would often meet up with Brian Eno for tea. "I asked him, 'Do you know any producers who could help us to get better as a band?'" said Chris. "And he said, 'Well, I don't mean to blow my

own trumpet, but I might be the man.'" Brian Eno's approach to recording and creating music was very different to what they had experienced before.

The band's initial conversations with Eno meant facing up to some hard facts, however. "Eno said, 'Your songs are too long. And you're too repetitive, and you use the same tricks too much, and big things aren't necessarily good things, and you use the same sounds too much, and your lyrics are not good enough,'" said Chris. The singer agreed. "You can either sit 'round, look at your platinum discs and say: 'Fuck you, you're all wrong,' or you can go: 'OK, he's probably got a point.'"

Eno brought a new attitude, a new philosophy as well as an effective working schedule of two weeks off, two weeks on. "Some people say we're talented and some say we're the worst thing ever to happen to music, and it's a bit confusing being in the middle of that," remarked Chris during this period. "So, we were like, 'Fuck it, we'll make a record that really reflects what we listen to, and it doesn't matter what category it comes from.' And that was part of Brian Eno's philosophy: You have to ignore all the noise around you and just have as much fun as possible when you're in that room for the 300 days of the year when no one is watching. It's not about who sold the most records, as much as it's about who's enjoying their Thursday. He helped us to enjoy being in a band rather than just feeling under pressure to keep share prices up." Thursdays actually became the one day of the week where the band would dress smartly, in suit and ties, to attend to business.

ABOVE Will, Guy, Jonny and Chris' mad dash to the c-stage is always worth the run. Pictured here performing at the *Manchester Evening News* Arena, December 11, 2008.

OPPOSITE TOP Brian Eno with Jonny, Guy and Will at The Bakery studios.

OPPOSITE BELOW String arranger, composer, musician, collaborator Davide Rossi with Chris.

> **"** I always thought that if you were a 16-year-old and liked Coldplay you'd keep it quiet. We aren't cool and never will be. But I hope after this album, 16-year-olds will feel proud to like Coldplay. **"**
>
> Chris

ABOVE RIGHT *Viva la Vida* tour laminate.
BELOW *Viva la Vida* photoshoot, London.

OPPOSITE Chris and Will at the 2009 MusiCares Person of the Year Tribute to Neil Diamond, Los Angeles Convention Center, February 6, 2009.

OPPOSITE BELOW Jonny and Guy share a moment on stage at the Home Depot Center, Carson, California, July 18, 2009.

Early in the process, Eno suggested the use of hypnotism, alongside other less traditional strategies to get the band thinking outside the box. "Brian knew a hypnotist and we thought it might get some interesting results. He got us into some strange kind of trance," said Jonny.

"It did work, actually," said Chris. "We came up with a lot of interesting noises, which we used. I think the whole process of getting our own place and working with Brian has been really liberating for us. Because it was starting to become a little difficult to be in Coldplay – there's so much opinion, expectation, and criticism. We wanted to be free from that for a bit, to try things and just be a group. All these crazy experiments that he tried with us was just an effort to say, 'It's OK. Not everybody hates you because you're in Coldplay. Just play some music and don't worry about it.' After about a month of working with him, we literally forgot that we'd ever been on tour or had any other records out."

Eno and Markus Dravs both brought very different qualities to the recording and writing process. There was discipline and focus from the get-go, something that had been missing on *X&Y*.

"I wanted the band to be as prepared as possible before going

into the recording process," said Dravs, "so even when Chris was away I spent a fair bit of time running through arrangements with the other band members, trying different ideas, rehearsing their parts, exploring sounds, arrangements and so forth."

Dravs pushed them to the point where they could record a lot of the album live. "He worked us like dogs," said Jonny. "Everything had to be done to his exacting standards."

Eno wanted to free up Chris from playing keyboard and he suggested that Jon Hopkins, an ambient musician and producer, come to work with Coldplay for a day. Hopkins' track 'Light Through the Veins' provided the foundation for the band's all-important opening song, 'Life in Technicolor.' Hopkins played Chris the track in "an opportune moment" and that was that. "That's got to start our album, we've got to work together on this,' said Chris.

A SERENADE OF SOUND

The record evolved from the band playing live and exploring a song in the room, rather than assembling it on a computer. A lot of time was spent "simply just jamming", said Dravs. "About 80 per cent of this album was recorded with the four of us playing simultaneously – that's very rare for a band these days," said Chris.

In June 2007, the band revealed on their website that 25 tracks had been recorded during the sessions. "We spent a lot of time trying different arrangements with the whole band constantly playing before actually recording them," said Dravs.

Parts of the song 'Violet Hill' had been around for a long time.

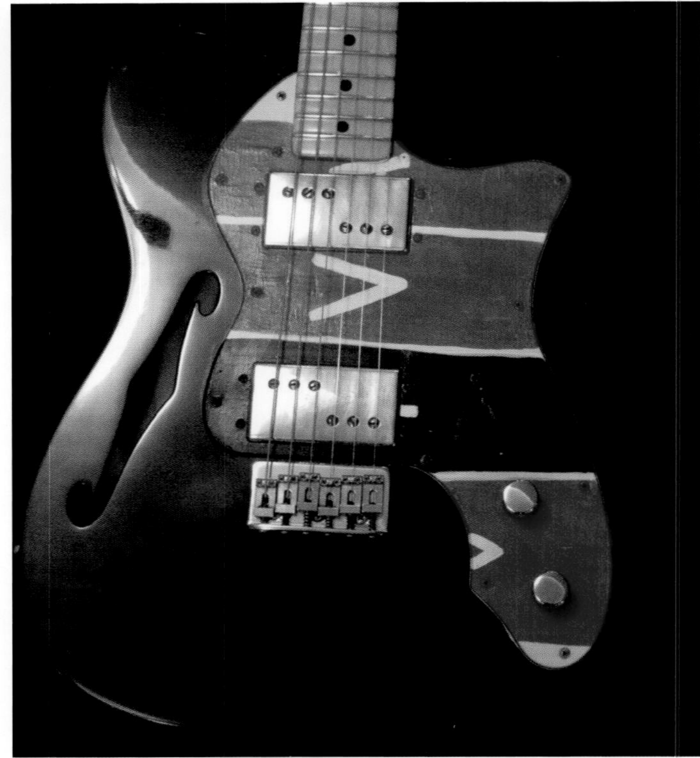

ABOVE Will's painting of the *Viva* logo on The Bakery walls and the guitar used on the *Viva* tour, hand-painted by Vicki Taylor.

ABOVE LEFT Chris' piano, hand-painted by band assistant Vicki Taylor.

In 2016, Chris revealed that the opening lyric of 'December', which Chris and Jonny wrote in 1997, is why Guy initially joined the band. The same lyric now formed the first line of 'Violet Hill', the album's first single. The 7-inch single was given away with the *NME* and as a free download on coldplay.com. By now, free content online had become commonplace, and the band were keen to be part of that evolution.

Talk began to turn to the colour and shape of the record. Will's

desire to see artwork flourish at the studio became a reality. He painted the red and black vertical lines of *Viva*'s album art on the wall of The Bakery's lounge area (and another set, purple and yellow). He also painted the walls of the live recording room.

The band also customized their instruments. "All of our instruments have been painted by our lovely assistant Vicki," said Will. "She's a very talented artist." Vicki Taylor, who has a fine art degree, responded to Chris' brief. "Having lots of colour was really important. Chris had really gotten into Frida Kahlo and decided that's what he wanted the theme to be. There was an illustrated book of her diary with little sketches she'd done and Chris really loved it. He said it'd be great if we did this on the instruments. The first guitar I painted was Chris' acoustic with 'No Me Llores' ('Don't Cry For Me') written in brush strokes. After I'd done one, Chris asked if I could paint them all."

ABOVE LEFT Guitar hand-painted by Vicki Taylor.

ABOVE RIGHT Keyboards hand-painted by Vicki Taylor.

LEFT Viva Latin America tour itinerary.

LEFTRIGHTLEFTRIGHTLEFT

In May 2009, as a thank you to fans, it was decided to hand out a live album at the end of every concert. *LeftRightLeftRightLeft* was then made available online as a free download.
Chris said: "A lot of people who work at our record company just love music, so they're happy to be able to help us give something back. We've all got to make a living, but we've been really lucky as a band, so we can afford to manufacture an album and give it away. I think everyone we work with is happy that they've helped us get to a position where we can do that."

Miles Leonard, at Parlophone, supported the band: "Sometimes you have to bite the bullet and support it. This band have given us so much."

ABOVE The cover of the CD *LeftRightLeftRightLeft*.

ABOVE Chris' military-style jacket worn on the *Viva la Vida* tour.

RIGHT Chris shows off his *Viva* jacket, with a nod to newly appointed US President Barack Obama, at the All Points West Music & Arts Festival, Liberty State Park, New Jersey, August 2, 2009.

OBA
MAR
BCK

ABOVE Soundcheck of the first of two Crisis charity gigs at Liverpool's Royal Court. Fans waiting outside in the snow were invited in to watch and keep warm.

BELOW The Crisis charity hidden gig at the Tyne Theatre, Newcastle, England, December 20, 2010 – one of just two UK dates they played that year.

ABOVE Access All Areas pass for the Crisis show at Liverpool's Royal Court, 2010.

TOP The band perform 'A Message' live on television for the Hope For Haiti Now telethon, 2010.

ABOVE Vicki Taylor's spontaneous snap of Coldplay with The Killers, U2 and Gary Barlow in London, performing 'All These Things That I've Done', in February 2009 at the War Child gig.

Viva la Vida's heart was a song that arrived to Chris during one of his middle of the night writing sessions. 'Viva la Vida' not only gave the album a title and a killer track, it also gave them their first No.1 single.

"This little thing came into my head which went, 'I used to rule the world.' I thought that sounds like a big hit single to me and half of me said: 'Yeah, but we really should go to bed', and the other half of me: 'No, now go downstairs and work it out.' I went down to find a guitar and I recorded it and I'm very glad I did because it's an important song to us."

"It always tickles me that they came close to not putting 'Viva la Vida' the song on the *Viva* album," said Chris Salmon. "I remember listening to it on headphones plugged into Phil's laptop and getting such a rush of excitement because it was just so good. Then – I'm sure like everyone else who had the chance to hear it – I was like 'You have to put this on the record!'"

Looking back, Phil admits: "So much effort went into every single second on that album that I think we lost a little bit of perspective on what was and wasn't essential".

Inspired by Frida Kahlo, and a painting of the same name, 'Viva la Vida' went through many guises before finding a home, like all the songs on the record. "We went around the houses on it," said Chris. Davide Rossi had a crack at it. "We wouldn't have the string rhythmic riff of 'Viva la Vida' if I didn't come up first with the 'Rainy Day' part… it's strange and kind of unexplainable how things come out in the studio," he said.

The first version of the song was quite guitar-heavy, and its rock feel didn't fit in with the rest of the album. "As soon as I finished working on the song at The Bakery, I told Chris and Phil that this was going to be a No.1 song. Chris told me off: 'Don't say that, Dav!'"

REVOLUTION NUMBER ONE

According to Phil, one of Dave Holmes' "defining moments" started off as a very divisive suggestion. Holmes had a long existing relationship with iTunes, especially Jimmy Dickson – hired by Apple co-founder Steve Jobs. Apple had previously expressed interest in using new Coldplay music in a TV spot, but at the time Holmes didn't feel it was the right moment. As soon as *Viva* was finished, however, Holmes sent a copy to Dickson and Jobs.

The band had never done a commercial, and despite the band loving Apple and their products, they were hesitant when Holmes broached the subject.

The label were working the single 'Violet Hill' at the time, so Apple attempted a 30-second edit of the song to see if it would be effective, but didn't feel that it was. Apple suggested 'Viva' because they really loved the song.

It took three band meetings for Holmes to convince the band and Phil into at least turning up to see what would happen. On May 20 during *American Idol*, Apple iTunes aired a "teaser spot" of 'Viva la Vida'. Shortly after, Phil remembers, "I opened up iTunes and saw the song was No.1 basically everywhere across the world. Dave had made it the 'instant grat' (a free track if you pre-order an album). It was a masterstroke." The commercial was a deciding factor for it becoming a single. Despite the band's initial resistance, Holmes is proud of his persistence, "Being right about that was a great feeling for me. I think they saw that I was willing to lose my job... I don't know if it ever went there, but I was not letting go!"

Three weeks later, on June 12, 2008, the most-anticipated album of the year was released. It sold 125,000 copies on its first day and in its first week reached No.1 in 20 countries, and it became the best-selling release on iTunes.

Viva la Vida was about to beat many sales records. It was the most pre-ordered album from online sale websites, and on June 23 'Viva la Vida' scored the No.1 spot both in the UK and US. It was the first time this had been achieved by an artist since Rod Stewart in 1971 with his song 'Maggie May'.

The 'Viva' campaign had more colour visually than the black/white palettes of the previous albums. It was inspired by the French romantic painter Eugène Delacroix, whose *Liberty Leading the People* hangs in the Louvre, Paris, and offers the central visual on the cover of *Viva la Vida*. The band also helped create their own costumes – a very home-made military look with a spectrum of pastel hues – alongside designers. "We really like them – it's better than the old look. When we put them on, we feel like we're in a proper little gang," said Chris.

They headed out on their world tour. "We're not a stadium band yet," said Chris at the start of the tour. "I think we're still trying to figure out how to make a room full of 10,000 people as exciting as possible, let alone a stadium. To me, an arena feels like the perfect-size canvas, so we're trying to master that." In 2009, after 16 months on the road, the band finally expanded into stadiums.

"They like to keep an intimacy where possible, and they really enjoyed theatre and arena experience because they felt they had a real connection with their fans," Steve Strange said. "As things got bigger, they actually turned the stadiums into an intimate environment as well."

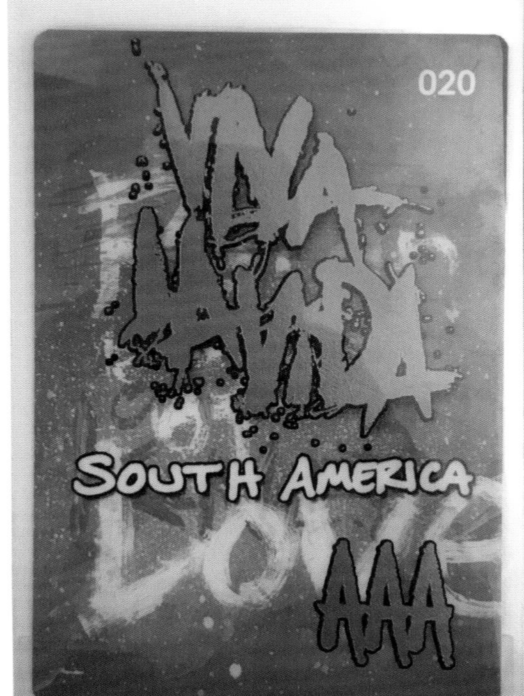

ABOVE Coldplay perform 'Viva la Vida' at the BRIT Awards 2009, at Earls Court One on February 18, 2009.

RIGHT Latin American *Viva la Vida* tour Access All Areas laminate.

As usual it was important for the band "to make sure that people who spend their money get entertained. We think about how every song looks and what the ideal place to be is, and who will see this best from which place. We probably get a bit too obsessed with it, to be honest," said Chris.

Shot from confetti cannons, "The butterfly confetti was wonderful, because you always knew that as long as the bloody machines worked people would gasp and it would be a really great moment," said Phil. As a performer, Chris put it even more bluntly: "Even if the show's going shit, I know that there's two moments that'll be fine. The song 'Viva la Vida' – and when the butterflies glow in the dark."

Puppet versions of the band members were made for the video for 'Life in Technicolor II'. They didn't particularly bear a striking similarity to Jonny, Chris, Will and especially not Guy but they became something of a gimmick on the Viva tour in a 'Wish You Were Here' feature.

LEFT Coldplay puppets chilling with friends in Guadalajara, Mexico. March 2010 .

BELOW The stage set for the video shoot of 'Christmas Lights'. South Bank, London.

BELOW RIGHT 'Christmas Lights' CD sleeve.

OVERLEAF Jonny and Chris walk among the crowd at the 2009 All Points West Music & Arts Festival, Liberty State Park, Jersey City, New Jersey. August 2, 2009.

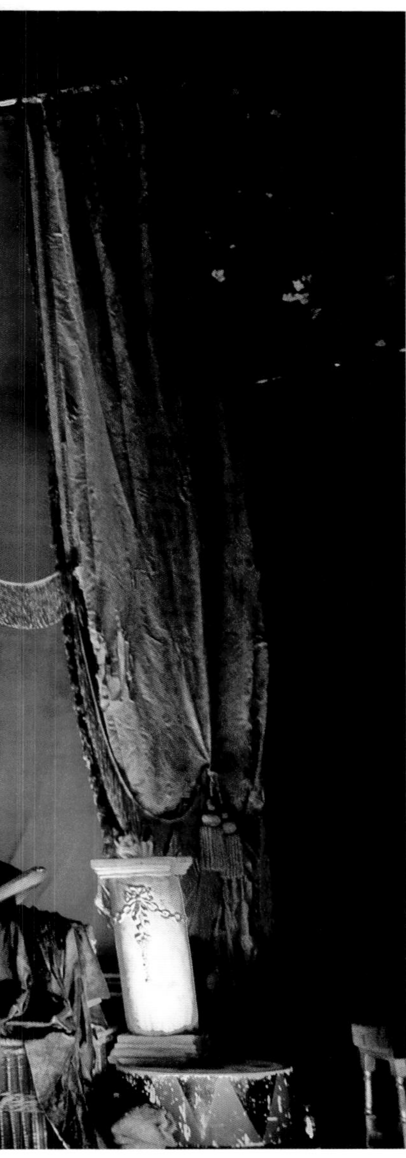

CHRISTMAS LIGHTS

Although a sneak preview of 'Christmas Lights' was shown back in 2008 on the *60 Minutes* TV show, the single was finally unveiled on December 1, 2010. The band had managed to keep the project – code name 'Snowy Owl' – under wraps, which considering the video was shot out in the open, was impressive. Production designer Misty Buckley was in a band meeting discussing ideas for the next album when the conversation turned to 'Christmas Lights'. "It was mid-November," Buckley recalls, "and they wanted to put a music video together to be released in time for Christmas.Chris turned to me and said, 'How do you fancy designing a set for us for the video? It should look like a travelling theatre and will need to be somewhere in London.'" Misty agreed and it was no surprise when she asked Chris when he wanted it for, he replied, "Oh, next week... !"

With that, they all jumped in a taxi and drove round London, looking for the perfect site for the shoot. They decided on the South Bank, so they could capture London at Christmas by the river.

Mat Whitecross – who was by now accustomed to receiving last-minute calls from the band – was asked to direct the video and a mere seven days later, the set had been designed, modelled and built. On the evening of filming, temperatures were expected to drop below zero. "My team and I were there all night until 5 a.m., shooting the video," said Buckley. "The band were freezing... and poor Phil Harvey and Simon Pegg were appearing in the video in paper-thin, Lycra Elvis costumes."

They were exhausted and frozen to the bone, but the results were amazing.

"As we packed up and drove home from the set at 7 a.m., I got a message from the band. 'Well done. We loved it. See you on the tour.'"

A little bit of subterfuge was applied when inviting a select few fans to a staged boat party on the Thames on November 25; they were going to be extras in the video.

"It was a lot of fun coaxing some fans onto a boat on the Thames with Debs on the pretext that we were having a Christmas boat party," said Chris Salmon. "I remember having to play the fans the song for the first time via my phone, and then teaching them the 'Oh-oh-ohhhhhh' bit we'd all have to sing, which you can hear on the video. It was a very cold, very surreal but very fun night."

“We wanted to make a record which people couldn’t pigeon-hole too easily. We don’t want to be thought of as one-trick ponies.”

Guy

WILL CHAMPION

Will Champion's potential as an aspiring guitarist was cut short when he spontaneously sat behind the drumkit at Coldplay's first rehearsal. With one drum roll, Will was appointed to the drum stool, making the group officially complete. But, as the band were quick to find out, Will was much more than a drummer...

"Will's the one I have to impress," said Chris in 2002. "If Will goes 'Ugh', then I have to acknowledge the song's no good. It's one of my great hobbies in life to try to convince Will that my songs are any good. If Will really doesn't want to do something, he's probably right." Chris summed up his bandmate: "When I think of him, I think of something heavy and granite-like. Like the base of a statue. Without that, the thing topples."

So, when it comes to requiring a critical voice of reason within the band, Will's role as "trustworthy" (Guy's word) is something the band all agree on. "Will has a very sensible head on his shoulders and when it comes to making band decisions he's really good at putting valid points across and keeping everyone focused. He frequently has the casting vote and his decision can sometimes override the consensus!" Jonny says. As Chris has repeated several times: "Coldplay are all just working for Will Champion."

MUSICAL DNA

Will's musical ability runs deep in his DNA. Parents Sara and Tim were both lecturers in Archaeology at the University of Southampton. Tim also used to DJ on campus grounds, and around the city in local pubs, under the moniker Champion Tunes. Will's mother taught him how to play the guitar.

Born on July 31, 1978, Will grew up in Highfield, Southampton, and attended Portswood Primary School ("It was quite rough") and secondary school at Cantell Maths and Computing College, and Peter Symonds College. At University College London, he attained a 2:1 Bachelors degree in Anthropology. As he was growing up, the music constantly on the stereo at home – anything from Tom Waits and Nick Cave to traditional Irish folk – imprinted heavily on Will's mind. Not content with just listening, Will picked up playing the piano and violin relatively easily before he was eight, and the guitar when he was 12, not forgetting the bass and tin whistle.

"I started doing lessons on various instruments," Will recalled, "but I didn't enjoy doing them because I couldn't read the music. Instead, I would play songs from memory. I watched my teacher's hands on the piano, memorized it, and ended up doing it myself.

"I think music first clicked as a creative pursuit when my mum taught me how to play three chords on guitar," he remembered. "At the time I had the ability to listen to a song and work out how to play it instantly. I think the guitar is a really easy thing to do that on. That's when I realized most songs revolve around three chords anyway." For the remainder of Will's youth it was the guitar, his beloved football team Southampton FC and playing cricket for Chandler's Ford CC (along with his older brother) that stole the teenager's time. "I was never really in bands (apart from his first group, Fat Hamster); my friends were always playing football instead," he said. "I used to play music by myself, really." When Jonny first heard Will play the guitar he was astonished by his talent. "He's probably a better guitarist than me. He's sort of a multitalented, Swiss Army drummer."

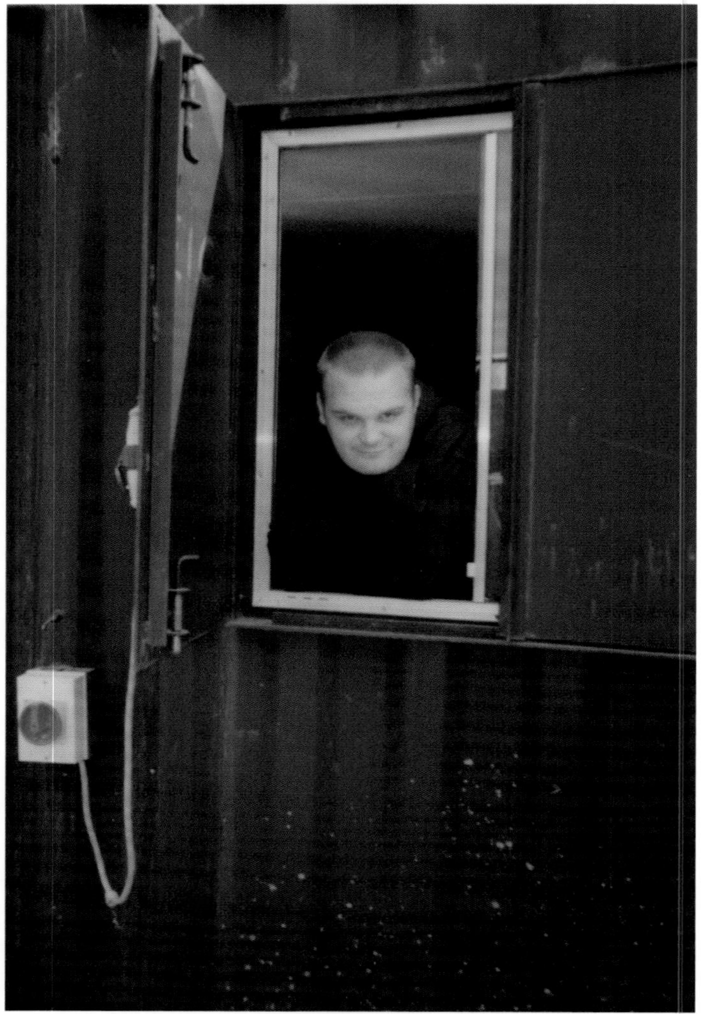

TOP Rockfield Studios, during the recording of *Parachutes*.

ABOVE Backstage at Rockaforte Festival, Verona, Italy, July 2000.

RIGHT The opening night of the *Viva la Vida* tour at the Grest Western Forum, Inglewood, California, July 14, 2008.

HUMAN JUKEBOX

"My next door neighbour when I was growing up had a drum kit and I occasionally played on that, and also during music lessons at school," Will said, "but then I started playing other instruments when I was about 14 and didn't really look at a drum kit. I'm very glad that I played other instruments before the drums. It allowed me to have a different perspective on drumming in music. It's one thing to be a technically brilliant drummer, but knowing the difference between the major and minor key is very important too, and I was lucky to learn all that before I was playing drums. That has more to do with the feel of a song, knowing what's right for the song, instead of knowing how to play powerfully for a second or two."

Chris remembers Will from the early days: "Me and Will used to sit on the stairs at our hall of residence and he'd know more songs than anyone. You name it, he'd play it. He is like a human jukebox." While this musical experience was to be repeated between them throughout their first year of university, it wasn't until year two that the four members started to come together. Before that, Will spent his time hanging out with his new friends, enjoying the delights of UCL's student union, and drinking beer with Guy and Jonny. "I feel that it is important to base a band around a group of friends. Chemistry between bandmates is something that you cannot overestimate. It's more important than technical ability in my opinion," he said.

Kris Foof, a long-time friend of the band and UCL student, remembers Will during this time: "In years two and three, me and Champs used to work a lot in ULU [University of London Union] where (at the time) Ricky Gervais was working. We would work behind the bar for less than £3 an hour, but we would also work as events staff, which meant getting to watch numerous up-and-coming bands that would play the ULU venue. Sometimes we would get paid to watch the touring bands' gear overnight, and we would just be playing on these really great instruments through the night."

> " If we were just hired guns, if it was just the Chris Martin Band, then I wouldn't care. I'd be at home and letting Chris get on with the record. But it's our thing. It's all four of us. We're in it together. "
>
> Will

THE DRUMMERS' DRUMMER

"Coldplay and drumming arrived simultaneously for me." It took the budding drummer quite a long time to feel comfortable. "I was nervous," Will remembers of first rehearsing with the band. "Right off the bat I didn't have the confidence to play loud or heavy, I just was focussed on not fucking up basically! I never felt I was good enough to show off, so that's partly where my style has come from – just wanting to support the song as much as possible – whether that's by not playing for 75 per cent of the song, or by playing something very simple. That's my trademark – wait. Keep waiting... keep waiting... and then at the last moment possible come in and steal the limelight at the end. I'm not one for big fills and flashy rolls. I try and listen to the song and only play when it is really necessary. It is just as important when you don't play as when you do."

Will has always maintained that his ability to play drums stemmed originally from his musical education at home, where he was encouraged to play a multitude of instruments. "Playing the piano did help, because it gave me coordination for my hands and feet, and a different perspective from other drummers. There's hundreds of other drummers who are technically brilliant, but my favourite drummers are people who played in great bands and complemented a great singer. Dave Grohl, Ginger Baker and John Bonham are perfect examples: they're people who are original with their own style, but perfect for the band they played in." At the HFStival in Washington, D.C., in 2001, Chris remembered Dave Grohl going up to Will and telling him he was a great drummer. "That changed Will's life," said Chris.

Debs Wild on Will: *"When someone is born with a surname such as Champion, it would be a waste not to live up to it. Will has, and then some.*

He may be seen as a force of nature, but the only force on display is that with which he hits his drums. He's often accused of being the scary one who makes all the decisions, but it's just that he says 'no' more than anyone else. That's why he's the sensible anchor; any 'no' comes from a place of wanting to do the right thing for the greater good, he always puts other people before himself. Will is a gentle tower of strength."

> "Nobody really tells you how to be a band. You don't go through a schooling system where people tell you how to act and how to behave. But I think we got used to playing together and through the amount of practice we did and the amount of gigs we played, we started to find our voice."
>
> Will

ALL YOUR FRIENDS

As for being famous, Will remains consistently nonchalant about the whole experience. "I've never felt like fame is getting in the way of me living the way I want to, which in certain circumstances it really can for Chris. It would be foolish of me to pretend that I was the band's driving force. Chris is single-minded, he's focused 24 hours a day. I've got a short attention span and want to switch off when I get home. Part of me wants to remain hidden – but that puts a lot of pressure on Chris." He does get recognized in the street more these days. "About once a month, a stranger will say something to me. I was walking down near where I live and I just heard someone on a building site go: 'Oi, drummer of Coldplay!' I loved that. I felt like saying: 'Hello, builder of houses!'" As the band emerge into their 20th year, Will, as ever, is about to tackle it head-on. "We're not an emerging band anymore. We're no longer a new band. And we're certainly not quite that sort of heritage value."

LEFT Forever focused on the target, Will performs at Ahoy, Rotterdam, Netherlands, December 17, 2011.

RIGHT Will performing 'Viva la Vida' during the *A Head Full of Dreams* tour at the MetLife Stadium, East Rutherford, New Jersey, July 17, 2016.

LOVE
IS EQUAL

CHAPTER FIVE

GLOWING IN THE DARK

MYLO XYLOTO

Released: October 19, 2011
Recorded: November 2008–September 2011
Producer: Markus Dravs, Rik Simpson, Daniel Green
Tracklisting:
Mylo Xyloto
Hurts Like Heaven
Paradise
Charlie Brown
Us Against the World
M.M.I.X
Every Teardrop Is a Waterfall
Major Minus
UFO
Princess of China (feat. Rihanna)
Up in Flames
A Hopeful Transmission
Don't Let It Break Your Heart
Up with the Birds

ABOVE The *Mylo Xyloto* CD cover.

OPPOSITE ABOVE Commemorative disc for *Mylo Xyloto* sales, personalized DW for Debs Wild.

OPPOSITE BELOW The *Mylo Xyloto* tour programme.

Writing sessions for the fifth album began almost on the same day as *Viva la Vida* was handed over to the label. The band's initial plan was to record a more acoustic album. Indeed, an early incarnation of the track 'Charlie Brown' (then called 'Cartoon Heart') even featured Will playing accordion, prompting Guy to suggest they needed to "plug in again". When the band realized they were holding back some of the best songs that didn't fit with an acoustic direction, they decided instead to simply work on those and see what happened.

BEAT FROM MY HEART

Despite Chris claiming (once more) that, after *Viva la Vida*, the band might never record again, and that "I don't think bands should keep going past 33," they couldn't wait to get back in the studio. They had some songs that were three years old and some three weeks old.

"It was time to start thinking about how we could better it, or do something different," Jonny said. This was highlighted by a letter Brian Eno wrote to the band after recording *Viva la Vida*:

> "Dear Coldplay. I really think we've made a good record here. But I do think we can do a lot better, and I feel we all need to get back to work as soon as possible because I feel like Jonny especially is on the route to something, and he hasn't got there yet. *Eno.*"

"First and foremost, we do anything Brian says," said Chris. "That goes a long way with him. So, I'm secretly using him as much as he thinks he's using us, you see – by letting him do whatever he wants, we're actually gaining."

Guy revealed that *Mylo Xyloto* almost existed as an animated film, (the characters ultimately went on to star in their own comic book revealed at Comic Con, San Diego, July 6, 2012), but the film was put on pause and *Mylo* became a concept album of sorts.

"We got quite far down the line with designing characters and then we abandoned that idea and moved into a different direction, retaining elements of the acoustic album and the soundtrack album, so what we've ended up with is an album that we arrived at in quite an unusual sort of way," said Guy.

"It was supposed to be about two people who grow up separately in a very big oppressive city, and they each are a bit lost in their lives, a kind of love story so all the songs fit together," said Chris.

One of the bravest decisions for the group was the title. The band wanted to come up with new words. Something completely original. The title "*Mylo Xyloto* might sound silly now," said Chris

THE SIX COMMANDMENTS

In May 2010 the group asked Eno to write Ten Commandments for them to live by. He wrote six.

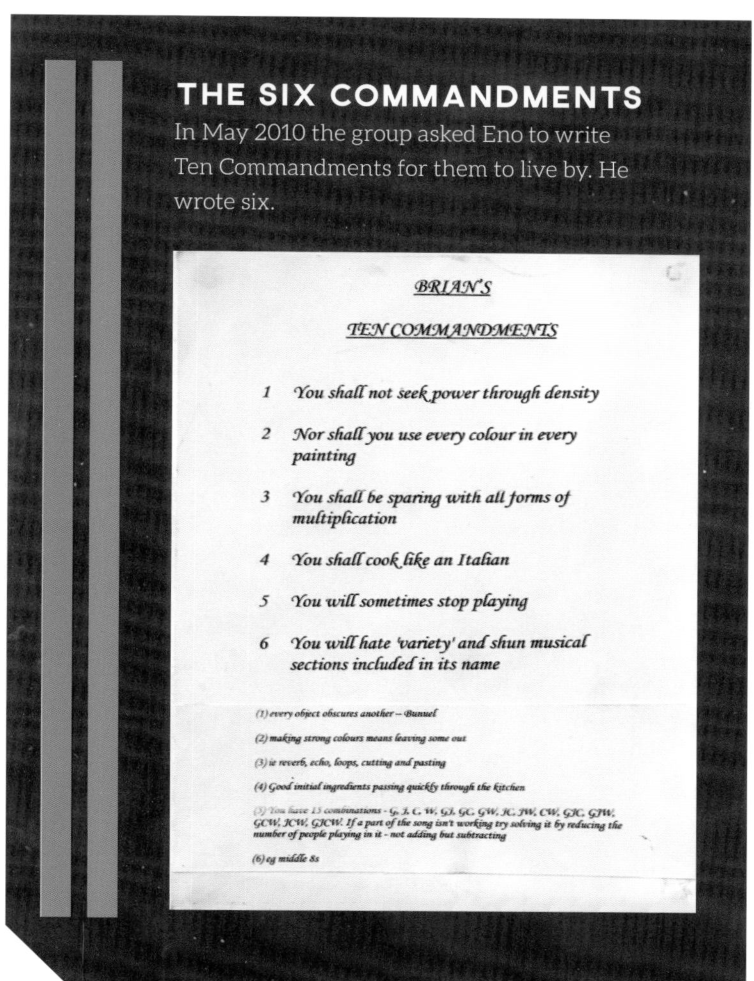

BRIAN'S

TEN COMMANDMENTS

1 *You shall not seek power through density*

2 *Nor shall you use every colour in every painting*

3 *You shall be sparing with all forms of multiplication*

4 *You shall cook like an Italian*

5 *You will sometimes stop playing*

6 *You will hate 'variety' and shun musical sections included in its name*

(1) every object obscures another – Bunuel

(2) making strong colours means leaving some out

(3) ie reverb, echo, loops, cutting and pasting

(4) Good initial ingredients passing quickly through the kitchen

(5) You have 15 combinations - G, J, C, W, GJ, GC, GW, JC, JW, CW, GJC, GJW, GCW, JCW, GJCW. If a part of the song isn't working try solving it by reducing the number of people playing in it - not adding but subtracting

(6) eg middle 8s

promoting the album in 2011. "But one day I don't think it will." The band wanted to come up with a new couple of words. "When we called our band Coldplay everyone was confused, so we thought we'd try that on an album title," Chris remarked. "We thought it would be nice to have something that didn't mean anything else except what your imagination wanted it to."

Eno was once again on board as, according to Will, "more a sower of seeds". Eno even invented the term "enoxification" to define his own input during this period. "He was more of a band member this time around," Chris said. "He loves to just stand in the circle and play with the band."

One of Eno's most effective techniques was telling the singer to go away. "Eno said to me, 'You need to fuck off for a bit, and then the end result will be much more about the chemistry of the band than the ramblings of a dictator," said Chris. The singer was dismissed for two weeks, effectively ensuring Jonny, Guy and Will would step up to the mic.

"Jonny is a naturally shy person, but after spending time with Brian, he was much more prepared to take the lead role once we started putting songs together, which was great news for me," said Chris. "Jonny is coming out of his cocoon. We're trying some risky things. I feel very proud of Jonny. He's pushed himself a lot," said Chris.

Dan Green, long-time sound engineer, was always writing ideas on his laptop, some of which he played to Chris. One of those ideas became 'Up with the Birds', which led to Chris inviting Green to share production responsibilities with Markus Dravs and Rik Simpson.

"One of the brilliant things about the guys is they have a really good eye for choosing a person to do a specific job, there's very little overlap. Within that, everyone just works together," said Green. "We are all aware of not treading on anybody else's toes. Everyone is really respectful of each other's roles. It's the same within the band, they're like that too."

> “It really fees like a gang travelling the world. It feels like a family. Kind of a circus family I suppose.”
>
> Jonny

ABOVE Jonny on stage at an early show on the *Mylo Xyloto* tour, Verizon Center, Washington D.C., July 9, 2012.

RIGHT A part of Coldplay's live show since 2002, lasers wow the audience at Verizon Center, Washington D.C., July 9, 2012.

"Dan and I have a great working relationship," added Simpson. "Markus dipped in and out more. It refreshed the creative spirit." Towards the end of the Viva tour, the band acquired a second recording studio, The Beehive. Located near to The Bakery, The Beehive is a very different workspace. Inside there are offices and writing suites and a basement that morphs into whatever is needed, as and when. The jewel in the crown is the vast open-plan live room.

"There's no control room in The Beehive; it's a large open space – like a hall with lots of natural light." said Simpson. "It's great for communication. If there's glass between you're removed from it." Photos of inspirational people began to adorn the walls, just as they had at The Bakery during *Viva la Vida*.

Dravs also felt the band were better at knowing when to work with which person and on what, helping the album develop organically but also uniquely. It's perhaps why 'Us Against the World' and 'Princess of China' may sound like the offspring of two different bands, but yet share a common connection within one.

TURN THE MUSIC UP

Historically, Matt Miller has been responsible for recording all the sound checks when the band are on tour, and he maintains an iTunes library of anything that might eventually end up as a new song. Anything "from Will playing a drum pattern that works with a funny slapback echo in the venue, to the whole band playing through a song that's been in the works for months." Similarly, in the studio, there is a music library that contains all of the ideas and works in progress.

The evolution of the songs continued. 'Lost' began as a very fragile-sounding piano piece and ended up swaggering and full – but the chords, words and melody remained almost the same as the original.

"There were occasions at the beginning of *Viva la Vida* when we would have three versions of the same song and maybe more emphasis on Brian and myself agreeing on which version to further," said Dravs. "For *Mylo*, it was more fluid. We would cherry-pick from different versions in a more organic way."

Even though the album changed course, Simpson felt it was "very organic whilst not veering off to anything extremely different sonically". The album begins with a crescending instrumental that

runs into 'Hurts Like Heaven', which was designed with large shows such as Glastonbury in mind. "They warm us up, help us get fired up. It's callisthenics musically for us," Chris said.

The band's aspirations to be more experimental with videos, stage design and aesthetics truly came to life during the *Mylo* era. With the first single, 'Every Teardrop Is a Waterfall' (released June 3, 2011), *Mylo Xyloto* positively burst into vivid neon. Everywhere the band had travelled they saw street art. Chris said they "loved the freedom of expression. You can paint anything yourself, and you don't have to be a grandmaster. The idea of the record too is to find colour within darkness and depression."

The group also wanted to dramatically change their stage design for the new tour.

Paris, a Bristol-based graffiti artist, got a phone call out of the blue from Misty Buckley, asking if he'd like to work with a band. Paris didn't know their identity until he went to meet them.

With Paris' assistance the band eventually made an enormous graffiti wall – nine individual panels that became an integral part of the campaign's artwork. Paris told Chris Salmon: "The band had a lot of stuff they wanted to put on the wall," Paris told Chris Salmon. "I showed them how to do it and then I added my flavour to it as well. Guy mentioned they wanted to do paint bombs, so the next day I had loads of balloons with paint in to throw at the wall. And then we'd be scratching into it. The wall was incredible."

Paris was also called in to work on Mat Whitecross' stop-motion animation video for 'Every Teardrop Is a Waterfall', where

Paris and his team would be painting the blank walls of the site at Millennium Mills, London. "There was a theme and it was very tightly planned, but we were also given the opportunity to interpret things for ourselves. We were told what had to happen – like the pulsing heart – but how we did it was up to us. It was three days of non-stop work," Paris said.

RIGHT Access All Areas laminated tour passes for the *Mylo Xyloto* tour.

BELOW Miller's photo of Coldplay's famous Xylobands in all their glory, as the band walks to the stage in Stockholm.

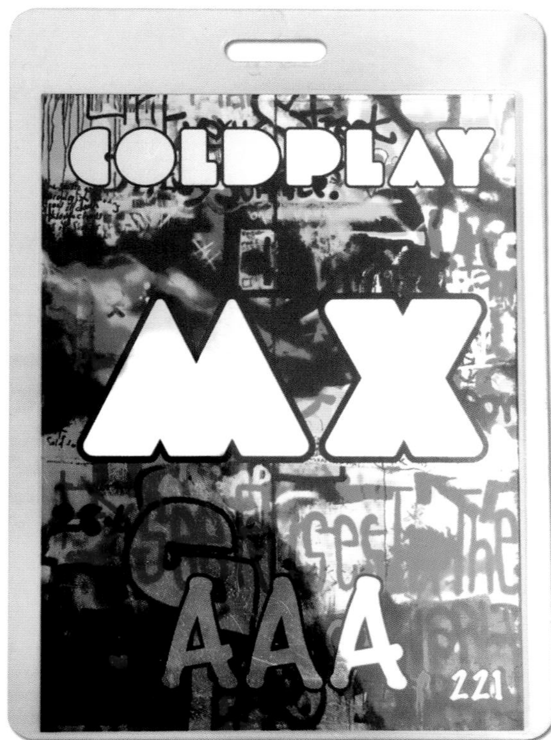

As they finished painting in one room and moved onto the next, immediately after filming another team of people followed behind, whitewashing over it.

The second single, 'Paradise', generated more than a billion views on YouTube thanks to its wonderful video, and became the best-selling download of 2010 in the UK, with more than 410,000 copies. "It's the song you can build everything else around," Chris said. "You need to have one of them, at least, on every record. They give you a reason to write the others."

Phil casually passed on a request to Chris from the *X Factor* producers that he write a song for that season's finalists. Phil witnessed Chris sit down at the piano and out came 'Paradise', fully formed. Coincidentally, a year later, the band would perform the song live on the show, a week before the song went to No.1 in the UK charts.

"Very early on in the process of recording this record, we were playing a lot of acoustic instruments and we had it in our mind that we might try to record a small-sounding, intimate, reflective record. Then 'Paradise' came about, and it dawned on us that we couldn't play it in that acoustic style. So we thought, 'OK, we'll finish this one and then we'll do another record,'" said Will, who was behind the decision for the band to keep the song for themselves.

WELCOME TO PARADISE

Getting the right video for 'Paradise' had proved difficult: two had already been rejected. With time running out, Chris called on Mat Whitecross and asked him to do it. At very short notice, Mat managed to pull everything together to make the best video ever to feature a unicycling elephant – a concept that Chris had originated.

The video follows Chris, dressed up in an elephant's costume, escaping from Paradise Wildlife Park in London, travelling on the Tube, flying to South Africa and then unicycling to meet the band, also dressed up in elephant costumes.

Chris had learned how to ride a unicycle as a child ("We didn't get bicycles in Devon until 1996, so we had to make do with what we could," he joked) but he wanted to keep his identity a secret throughout the shoot. He went unnoticed on the London Underground, but temperatures got so high in South Africa, he removed his elephant head.

Inspiration for *Mylo Xyloto*'s third single, 'Charlie Brown', came from an entirely different direction.

"I had my scooter nicked, and it got me thinking what journey would that bike go on, with the kid that stole it. So 'Charlie Brown' started out about that," said Chris. "'Charlie Brown' was the centrepiece of this other record we started first. We were playing the riff on an accordion and Guy came in one morning and said, 'I'm afraid I have to put my foot down. I don't want to speak out of turn, but I will not allow this song to be played on an accordion.'"

The record's fourth single, 'Princess of China', was a dream come true for Coldplay. As the song's female character developed,

ABOVE Opening with 'MX' and incredible fireworks, Coldplay play the Pyramid Stage at Glastonbury Festival, Worthy Farm, Pilton, June 25, 2011. This performance was later voted the best Glastonbury moment ever.

OPPOSITE Miller photographed the band taking a break during filming of the 'Paradise' video in South Africa.

Chris had Rihanna in mind to sing the part. "We did a show in Las Vegas and I met her and said, 'Do you think there's any chance?' I was very Hugh Grant-like and spluttering about it. To our great surprise, she said OK."

"I found that with *Viva la Vida*, I enjoyed writing from someone else's perspective to actually get out what I was feeling," said Chris. 'Princess of China' is from a girl's perspective. I wonder what that says about me?"

Mylo Xyloto was bursting with upbeat anthemic pop songs. "The album sounds colourful," said Chris. "I don't know whether they're good colours or bad colours, but they're definitely different colours."

In May, the band also began teasing lyrics from 'Every Teardrop Is a Waterfall' before finally announcing its imminent release. There was a secret show at the Forum, the London venue the band had occasionally used for production rehearsals since their humble beginnings there in 1999. It gave them a chance to play in front of an audience, albeit a small one, before they went to Europe.

The band also found a new way to insert colour into the live shows courtesy of Jason Regler, who had been invited to the Forum. Jason made a winning bid to meet the band at their Crisis charity show in Newcastle, but heavy snow halted the trip. "He wrote me a letter telling me his son was a big fan," said Phil. "I can't begin to explain why I actually replied and said he could come along." In an opportune moment, Jason told Phil, "'Oh by the way, I'm an inventor and I had this idea of having wristbands with lights on' and it just clicked in my head: 'That's a brilliant idea.'" Phil said.

Phil and Jason's team, with ideas from the band, began work on making Xylobands a reality for their upcoming tour. The invention came to embody the innovative and multicoloured spirit of the band.

GLASTONBURY – PART FIVE

The band were scheduled to play Glastonbury in June. Unlike 2002, when they felt panicked at playing before the new album's release, they made the decision this time to play their new songs at many of the summer festivals. 'Every Teardrop Is a Waterfall' and 'Charlie Brown', like 'Viva la Vida' before it, were big bouncy numbers that particularly lent themselves to the live shows. They were made for festivals.

On June 25, 2011, Coldplay headlined Glastonbury for the third time. "I'll never forget the atmosphere in the dressing room after the set," said Chris Salmon. "They put so much into that show, and it really couldn't have gone any better. There was an atmosphere

> “I would love it if in 20 years I would look back on this and think that’s when I feel like we started to become really good.”
>
> Chris

of pure, unadulterated joy from the band and the whole team. It was a lovely thing to witness.”

Two years later, in 2013, Coldplay’s performance was named as the favourite Glastonbury moment of all time by BBC radio listeners. The band’s long-term friend Jo Whiley was there. “Knowing how much it meant to them – to be headlining a festival they grew up with and that they performed at in their infancy as a band – it was probably the biggest, most important gig of their careers and lives. I could not have been happier for them. It was the perfect Pyramid headline set.”

Misty Buckley, creative director of Glastonbury’s Park Stage, designed Coldplay’s stage, “Coldplay are family to the festival, so it is extra special when they perform there. The *Mylo Xyloto* show at Glastonbury was off the scale.” The pyramid had never been projected on to before, and it looked incredible as it lit up. The lasers reaching across the audience, connecting everyone in that field, was just extraordinary.”

The Xylobands finally got their first appearance at the *Mylo Xyloto* album launch gig on October 26, 2011. The bullring venue, La Plaza de Toros de Las Ventas, Madrid, provided the perfect backdrop to showcase the spectacle.

The first incarnation of wristbands were on a timer because, given that the Madrid show was broadcast live, the exact start time was known. It was a nerve-racking situation with a product that was untried and untested. Regler was under enormous pressure and show day was not without its problems, but he remembers: "The crowd, the noise, the intensity. It was crazy." To see the Xylobands in all their glory brought him a "massive sense of relief".

The effect was breathtaking. "There's nothing like it. The sheer rush of energy and joy you get when they switch on and the sense of bringing the audience together as one," said Phil.

"When the wristbands light up, I feel this is one of the greatest things I've ever seen, and I feel extremely grateful," agreed Chris.

ABOVE Debs' photo of Will with video director Mat Whitecross.

OPPOSITE The band play 'Paradise' on Jonathan Ross' chat show, London, October 15, 2011.

LEFT Debs' photo of Gavin Ahern, Naomi Hilton, Jonny and John Hilton.

BELOW AND OVERLEAF Showing just how far they've come at the 2015 iHeartRadio Music Festival, MGM's Grand Garden Arena in Las Vegas, Nevada, September 18, 2015.

iHeart
RADIO

iHeart
RADIO

675461
COLDPLAY
COLDPLAY
085
VIP
COLDPLAY
EVERY
SURFACE
275
AAA
CUBEPASSES.COM
COLDPLAY
465
VIP
COLDPLAY

" By the time we're finishing an album, I'm so keen to get back to playing live, but when we're 18 months into a tour, all I want to do is get into the studio. "

Will

"We'd been sort of searching for something like Xylobands since doing the Viva tour of playing very big places, trying to get everybody involved and everybody as part of the concert, and hadn't come up with anything anywhere near as good," said Jonny. There was something magical about the marriage of *Mylo Xyloto* and the Xylobands. "The start of the show worked so well with wristbands. It was euphoric and beautiful," said Regler.

Money was spent developing the Xylobands over the next few months, as the band were preparing once again to go out on the road. "Phil was instrumental in working on ideas for how to bring that to life at shows. He would constantly be searching the internet, different publications, theatre, movie, press and just everything, to try and find interesting new ideas and technologies that we could use," said Will. "We like the idea of working with people that have fantastic ideas to do things that nobody else has done before."

OPPOSITE TOP Wristband and laminated tour passes for the *Mylo Xyloto* tour.

OPPOSITE The authors of this book brandishing their Xylobands at London's Emirates Stadium, London, June 2, 2012.

BELOW Fans at the Lanxess-Arena in Cologne, Germany are treated to confetti, December 15, 2011.

"I always try to imagine what it's like for the person who's at the furthest seat," said Phil. "And when we're on tour I very often go up to the back to watch the show, just to see what experience people are getting up there. It can be hard to make that person feel like they're close to the band, but that's a big part of what we're trying to do. On the *Mylo Xyloto* tour, we went out into the audience and played some songs out there on what we call the C Stage. We just feel extremely grateful to anyone who buys a ticket to one of our gigs and we do not take it for granted, not for a second. We want to make sure they feel appreciated and have a great experience."

The Xylobands ensure an inclusive feeling at every Coldplay show. "Since we got our wristbands you can see everyone literally light up!" said Chris. "We just feel like we're the house band, facilitating this big singalong." Regler explains his initial vision, "We are going to make a lot of people happy and bring this big unity to music. That was the dream, that was the plan and that's where we were heading with it. Phil Harvey – he's the one that saw the potential and took the chance." The plan succeeded.

At the end of such a huge tour, "there's a weird hollowness at the end of it," said Chris. "You've got two years of being needed every night, a lot of energy coming at you, then it's all gone and you have to see what's happening in your personal life. So, a lot of things were just… not there."

That personal life would be laid bare on the band's next, more subdued, project.

“We’d be shooting ourselves in the foot a little bit if we made music which wasn’t particularly suited for playing in arenas, or perhaps even stadiums.”

Guy

ABOVE Chris, moments before the band perform 'Princess of China' at the 54th GRAMMY Awards at the Staples Center, Los Angeles, California, February 12, 2012.

LEFT The band bring the house down in Madrid, Spain, at the Vicente Calderón Stadium, May 20, 2012.

PARALYMPICS CLOSING CEREMONY

On September 9, 2012, the band performed a 16-song set in front of 80,000 people at Olympic Park stadium, London, while also enlisting the help of Jay-Z and Rihanna... and a supporting cast of 1,200. Coldplay's live performance was at the centre of an incredible tableau of dance, musical and theatre performers, including Candoco, Charlie Hazelwood's Paraorchestra, Help4Heroes and paralympians, who had trained to perform at the ceremony as well. "It felt like quite a heavy responsibility, not just because it closed the games but for the paralympians," remembers Phil. "It felt like that year the Paralympics had made a break-through in terms of recognition and awareness, and we didn't want to let them down. I only have good memories of that. I remember being really proud of the band."

Before the start, however, a technical emergency was being averted.

"It was an unforgettable experience for anybody who was there, but I'll never forget the stage power going down twice in the hour leading up to their set," said Will's drum tech, Bash. "The electricians saved the day."

Dan Green remembers the panic, "Almost as the band were walking towards the stage, the power went. We thought it wasn't going to happen. There were people going crazy trying to plug things in, things were blowing up, there's literally people falling through the holes on the stage and things like that. It was a real *Back to the Future* moment. Everything in that performance was live and that was pretty ambitious to do on such a big scale."

The band were paid £1 for their performance. Debs Wild remembers the immensity of the production. "There was so much going on, I didn't know which part to watch! It was the most spectacular thing I have ever seen. A proud moment for everyone."

"We can't actually imagine a bigger honour. This will be the biggest night of our lives," said Chris.

BELOW Debs' photo of fireworks filling the sky following Coldplay's epic performance at the closing ceremony of the London 2012 Paralympic Games, Olympic Stadium, on September 9, 2012.

OVERLEAF Jonny and Chris perform an intimate acoustic gig to support the MENCAP charity at Little Noise Sessions at St John-At-Hackney, London, November 24, 2011. They played ten songs, with 'Fix You' as the closer.

ABOVE Debs' photo of one of the most incredible nights of British sport in history – and Coldplay were at the heart of it.

BELOW Rihanna and Coldplay during the closing ceremony of the London 2012 Paralympic Games, Olympic Stadium, on September 9, 2012.

CHAPTER

SIX

CALL IT MAGIC

GHOST STORIES

Released: May 19, 2014
Recorded: February 2013–March 2014
Producer: Coldplay, Paul Epworth, Rik Simpson, Daniel Green, Jon Hopkins, Tim Bergling
Tracklisting:
Always in My Head
Magic
Ink
True Love
Midnight
Another's Arms
Oceans
A Sky Full of Stars
O

A SKY FULL OF STARS EP

Released: June 29, 2014
Producer: Coldplay, Paul Epworth, Rik Simpson, Daniel Green, Jon Hopkins, Tim Bergling
Tracklisting:
A Sky Full of Stars (Radio Edit)
All Your Friends
Ghost Story
O (Reprise)

The band's sixth album, *Ghost Stories*, was unlike any album that came before. Like an interlude, an unexpected surprise, it arrived without much warning. An open and honest record about the trials of love, and the changes that can tear it apart. This album reflected a difficult period in the singer's life. "Everyone in their life goes through challenges, whether it's love or money, kids, or illness," Chris said. "You have to really not run away from that stuff."

TURN YOUR MAGIC ON

As ever, new song ideas were put down following the completion of the *Mylo Xyloto* world tour.

Chris called this particular period "a realization about trying to grow up". "He set himself a road map for getting out of his hole," Phil said. "He gave himself a framework to get himself enjoying life again." It is this framework that saturates the group's seventh album, *A Head Full of Dreams*, with so much positivity and colour. But in order to see the light, the band knew they must encounter the dark.

Ghost Stories is an understated collection of songs in collaboration with a wide range of producers, including Paul Epworth, Avicii and Jon Hopkins. On first play, a listener could be forgiven for thinking it downbeat and introspective. Listen again – there are themes of colour bursting through the darkness.

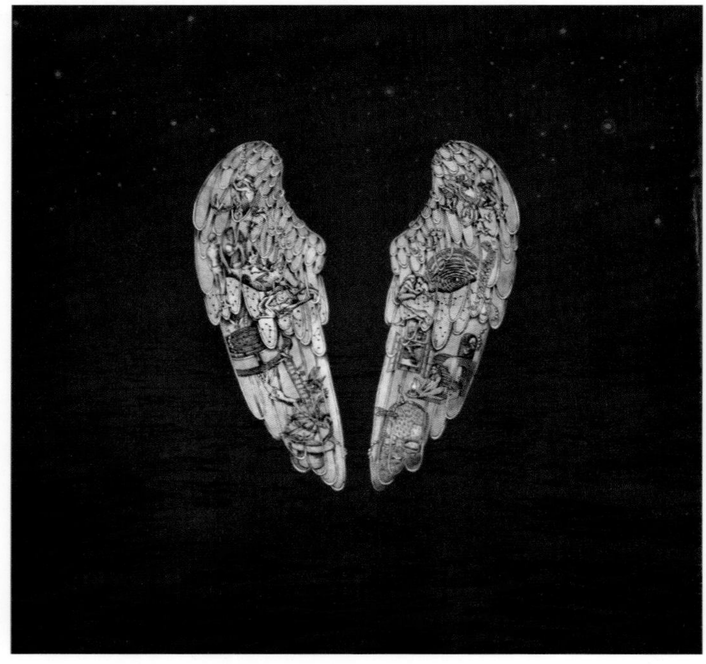

ABOVE Mila Fürstová with the band.

LEFT The *Ghost Stories* CD cover.

RIGHT The original etchings idea for the *Ghost Stories* cover by Mila Fürstová.

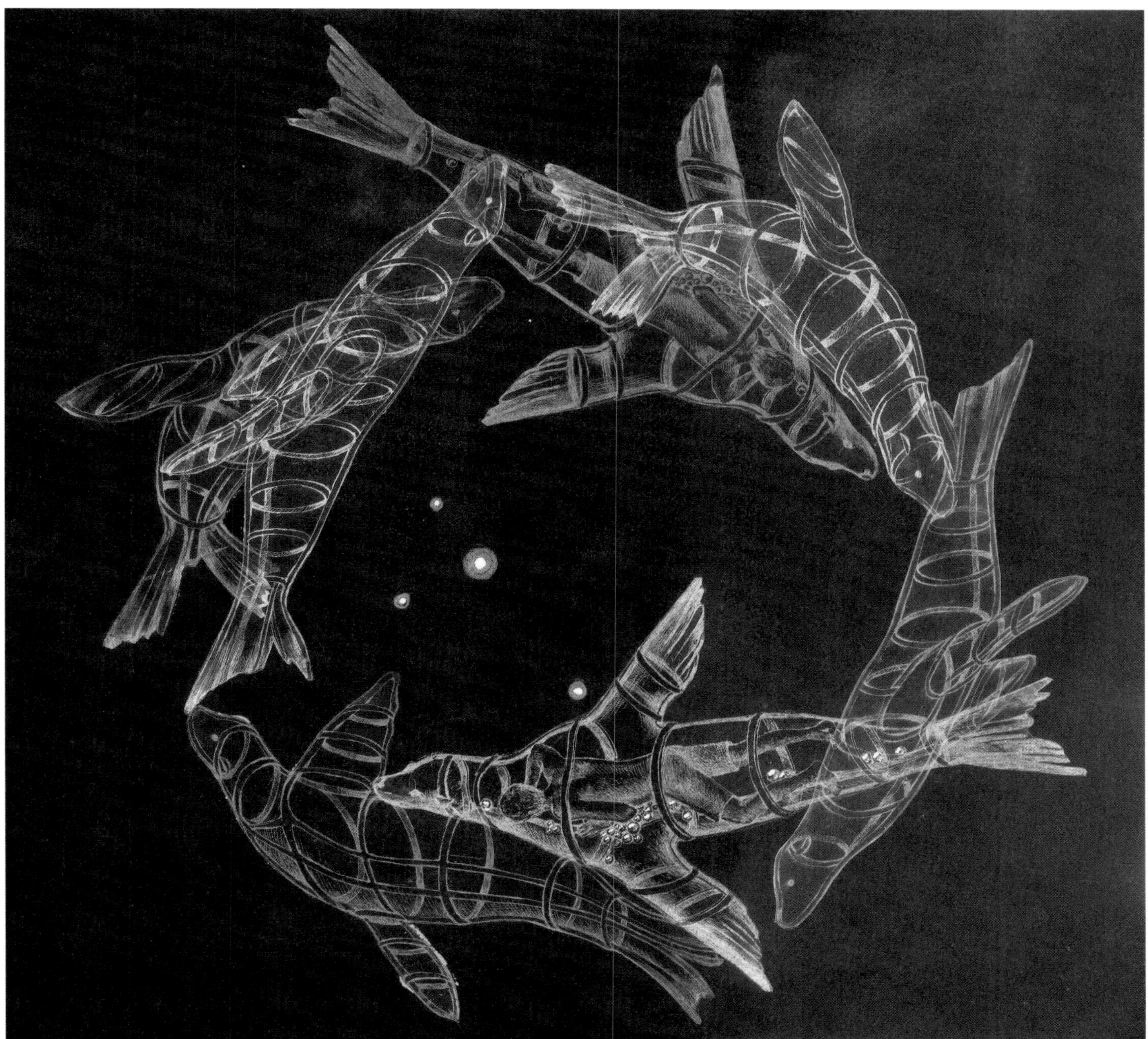

Things had changed, rather publicly, in Chris' personal life, but the singer didn't want to go through life "being scared – of love, of rejection, of failure". Inspired by alchemy (at one point a proposed title for the album – the process of turning metal to gold), the group turned negativity into positivity.

Recording sessions began in February 2013. For *Ghost Stories*, so many songs were arriving "from the universe" that the band didn't want to stop recording. The band met at Guy's house for a few weeks. The intimacy of these initial surroundings would influence the album's tone. "For a lot of *Ghost Stories*, we were in Guy's living room," recalled Chris. "Not even a living room, a big cupboard – and we put in a piano and a mixing desk and we started in there." The room was so small, Will and his drumpad (there wasn't space for a drum kit) had to be in another room on his own. "It was very productive," recalls Guy. "We weren't surrounded by familiar rooms or lots and lots of equipment. It was very reminiscent of when we first started the band, which was basically in Jonny's bedroom."

The bass riff that opens 'Magic' was one of the first things to come from those sessions. "I'd been begging the band: 'Please, could someone else start a song," said Chris. "Then one day, Guy very quietly came over to me in the studio and said: 'Chris, you know we did this jam yesterday? I think you should listen to it' and it was the beginning of the song 'Magic'. I was so grateful; it made me so happy."

Joining Rik Simpson and Dan Green in The Beehive on production duties was Paul Epworth. He was best known for collaborating with Adele, but the band had loved his work with the Futureheads. *Viva* collaborator Jon Hopkins is also credited on the album's lead single 'Midnight'. A noticeable departure for the band, 'Midnight' emerged out of 'Amphora', a 2003 track by Hopkins. "It is similar to 'Magic' in that the original music didn't come from me," said Chris.

'Midnight' came about by accident. During a writing session at The Beehive with Jon Hopkins, Rik Simpson and Dan Green, Chris asked Green to load up a Hopkins track they had been working on a few nights earlier. As that session hadn't gone particularly well, Green misunderstood and instead loaded up something they'd started work on a year before, a track Chris had forgotten about but was immediately excited by. "Chris had been working with this harmonizer sound that had nothing to do with me," said Hopkins. "My track was playing in the background and he just quickly wrote that whole bit on top. It was kind of really an amazing moment, because we all had a feeling that there was another seed of a great song being born."

COLDPLAY

✦

GHOST STORIES

A BIG thank you for accepting the **TOP SECRET** mission to hide the enclosed sealed envelope for us in a book in a library in your city. Here are your instructions!

1. On Monday 28 April (or soonest day afterwards if you can't do that day) please take the sealed envelope to the main/biggest public library in the city where you live.

2. Find a book which could be described as a Ghost Story - ie a story which has some spooky, spirit-y element. It could be Charles Dickens' A Christmas Carol or Shakespeare's Richard III or Edgar Allen Poe's The Raven, or a book of local spirit tales or even just a book of children's spooky Halloween stories. Anything which is vaguely spooky. If you can't find one of your own, just use one of the above, please.

3. Place the sealed envelope in the middle of the book. Please make sure that nobody sees you doing this.

4. Don't forget to make a note of the title and author of the book that you placed the envelope in. We will need this in order to give clues to the location.

5. If there is nobody around, then please take a quick photo of the book on its shelf with the cover facing out, before you put it back.

6. Put the book back and walk away looking innocent!

7. Email us at [illegible] as soon as you can, to tell us the name of the library and the street it's on, plus the name and author of the book where you left the envelope.

Remember, nobody must know that you're doing this!
Please don't tell a soul or post anything online about it!

THANK YOU!

ABOVE A letter from the treasure hunt where Chris' handwritten lyrics for the *Ghost Stories* album were hidden in libraries across the world.

BELOW Debs in pre-stage huddle before the band take the stage at the Casino de Paris, 2014.

RIGHT Fan photos from the 'A Sky Full of Stars' video shoot in Australia.

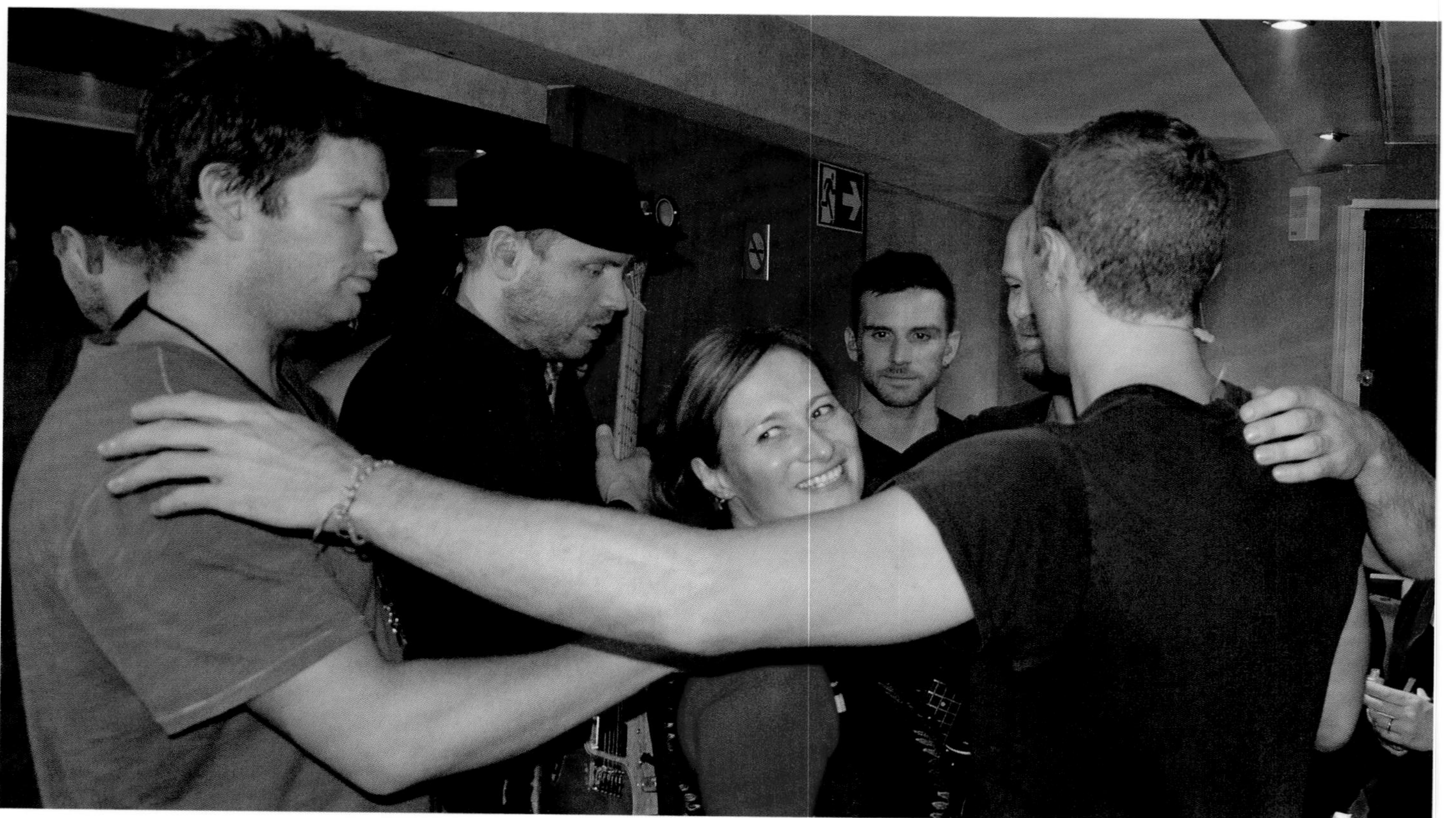

Everyone agreed 'Midnight' should form the foundations and be the main sound of *Ghost Stories*.

Rik Simpson would describe these unplanned collaborations as "creative bubbling. I felt my role was more of curator. All those different palettes coming together. It was very satisfying."

'Magic' was the first official single, released March 3, 2014, with Chris playing both the protagonist and villain in the supporting clip filmed in black and white, directed by Jonas Åkerlund. Chris was taught magic tricks on set by magician Joe Labero.

LEAVE A LIGHT ON

If 'Midnight' represented the "darkness before the dawn", then 'A Sky Full of Stars', the penultimate track, is the light at the end of the tunnel. Usually when the band get to a creative impasse, where they don't agree, they debate, discuss and vote on a song's inclusion. One song that divided opinion during this period was 'A Sky Full of Stars'. It had only Chris' vote; the others were uncertain.

There is no doubt that the song doesn't feel like a natural fit alongside the gentleness of the other tracks. It could have been a hidden track, but Chris was adamant that it took its place centre stage. It wasn't that the band didn't like the song, Dan Green noted, "it was the first time a finished song had come back and been presented to the guys," an act Chris considered as cheating on the rest of the band. "I was at the piano and this song just fell out [in seven minutes!] and came right through. The rest of the band weren't here, and a bit naughtily I called Tim (Avicii) and asked if there was any way he could set up and record a demo of this," said Chris. "He just made these great piano and synth sounds."

Despite the circumstances surrounding its inception, the band were happy with *Ghost Stories*. It was the album they set out to make. Chris said it was the first time that had happened since *A Rush of Blood to the Head*. "The way I would describe *Ghost Stories* is the journey of going through a challenge or an ordeal to come out a little bit stronger and happier at the end. Not letting it break you, but letting it make you," said Chris.

Miles Leonard stated the importance of *Ghost Stories*: "I always knew that it was a hugely important album. At the time, they were so big and to bring it all back down to something more intimate..."

A video had been shot for 'A Sky Full of Stars', but the final result didn't meet with the band's approval, so they once again called upon Mat Whitecross to step in at the last minute. Phil posted a tweet asking locals to appear as extras in the video that was shot on June 17 in Australia, during the band's small tour: "250 fans needed for #ASFOS video tomorrow (Tues). Meet 11.30am at Courthouse Hotel, 202 Australia St, Newtown, Sydney. Bring a smile. PH". The scrapped video makes a tiny appearance on TV screens inside a shop, as Chris passes by during filming of the new video.

A HEAVENLY VIEW

Even before recording began, Coldplay commissioned the Czech Republic-born artist Mila Fürstová for their album's artwork. A few years before Mila met Coldplay, she received devastating news that her partner, Jan, had suddenly collapsed and died.

> "We weren't surrounded by familiar rooms or lots of equipment. It was very reminiscent of when we first started the band."
>
> Guy

Later that evening, her friend, Katerina, opened her laptop and said, "Listen to this". It was *Viva la Vida*. Mila said: "I suddenly felt as if something bigger was touching me on my shoulder and then an embrace of calm and love spread through my body."

Her experience was so profound that she considered writing to Coldplay to thank them but never did. "A couple of years later it was Coldplay who found their way to me," she said. The contact came about when Mila's agent spotted her work at Phil's home.

Phil felt Mila's art could visually express the ideas that are central to *Ghost Stories* and he filled the walls of The Bakery with her art. "When the band were forced to live with it, I think it got under their skin," she said.

Initially, Chris wanted to use her swimming sea lions piece as the central motif, as they have a feeling about them of ghosts moving weightlessly in the sea. He abandoned that idea when he became attracted to an etching called 'Blue Dream III', an image of a female head with wings woven in silver thread. The wings contained her journeys and her dreams.

Chris phoned Mila from LA and said that he would like to use the wings as a framework to tell the stories within the album. Mila was listening to the unfinished album over and over again. "I loved it immediately, but the more I listened the deeper in love I was falling," she said. "This was the right environment for the art to just flow out, just pure and heartfelt, made from love."

Trunk Animation took Mila's artwork and brought it to life. The week before *Ghost Stories* came out, the album was available to stream, accompanied by full-length animations for each song.

GHOST IN THE MACHINE

Rather than plan a large tour for this very personal record, the band instead embarked on a six-date promotional tour in support of *Ghost Stories*, from April to July of 2014.

The most spectacular performance of the album in its entirety occurred at a custom-built amphitheatre at Sony Studios, in California, on March 23, 2014, in front of 800 fans. As they performed in the round, they also were able to incorporate 360-degree projections designed by Phil, Paul Normandale and Misty Buckley. Stefan Demetriou, responsible for all the visual projects at the band's record label

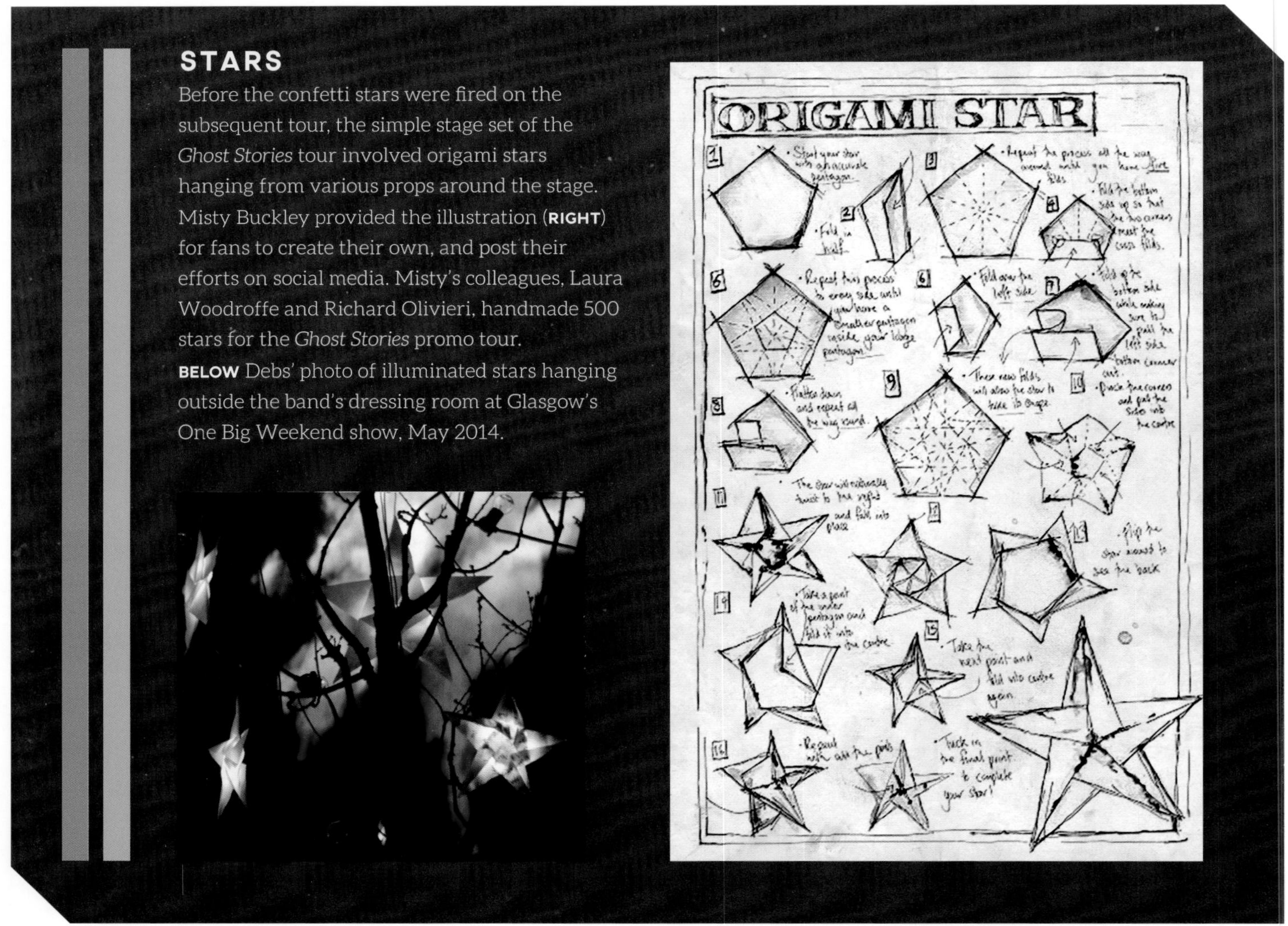

STARS

Before the confetti stars were fired on the subsequent tour, the simple stage set of the *Ghost Stories* tour involved origami stars hanging from various props around the stage. Misty Buckley provided the illustration (**RIGHT**) for fans to create their own, and post their efforts on social media. Misty's colleagues, Laura Woodroffe and Richard Olivieri, handmade 500 stars for the *Ghost Stories* promo tour.

BELOW Debs' photo of illuminated stars hanging outside the band's dressing room at Glasgow's One Big Weekend show, May 2014.

until late 2017, was on set. "There was so much work done for it that was never seen. There were films done for every single track."

"We had a slightly mad idea to have a 360-degree stage with a magic ceiling and magic walls where there was going to be video content all around the audience and the band, and above the band," said Phil. "It was technically a huge challenge and cost a ridiculous amount of money to bring to reality. It's one of those moments of 'shit, did we actually do that? How come nobody stopped us?!' I really enjoyed it. I thought it was really beautiful and original. There was no way it was ever going to go on the road. It was not something that could be toured."

Despite this, the show was still visually stunning with a simpler yet effective production. The band also introduced two new toys: Guy played a colourful laser harp, and Will played the Reactable – instruments that would appear again at their live shows.

Steve Strange said, "We always knew that this was going to be more of a studio album experience as opposed to having a full-on live campaign. We chose to earmark specific key cities that we could go and do shows in."

Two nights in July 2014 at the Royal Albert Hall proved to be the perfect setting for the band to perform the *Ghost Stories* tour in the round when they returned to UK soil.

A spectular *Ghost Stories Live* DVD, directed by Paul Dugdale, was released. It captured the intimacy beautifully.

Twelve months after *Ghost Stories* was released, on May 12, 2015, with no speculation and no rumours, there was an announcement that the title of album number seven would be *A Head Full of Dreams*. The news would see the band shake off the blues of *Ghost Stories*... and head into the kaleidoscopic light of the future.

> "It's one of those moments of 'shit, did we actually do that? How come nobody stopped us?!'"
>
> Phil

BELOW Debs took this photo from the side of the stage at Glasgow's One Big Weekend show, May 2014. Knowing the set so well helped to capture the shot.

OVERLEAF The band taking their final bow after playing at London's Royal Albert Hall.

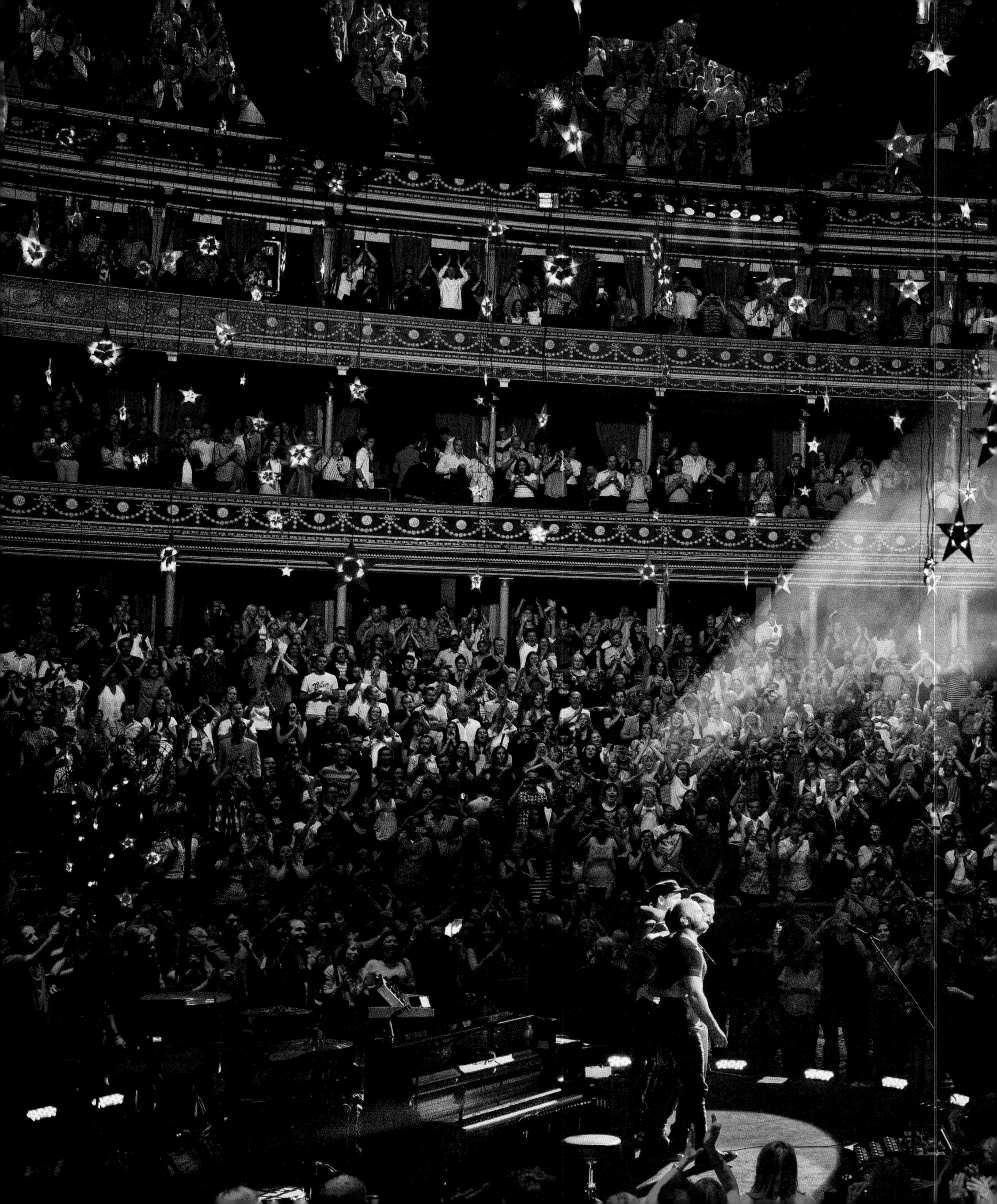

CHRIS MARTIN

Chris Martin has a unique perspective on life, which for 20 years he has shared through his songs. As the mouthpiece of the world's biggest band, he carries the responsibility and expectation on his shoulders. With the band entering the next phase of their career, it is clear that the confident singer we see in front of us today is the real Christopher Martin, at peace with himself, if not with the state of the world.

"I don't want to change places with any person in history. I like being me."

WAITING IN LINE

Growing up in Whitestone, near Exeter in Devon, he "grew up listening to cheesy stuff," said Chris. "It wasn't until I roomed [at university] with Jonny and our friend Tim, that I discovered things." Like Jonny, the pair grew up in small, quiet communities. "I didn't have a clue about anything that went on outside of my own town. Until I went to London, I didn't really know anything," Chris admitted.

Chris' musicality began at Exeter Cathedral school. That's when music became Chris' driving engine. He experienced his first public appearance in a school concert when he was 11: "I sang a song I had written about newspapers. Some people really dug it. Others didn't. I remember these two girls came up to me afterward and said, 'We heard you singing,' and then they both giggled and ran off, as if to say, It was shit. And my whole life has been that day repeating ever since."

In 1990, Chris met Phil, at Sherborne, a public boys' school in Dorset. Both were aged 13 and the two became inseparable, bonding over a shared love of U2's *Achtung Baby*.

"We always dreamed about going into music together when we were older," said Phil. "My initial ambition was to play music with Chris, but it became apparent I didn't have the requisite talent to play."

It was a few years later that Chris' bug for performing returned. "I forgot about singing for a while, then some friends wanted to play 'Sweet Child o' Mine' in a concert at school. I said, 'Wow, let me sing it.' At the end, this guy Tom said to me, 'Chris, could you

> **"** When you're born into a middle-class white family in the county of Devon, there are things that you feel like you're not allowed to do. Like be a pop star or grow your hair long. **"**
>
> Chris

ABOVE Chris and Phil rehearsing as the Rockin' Honkies. Of the band, Chris said, "There are some terrible things that could turn up. My friend Rob [Eaglesham], who I used to be in a band with, if I ever upset him he could really destroy our career."

BELOW Chris during the recording of *Parachutes* at Rockfield Studios.

ABOVE Another live photograph taken by John Hilton, circa 1999.

sing it a little less like Tina Turner?' And I was like 'I wasn't! I was trying to sound like Axl Rose!'"

The arrival of a new music teacher at school, Stephen Tanner, reignited in Chris a desire to play keyboards. He had initially taken piano lessons aged seven. "Our music teacher before Mr Tanner was very classically based," recalled Chris. "But Stephen told us that music was for everybody, and just because you didn't have classical training doesn't mean you can't play. Which was incredible. No one ever told us that was possible. He dismissed the idea that you had to be some kind of miniature Mozart to enjoy music." Tanner bought keyboards for the school. "They were very easy to work, everyone could have a go. You could play with one finger and have a tune, so we did. That was the first band I was in."

Chris would later pay homage to his former music teacher by awarding him the 2016 Love Button Super Soul Award. The award is inscribed with a message from Chris. "To my powerful music teacher: When I was 11, you purchased 11 electronic keyboards that opened up new possibilities unto my life. I am forever grateful."

The young musician's discovery of keyboards and songwriting came at just the right time. "I don't think being 13 to 15 is an easy time for any boy. It's like a big puberty race, and if you're coming in last, it's not such a great race to be in. I was a hyper-religious, quite naive and very judgmental kid," said Chris. "I was unpopular for three years, and then it all kind of switched. I'm very grateful for that period of challenge, facing the blinkeredness of that kind of schoolboy mentality."

It was at the age of 16 that school life got a little easier for the singer. Again, it was the keyboards that saved the day. Entering a Yamaha songwriting competition made the young composer hone his burgeoning keyboard skills with his lyrical mind and encouraged Chris' natural ability to write melodies. "It was such a good thing to be involved with. It's about songwriters and performance. It was suddenly like 'Come to London and do this,' and I was like 'Wow, what me, from Devon?' It gave me the feeling, 'Oh wow, maybe you really can do it'." Chris was invited back to judge the competition some years later.

During his time at Sherborne, Chris spent his late nights in rehearsal rooms, hammering away at the piano. "But like every keyboard player, I desperately wanted to be the frontman." From that point on, Chris was in a bunch of bands – Identity Crisis ("a pre-pubescent Pet Shop Boys"), Floating Insomnia and The Rockin' Honkies.

The Rockin' Honkies – fronted by Rob Eaglesham, with Phil Harvey on bass – were on the lookout for a keyboard player. Phil suggested Chris. Eaglesham thought "Chris had a real joy to him that he brought to the stage. He had an air of confidence that no

one else in the band had. At some point Phil asked me, 'Do you think Chris could be a star?'"

Phil gradually got demoted through the ranks, until he fell into a behind-the-scenes role. By contrast, "Chris was prodigiously talented, even at 13," said Phil. "He was just sensational. It was the reason a few years later when I told my mum and dad that I was going to drop out of Oxford halfway through my course they didn't freak out because they'd seen how good he was. They got it."

LOOKING FOR GOLD

Little is known of Chris being rejected from one university for an application that said he wanted to study English 'because it'll help my lyrics'. Had he been accepted Coldplay would never have come to exist.

"I went to London like Dick Whittington looking for gold," Chris said of his move to the capital. "I didn't have a cat, but I did have about 12 bags and my dad had to drive me there. I arrived at this big place called Ramsay Hall and I met Jonny and everything changed."

It was at his halls of residence that the musician met all of his future bandmates among "500 kids with guitars who came to the university looking for the same thing we were. We were just four of them, and so it happened that we found each other. I don't know what I'd be doing if I hadn't met the boys," said Chris.

> **"** You can't fool the rest of your band. I can walk into a room now and be Chris from Coldplay, be all detached. But Will's seen me running round in my pants backstage, doing an impression of Frank Spencer. **"**
>
> Chris

Kris Foof remembers a particular moment at the Student Union bar. "Chris had re-recorded the song 'Smells Like Teen Spirit' on his 4-track with the lyrics, 'Please leave the bar, leave it now. We don't want you to stay...' and handed it to the bar manager to put on when she was trying to clear the bar at the end of every night."

Over the course of 20 years, Chris has evolved and is finally comfortable in his own skin. As Phil explained recently, "Now, Chris is just like, 'Fuck it. This is where I am.' I think over the years, he's released himself from the shackles of worrying what people are going to say."

Debs Wild on Chris: *"Singer songwriter frontmen always attract more attention than their fellow bandmates. By the nature of that position, they are often more complicated characters and sometimes accidentally invite controversy in.*

Chris never courted the media attention and it wasn't something he craved or relished – that's just not who he is. He did accept it though and very rarely complained. Out of all the band members Chris has probably been exposed to an even higher level of celebrity status and shouldered attention beyond our comprehension.

The grace and manner in which he has held himself is admirable. I can't even begin to comprehend that level of intrusive invasion or media scrutiny into one's private life. Regardless, Chris remains true to himself and his values. He's navigated some rough seas but still has the desire to learn and grow and a steadfast commitment to – where he can – make a difference to the world from his position. All with his incredible sense of humour. He's one in a million."

OPPOSITE Chris takes flight during the *Mylo Xyloto* tour at the Emirates Stadium, London, June 1, 2012.

LEFT During the Twisted Logic world tour, at the Rod Laver Arena, Melbourne, Australia, July 1, 2006.

BELOW Rock in Rio Festival, October 1, 2011. Chris thanks the massive crowd. It is the first Rock in Rio gig in a decade.

C H A P T E R

S E V E N

UP AND UP

A HEAD FULL OF DREAMS

Released: December 4, 2015
Recorded: December 2014–August 2015
Producer: Rik Simpson, Daniel Green, Stargate (Tor Erik Hermansen and Mikkel Storleer Eriksen) and Coldplay
Tracklisting:
A Head Full of Dreams
Birds
Hymn for the Weekend
Everglow
Adventure of a Lifetime
Fun (feat. Tove Lo)
Kaleidoscope
Army of One
Amazing Day
Colour Spectrum
Up&Up

KALEIDOSCOPE EP

Released: July 14, 2017
Tracklisting:
All I Can Think About Is You
Miracles (Someone Special)
A L I E N S
Something Just Like This (Tokyo Remix)
Hypnotised

“On stage I don't have any doubt about who's the best fucking band in the world. But only for 90 minutes.”

Chris

OPPOSITE The Flower of Life. Their adaptation forms the basis for the cover, artwork and tour design for *A Head Full of Dreams*.

If *Ghost Stories* was considered a “night” record, then *A Head Full of Dreams* saw the group emerge into a bright, sunny day. After the relatively short, and emotional, *Ghost Stories* period, the band knew immediately what kind of record would be following the downbeat intimacy of its predecessor. “It's quite a hippie album,” said Chris of *A Head Full of Dreams*. “All of our records were a journey to get to this one.”

ALIVE AGAIN

Chris had discovered a poem by 13th-century Persian poet Rumi called 'The Guest House', a metaphor for humans receiving emotions as unexpected guests. “The poem kind of changed my life,” said Chris. “It says that everything that happens to you is OK. It's about accepting the negative along with the positive. It's about every feeling that you have being a gift. Self-doubt and depression, as well as all the joyful feelings, are all useful if you can harness them.”

And harness them they did. The record saw the band stretch their wings and become at ease with who they are. Finally. “If you're a Coldplay fan, you'll love it,” said Chris, “And if you don't like us? Don't worry about it. It's OK.”

With Chris and Phil residing in Los Angeles, and Guy, Jonny and Will in the UK, Coldplay found a routine that worked logistically.

A SKY FULL OF STARGATE

The writing process for *A Head Full of Dreams* was slightly different from previous albums. “With this one we're trying to do our whole spectrum,” said Chris. “The colours we're missing within the band we tried to bring in with guests and other producers.”

As the record evolved, Chris was handing over demos – a process he likened to auditioning – to Stargate, the renowned Norwegian pop record producers and songwriting team. “They need to know what they're getting involved with in terms of the songs, at least,” said Guy.

The decision to bring in pure pop producers was questioned at first. “Everyone was very sceptical – including me,” said Chris. “I think the rhythm section was much more sceptical,” agreed Jonny.

According to Will, the group were all mindful of what they termed the “Poochie effect” – the possibility that the band might look too desperate to try to reach a new audience by using the on-trend producers of the day. “There were some real pop songs that were like, 'That's too much, we've gone too far!'” said Chris of some of Stargate's iterations of their songs. “And then there were songs that were too much the other way – where Stargate were like,

CHARITY BEGINS AT HOME

The first time the band received a significant pay cheque, Chris made a proposal that they should set aside ten per cent of anything that came in for charitable purposes. It was a concept he took from childhood, as his mother insisted he gave ten per cent of his pocket money to charity.

They have supported many causes such as Oxfam and Client Earth... and they're currently setting up a North London project to help vulnerable children from difficult backgrounds.

Dave Holmes observes, "They certainly haven't changed as far as individuals. They're still just as kind and unaffected by fame as ever. They still have a sense of gratitude for the life we get to live, and none of us ever take it for granted."

"It's become an important part of the band's identity. They have a clear sense of how lucky they are. It gives them a real sense of social responsibility and the desire to have the most positive impact on the community and the world as possible," says Phil.

'Nah, that's a bit miserable.'" The balance resulted in the album's eventual spectrum of sound. "Stargate's biggest skill is finding space for things," said Will. "As a band, we tend towards thick and dense-sounding things. Their skill was boiling things down to a bare minimum."

"Stargate were very inspiring people to be around and work with," said Guy. "They work in a genre that isn't quite ours. And we were trying to go somewhere different."

The collaboration involved sending files back and forth. "We were all pushing in the same direction," said Will. "We could get on with something else while they did their little bit of magic. It was very fluid."

Rik Simpson and Dan Green were again on production duties. "It was great working with Stargate," said Simpson. "There was no ego."

"It was easy; we're just there to represent the boys, whatever that means," said Green. "Whoever it is, we're a team and we're just trying to get their vision across."

Midway through the recording process, Chris said, "It's our seventh album and the way we look at it it's like the last Harry Potter book. That's not to say there won't be another thing one day, but this is the completion of something. It's a very fun time to be in our band."

MONKEY BUSINESS

Written by Coldplay with Stargate, 'Adventure of a Lifetime' was a "fragile" track the band had been working on for a long time in the studio. "We had to keep pruning it," said Jonny. The lead single "started as a freeform musical session and was called, 'Legends'. It had a different chord sequence and different hooks and one-by-one things were taken away and things got added."

Inspired by the book, *Half the Sky: Turning Oppression into Opportunity for Women Worldwide* by Nicholas Kristof and Sheryl WuDunn, the track started when Chris dared Jonny to write a riff as killer as Guns N' Roses' 'Sweet Child o' Mine'. "I was asking the rest of the band to start something and I'll see if a song comes out from it, so not everything comes from me," said Chris. "It came from Jonny's riff. I was the last person on there."

The final version of the song was chosen as the first single. "I'm so happy it's the first song out there, because it's a real band piece,"said Chris.

On a flight Chris happened to meet Andy Serkis – who had starred in Mat Whitecross' film *Sex & Drugs & Rock & Roll* – and this led to a collaboration. Serkis had recently installed a digital motion capture studio called The Imaginarium, and the band were keen to use this technology to create an animated video. There were several character avatars to choose from and at first, they each chose a different one. Will's was a chimp and soon after, the rest of the band decided to be the same.

Serkis is king when it comes to this type of technology given his experience of movement and performance in *Planet of the Apes* and *Lord of the Rings*. He gave the band advice on how to move like monkeys.

The only problem was that the video, directed by Whitecross, was going to take six months to complete.

The post-production was such a lengthy process that Phil and the band were concerned that it would delay the already scheduled release date for the single. They had two choices: wait for the video or release 'Adventure of a Lifetime' with an alternative video. It didn't feel right to use the chimps for any other song, so the release was tailored to fit with its completion. The video was released on November 27, 2015.

> **"It was the most enjoyable album to make and I hope that comes across in the music."**
>
> Jonny

LEFT Chris during the 'Adventure of a Lifetime' video shoot.

ABOVE/BELOW Mat Whitecross filming the band during the 'Adventure of a Lifetime' video shoot; Chris in chimp pose.

ARMY OF MANY

A Head Full of Dreams was all about unity and togetherness and so, naturally, it made sense to make it an inclusive experience. Stargate were not the only new additions to the gang. "Everyone who got asked to sing on our album has an important part in our lives," Chris said of the album's key collaborations.

There were more guests on *A Head Full of Dreams* than any of the previous albums. Including Tove Lo, Merry Clayton and Barack Obama's heartfelt rendition of 'Amazing Grace' from his eulogy for Rev. Clementa Pinckney, a victim of a mass shooting in Charleston, USA, on June 17, 2015. An assortment of family and friends (and their children) also appeared on the album, notably as a choir on 'Up&Up'.

Two more of their favourite artists were invited to join the record: Noel Gallagher on 'Up&Up' and Beyoncé on 'Hymn for the Weekend'.

The band asked Noel Gallagher, the lead songwriter of Oasis, to come and play a little guitar. "I just happened to be in Los Angeles and matey boy [Chris] called us up and said, 'What are you doing tonight?'"

"I was pretty excited when Noel turned up in the studio," Jonny said. "I thought I've got to make my guitars sound good." For the song, both guitarists wrote lines in the style of each other. "It was really great that day when Noel and Jonny were duelling,"

said Chris. "They both were there showing each other licks and Noel was like 'Yeah that's alright, what about this?' And it came together over a few hours. It was lovely."

"They only looped this 12-bar bit, that's the only thing they would play me," said Gallagher.

Beyoncé had previously turned down a Coldplay hook-up despite their friendship and performing together at a benefit telethon back in 2010. With 'Hymn for the Weekend', Beyoncé knew it was the right project for her and agreed to record vocals for the track – at a makeshift vocal booth in Chris' LA home.

There were many takes and layers to the song. The intro was down to a happy mishap of Rik Simpson accidentally pressing play simultaneously on multiple versions of Beyoncé's vocals, creating an echo effect.

A BRAND NEW COAT OF PAINT

Created with Argentine artist Pilar Zeta, the album's artwork – yet again another symbol at the centre of the cover – came about when Phil saw her work featured in an email from her agency, Maaven.

Phil got in touch and they met to discuss ideas. As with *Mylo Xyloto*, the concept grew into a collaborative art project. Zeta came into the studio and set up a big space where there was a lot of experimentation with collage, photos, colour, painting and self-expression. Zeta, with the band's help, eventually made a huge canvas full of large and small details, including photographs of the band when they were children to make it more personal.

The kaleidoscopic feel was rolled out for the single's artwork. The "Flower of Life" became the central symbol and one to feature in the live show. It was also used to tease the album campaign. In October 2015, posters appeared worldwide with the symbol and a date: 04.12.15. Fans quickly worked out its significance.

On Friday December 4, 2015, *A Head Full of Dreams* was released. To mark the occasion, the band, along with fan and friend Radio 1 DJ Greg James, broadcast a live Q&A via Facebook from The Beehive. Ten fans were also in attendance, and had the opportunity to ask questions.

On January 9, 2016, the band came together to shoot the clip for what would be the second single, 'Hymn for the Weekend'. Filmed on location in Mumbai by director Ben Mor, the video had significant star power on screen with Beyoncé and Bollywood star Sonam Kapoor, plus the band. The video was the first glimpse into the vibrant rainbow colours that would soon fill stadiums around the world.

OPPOSITE Laminated *A Head Full of Dreams* tour pass: Access All Areas.

OPPOSITE BELOW Chris onstage in Cardiff, Principality Stadium.

BELOW RIGHT A ticket for Wembley; the band played four nights there.

BELOW European concert tickets, summer 2017, Brussels, Gothenburg and Paris.

GLOBAL CITIZEN FESTIVAL

Global Citizen is a movement to end extreme poverty by 2030. In February 2015 it was announced that Chris would curate the Global Citizen Festival until 2030. To mark the occasion, the band played a six-song set at the festival held in New York City. In December 2015, Chris visited India. The festival, and its ambitions, would later be celebrated in Mumbai on November 19, 2016.

On July 6, 2017, in Hamburg, Germany, Coldplay performed their third annual Global Citizen Festival appearance, during the *AHFOD* tour.

RIGHT & BELOW Coldplay perform on the Great Lawn at the 2015 Global Citizen Festival, Central Park, September 26, 2015, in New York City. Ariana Grande performed with Chris on the track 'Just A Little Bit of Your Heart'. The band closed the show with 'Amazing Day'.

SUPER BOWL 50

After months of preparation, the band performed to their largest viewing audience yet (an estimated 300 million) appearing at the Super Bowl 50 on February 7, 2016. The biggest challenge was how to present a spectacle during daylight hours, and Misty Buckley was on hand to help with the design.

In honour of the Bowl's 50th anniversary, they paid homage to some of the great performers that had been before and invited Beyoncé and Bruno Mars (with Mark Ronson) to share the stage.

Although it was a long process from planning to execution, sound engineer Dan Green took it in his stride. "Doing the actual event was relatively simple, it was all in the nine months' preparation before."

"It was a lot of pressure," said Phil. " I'm proud of what we did and proud of the message we put out there."

Later that month, the band accepted *NME*'s Godlike Genius Award, from friend Kylie Minogue. "Coldplay are one of the most famous bands Britain has ever produced," she said as the band took to the stage.

With that, the band departed for the road and began their global tour. It would become of the highest grossing tours in history.

DANCING ALL LIFE LONG

Not touring *Ghost Stories* meant the band were ready to get back on the road when the initial leg of their world tour started proper in Latin America – where it would also conclude some 20 months later, on December 12, 2017.

The production lavished upon this tour resulted in the band's dream show, both visually and musically. The stage design managed to bring to life the colour of the artwork, as well as the Indian influence by way of confetti mimicking holi powder and a backdrop of flowers. The "Flower of Life" took centre stage and aerial shots of the circular B Stage showed projections beamed back on to the huge screens.

The band's third single from the album, 'Up&Up', is an uplifting anthem. The supporting music video was devised and shot by Israeli artist and director Vania Heymann with Gal Muggia. It premiered on April 22, 2016. The surrealist video plays around with false perspectives, stitching together images. "The video is – I'm going to drop the mic here and say – I think it's one of the best videos people have made. Even if you take the music away," said Chris. "I can't believe that that's our video. If that was someone else's video, I'd be so jealous."

He explained, "'Up&Up' is kind of our defining credo and it's about a different way of looking at the world."

In the summer of 2016, the band returned to the UK and hosted four nights at Wembley Stadium. Their friend Simon Pegg was there. "They owned it, completely. They are first and foremost a live band, I think. They have a synchronicity which has grown out of their friendship, which makes playing live their natural habitat. If you're unsure of a particular song on any of the albums, listen to it live and not only will it suddenly make sense, it will become your favourite Coldplay song," said Pegg.

ABOVE Chris Salmon's photograph of Coldplay filling the stadium with colour for Super Bowl 50.

ABOVE An explosion of colour during a concert at BC Place, Vancouver, Canada, September 29, 2017.

RIGHT Debs posing with Chris' microphone after soundcheck, Lyon, France, June 2017.

BELOW Jonny during soundcheck in Lyon, France, June 2017.

ABOVE Misty Buckley's sketch of the stage set.

BELOW Liam Gallagher and Chris perform 'Live Forever' together, in unison with the loud crowd, at the One Love Manchester Benefit Concert, Old Trafford Cricket Ground, June 4, 2017. **INSET** A ticket for the event.

S.A.F.E.
SECURITY
कोल्डप्ले
कोल्डप्ले

S.A.F.E.
SECURITY
कोल्डप्ले

PREVIOUS PAGES Coldplay's performance was the centrepiece of the NFL's Super Bowl 50, held at Levi's Stadium on February 7, 2016, in Santa Clara, California.

ABOVE Coldplay light up the night at Estadio Unico La Plata, Buenos Aires, Argentina, March 31, 2016.

BELOW Chris Salmon's photograph of Chris lying on the stage in Argentina, 2017.

GLASTONBURY – PART SIX

Everyone in Team Coldplay always looks forward to Glastonbury, even if the band are midway through a tour. This time, June 27, 2016, they managed to bring even more magic. "We came here a bit scared about the state of the world... but you've made us realize people can do wonderful things," said Chris.

On Sunday, before the band's closing headline performance, word spread around the festival to find stewards wearing purple tabards, who would be handing out Xylobands. Jason Regler's vision from 2005, when he had the idea to invent the wristbands while watching Coldplay perform on the Pyramid stage, was about to become a reality.

Continuing with their habit to bring out guests on special occasions, the group invited Barry Gibb of the Bee Gees to perform 'To Love Somebody' and 'Staying Alive'. Michael Eavis also joined them to sing 'My Way'. However, the most poignant moment of the set came in Viola Beach's 'Boys That Sing'. Viola Beach were a young up-and-coming band who had tragically lost their lives earlier in the year. Coldplay gave them their posthumous Glastonbury moment in a very moving tribute.

"This is our favourite place in the world," Chris declared in 2016, when they performed yet again as headliners to support *A Head Full of Dreams*.

"One of the greatest and best performances I've ever seen them do. It was pretty special," said Miles Leonard.

As of 2018, Coldplay have now headlined Glastonbury festival more than any other artist, with the record arguably never to be beaten.

BELOW Miller's photo of Coldplay taking a final bow at Glastonbury, 2016.

GREATEST SHOW ON EARTH

The *A Head Full of Dreams* tour came to a head in December 2017. Chris wrote a speech that he delivered at the end of the finale: "Our friends, this is the end of the *A Head Full of Dreams* tour, right where it all began in Buenos Aires. Thank you everybody, all around the world, at home and abroad, for being the best part of our show and for keeping your, and our, heads full of dreams. This was our first chapter. From now on, we'll only be full of surprises. Believe in love!" The show ended with even bigger fireworks than usual. The tour closed with a bang.

As Chris said, "I think that one of the reasons why we're really loving this tour so much is that we're really grateful for everything. We're still the same band, and we're able to remember the shows when there was no one there... when I look back all I can think is, 'Wow, I never thought we'd ever get to this place.'"

Following the conclusion of the *A Head Full of Dreams* world stadium tour, the group's largest and most ambitious tour to date, the band were awarded with the accolade of the third biggest-grossing tour of all time. "How those shows come together is a bit of a mystery even to me," says Phil. According to *Billboard*, the tour grossed $523m (£376m), across ticket sales totalling 5.4 million and 115 performances at 83 venues. The *A Head Full of Dreams* tour proved that, as their agent Steve Strange said, "Their production has been fantastic for years, but it just keeps on getting better. They think outside of the box, they think how they can improve what they've already got.

OPPOSITE Chris making his way back to the stage at the London Palladium, November 2016.

LEFT Laminate for *A Head Full of Dreams* tour; close-up of a Xyloband.

BELOW The balloons are unleashed in Cardiff during 'Adventure of a Lifetime'.

OVERLEAF The band's nightly run to the c-stage has become a firm fixture in the band's stadium sets.

The state-of-the-art technology and production that they use from visuals to sound..."

The tour even prompted Jay-Z to comment, "If you get the chance to see Coldplay live, do it – you ain't gonna regret it."

"I think honestly what I'm most proud of is this tour," said Phil. "It was kind of crazy that we could take that stadium tour around the world – it's not the scale of it, it's about the intensity of feeling that was in that stadium every night. It was powerful and people were really into it. There was real joy and people really let go. That's not necessarily an easy thing to have happen in a sports stadium. For that reason I hope we get the chance to do it again. It's probably the thing I most look forward to."

With Dave Holmes saying that the band will "not be touring again, most probably, until 2021", Phil has time to contemplate the future. "When the subject comes up now, I have mild panic, 'Oh my god, how are we going to come up with any new ideas? We need to take a break and come back with something really special,'" said Phil. As with all ends, a beginning of sorts still occurs. Unsurprisingly, the band went straight into the studio to put new ideas down. Whether they will ever see the light of the day remains to be seen, but after 20 years together another chapter comes to a close.

"I've known the band for half of their lives. Even though I knew from Day One they were something special, I could never have predicted what they went on to achieve," said Debs Wild. "They have constantly amazed me and I can't wait to see what they come up with next".

"I just feel like we're right where we're supposed to be right now. This album, and the EP, and this tour marked the end of a chapter," said Chris. "It's our seventh album and it's the end of that first stage of the band. I think what the future holds is us doing things slightly differently, and trying to create music in ways that are graceful and honest. But we're still just trying to figure it all out – the next phase, and what that will be."

RIGHT Chris Salmon's photo of the band's final *A Head Full of Dreams* tour date in Argentina, November 2017.

BELOW Mat Whitecross' photo of Phil.

BOTTOM Multi-instrumentalist Will keeps an eye on Chris during 'Every Teardrop Is a Waterfall' at the Levi's Stadium, Santa Clara, California, October 4, 2017.

Buenos Aires Provincia
Buenos Aires Provincia
Buenos Aires Provincia
Buenos Aires Provincia
Buenos Aires Provincia
SALIDA
ESTADIO ÚNICO CIUDAD DE LA PLATA
SALIDA
EMERGENCIA
4000-8888
vital

> “I have no idea what’s going to happen. If one day we make another record, then that’s wonderful.”
>
> Chris

INDEX

123

A

B

C

D

F

PICTURE CREDITS

Key: T = top, B = bottom, L = left, R = right & M = Middle

p9 Debs Wild. Photos by Amy Leggett, p12 Kris Foof, p13-18 Coldplay, p19 Debs Wild, p20T Oz Cift (Private Collection), p20B Coldplay, p21 John Hilton, p22T&B Coldplay, p23T John Hilton, p23B Debs Wild, p24 Debs Wild, p25T Coldplay, p25B Kris Foof, p26 John Hilton, p27-28 John Hilton, p29 Authors, p30 Coldplay, P31-312T&L Oz Cift (Private Collection), p32R Debs Wild, p33TL Be Rozzo, p33TR&BL Coldplay, p33BR Debs Wild, p34T Debs Wild, p34B Gemma Fraser, p35 Coldplay, p36-38 Debs Wild, p39 Piers Allardyce/REX/Shutterstock, p42L Debs Wild, p42R Coldplay, pP43 Oz Cift (Private Collection), p44 James 'Pix' Pickering, p45 Kris Foof, p46 Jeff Dray, p47 Coldplay, p47B Rockfield Studios FEL LLP, p48-49 Jeff Dray, p50T Debs Wild, p50BL Pete Bryne, p50BR Jeff Dray, p51 Amanda Edwards/Redferns/Getty Images, p52L Debs Wild, p52R Danny McNamara, p53 Debs Wild, p54T Debs Wild, p54BL Jeff Dray, p54BR Debs Wild, p55 Debs Wild, p56 Amy Leggett, p57T Danny McNamara, p57R Debs Wild, p58T Amy Leggett, P58B Debs Wild, p59 Peter Macdiarmid/REX/Shutterstock, p60 Debs Wild, p61 Photograph by Chris Floyd, Camera Press London, p62 Richard Young/REX/Shutterstock, p63 Malcolm Croft, p64 Patrick Fraser/Corbis via Getty Images, p67L Jun Sato/WireImage/Getty Images, p67R - Shirlaine Forrest/WireImage/Getty Images, p68 Shane Wenzlick/Getty Images, p69 Quintin Lake, p72L Debs Wild, p72R Munawar Hosain/REX/Shutterstock, p73 Debs Wild, p74 Dave Hogan/Getty Images, p75 Debs Wild, p76 Jeff Dray, p77 TBC, p78 Nick Laham/Getty Images, p79 Vicki Taylor, p80T John Alex Maguire/REX/Shutterstock, p80B John Sault, p81TL Jeff Dray, p81TR Debs Wild, p81B Amy Leggett, p83T Jeff Dray, p83M Debs Wild, p83BL Jeff Dray, p83BR Debs Wild, p84 Eva Vermandel/Contour by Getty Images, p85 Photograph by Andy Cotterill, Camera Press London, p86-87 Debs Wild, p88 John Sault, p89 Photograph by Jason Bell, Camera Press London, p90 Patrick Fraser/Corbis via Getty Images, 94 Coldplay, p95 Debs Wild, p96-98 Vicki Taylor, p99-100 Debs Wild, p101 Action Press/REX/Shutterstock, p102-103 & p103T Vicki Taylor, p103BR & p104T Debs Wild, p104B Mick Hutson/Redferns/Getty Images, p105 Vicki Taylor, p106 Olaf Heine/Contour by Getty Images, p108 Patrick Fraser/Corbis via Getty Images, p110T James 'Pix' Pickering, p110B John Hilton, p111T Bob King/Redferns/Getty Images, p111B George Pimentel/WireImage/Getty Images, p112 Radharc Images/Alamy Stock Photo,p113 Rob Verhorst/Redferns/Getty Images, p117 Coldplay, p118-p119 Debs Wild, p120 Matthew Miller, p120B Davide Rossi, p121 Mick Hutson/Redferns/Getty Images, p122T Debs Wild, p122B Photograph by Dean Chalkley, Camera Press London, p123T John Shearer/WireImage/Getty Images, p123B Brian Rasic/Getty Images, p124TL Vicki Taylor, p124TR Debs Wild, p124ML Vicki Taylor, p125TL & TR Vicki Taylor, p125M Debs Wild, p126 Oz Cift (Private Collection), p127 Rob Loud/FilmMagic/Getty Images, p128TL&R Debs Wild, p128B Nick Pickles/WireImage/Getty Images, P129T&B Vicki Taylor, p130-131 Dave Hogan/Getty Images, p131B & p132T Debs Wild, p132-133B Sarah Lee, p134-135 Rob Loud/FilmMagic/Getty Images, p136 Patrick Fraser/Corbis via Getty Images, p138T Coldplay, p138B Jeff Dray, p139 Chris Pizzello/AP/REX/Shutterstock, p140 Rob Verhorst/Redferns/Getty Images, p141 Kevin Mazur/Getty Images for Atlantic Records, p144 & p145L Coldplay , p145R&M Debs Wild, p146 REX/Shutterstock, p147 Dave J Hogan/Getty Images, p148-149 Matthew Miller, p149T&B Debs Wild, p150 Matthew Miller, p151 Matt Cardy/Getty Images, 152 Christopher Polk/Getty Images for Clear Channel, p153LR Debs Wild, p153B Brian J. Ritchie/Hotsauce/REX/Shutterstock, p154 Ethan Miller/Getty Images for iHeartMedia, p156T Debs Wild, p156B Dan Moore, p157 Peter Wafzig/Getty Images, p158-159 Carlos R. Alvarez/WireImage, p159 Christopher Polk/WireImage/Getty Images, p160 & p161T Debs Wild, p161B Dean Mouhtaropoulos/Getty Images, p162-163 Hayley Madden/Redferns/Getty Images, p166 Coldplay, p166BR & p167T Quintin Lake, p168T Coldplay, p168BL Chris Salmon, p169 Helen Lu, p170BL Debs Wild, p170BR Laura Woodroffe, p171 Debs Wild, p172-173 Sarah Lee, p174 Patrick Fraser/Corbis via Getty Images, p176T Rob Eaglesham, p176B Coldplay, p177 John Hilton, p178 Richard Isaac /REX/Shutterstock, p179T Ryan Pierse/Getty Images, p179B Buda Mendes/LatinContent/Getty Images, p184 Mat Whitecross, p185 Sarah Lee, p186T Debs Wild, p186B Sam Neill, p187 Debs Wild, p188T Taylor Hill/WireImage/Getty Images, p189B Kevin Mazur/Getty Images for Global Citizen, p189 Chris Salmon, p190T Andrew Chin/Getty Images, p190B Phil Harvey, p191T Misty Buckley, p191B Kevin Mazur/One Love Manchester/Getty Images for One Love Manchester, p192-193 Harry How/Getty Images, p194T RMV/REX/Shutterstock, p194B Chris Salmon, p195 Matthew Miller, p196 Alex Fordham, p197T Debs Wild, p197B & p198-199 Sam Neill, p200T Mat Whitecross, p200B Steve Jennings/Getty Images, p201 Chris Salmon, p202-203 Sam Neill

Every effort has been made to acknowledge correctly and contact the source and/or copyright holder of each picture and Carlton Publishing Group apologises for any unintentional errors or omissions that will be corrected in future editions of this book.

AUTHORS

DEBS WILD has worked in the music industry since 1996. Starting as an A&R scout, she discovered and championed Coldplay from their first introduction. To this day Debs remains part of Coldplay HQ's trusted inner circle.

Debs thanks... Guy, Jonny, Will, Chris, Phil – you changed my life. I love you.

All at Coldplay HQ, with special mention to Dave Holmes and Chris Salmon.

My family, especially Mum and Dad, Jus and Ness.

My friends, advisers and distractors: Sophie, Suz, Jen, Vicki, Rhian, Dan, Stephen, Charlotte, Ahsan, Caroline, Jess, Malcolm, Rachel and extra special thanks to Siobhan and Moody.

This book is for my brother, Martin.

MALCOLM CROFT is a former music journalist, author and popular culture commissioning editor. Over the past 15 years he has spent time with many of the world's most popular bands and has written and published books across a wide range of subjects and genres. He and Debs met in 2007 when they bonded over a mutual love of music and champagne.

Malcolm thanks Roger and Zelda, Rachel and Indie.

The authors would like to thank...

Guy Berryman, Jonny Buckland, Will Champion, Chris Martin, Phil Harvey, Dave Holmes, Chris Salmon, Arlene Moon, Matthew Miller, Matt McGinn, Sean "Bash" Buttery, Jeff Dray, Dan Green, Rik Simpson, Vicki Taylor, Caroline (Elleray) Gale, Ian Ramage, Estelle Wilkinson, Gavin Maude, Kris Foof, John Hilton, Gavin Aherne, James "Pix" Pickering, Tim Crompton, Rob Eaglesham, Simon Williams, Andy Macleod, Dan Keeling, Miles Leonard, Keith Wozencroft, Stefan Demetriou, Chris Latham, Mike Walsh, Kevin McCabe, Steve Strange, Mel Brown, Ken Nelson, Pete Byrne, Markus Dravs, Nikki Rosetti, Mike Beever, Lisa Ward, Be Rozzo, Mat Whitecross, James & Alex, Jamie Thraves, Misty Buckley, Mila Fürstová, Davide Rossi, Jason Regler, Steve Lamacq, Edith Bowman, Danny McNamara, Simon Pegg, Maureen Pegg, Guy Garvey, Tim Rice-Oxley, Adam Tudhope

And to everyone who has given their free time, content and support.